A History of the Religious Education Association

A History of the Religious Education Association

STEPHEN A. SCHMIDT

Religious Education Press
Birmingham, Alabama

Library of Congress Cataloging in Publication Data

Schmidt, Stephen A.
    A history of the Religious Education Association.

    Includes bibliographical references and index.
    1. Religious Education Association—History.
I. Title.
BV1460.R6S35   1983   207   83-14005
ISBN 0-89135-037-3

Religious Education Press, Inc.
1531 Wellington Road
Birmingham, Alabama 35209
10 9 8 7 6 5 4 3 2

Religious Education Press publishes books exclusively in religious education and in
areas closely related to religious education. It is committed to enhancing and professionalizing religious education through the publication of serious, significant, and
scholarly works.

PUBLISHER TO THE PROFESSION

Contents

Preface

Till the Great Society is converted into a Great Community, the Public will remain in eclipse. Communication can alone create a great community. Our Babel is not one of tongues, but of signs and symbols without which shared experience is impossible.[1]

John Dewey, 1927

The first words of a book are, ironically, the last words written. At one level of understanding a preface is simply an introduction to a larger body of content, the book itself. Within the context of the worshiping Christian community, however, the Preface serves as a ritualistic doxological invitation to participate in the mystery of the Eucharist. The Preface of the Mass begins with the mutual blessing between the community and the celebrant and ends with the ancient Christian hymn of blessing, the Sanctus. The blessings shift from the people of God to the God of the people. These words and symbols introduce that which is to follow, the shared experience of Holy Communion.

The words of the Preface are some of the oldest and least modified of the entire Mass. The signs and symbols are ancient. There is no Babel here, only the sacred words of the Preface intoned with consistency and continuity since the second century of Christian experience. The communal nature of Christianity is most clearly symbolized in the Eucharist. Its ritualistic power is related to the sustained tradition of the liturgy. The Preface calls into memory the creative activity of God among God's people. It announces the unity of the communion of saints "with angels and archangels and all the company of heaven."[2]

At some level of human experience we all share the need for intimacy and community, individually and corporately. When there is an eclipse of the public (the community), we struggle to restore a sense of well-being in relationship. Our personal and shared stories are part of that

1

constant effort toward solidarity. I should like to preface this story of the Religious Education Association (R.E.A.) with a bit of liturgical ritual, moving from some personal signs and symbols to those more corporately shared by the subjects of this book. Like a Eucharistic Preface, the blessings flow from the individual participant to the larger community, then to the signs and symbols that one might call religious, or even revelational.

R. G. Collingwood once wrote that "history is for human self-knowledge."[3] Insofar as history deals with human story it must focus on personal understandings. I learned something of that truth during the five years I spent writing this book. I experienced dramatic changes in my personal and professional life. I was forced to leave the comfortable confines of my religious home of origin, The Lutheran Church—Missouri Synod. Personal losses included my own serious illness and the death of my mother. During these years I did some serious remembering. My quest took the form of conscious attention to my personal past as well as an objective search for the roots of my family of origin. Visits to the birthplaces of my grandparents in Northern Bavaria and Westphalia, West Germany, were journeys that touched my sense of self-knowledge. Ancient thirteenth-century parish churches, "pilgrim churches" the Germans called them, contained wondrous artifacts of my family's origin. Accounts of my ancestors' births, baptisms, marriages, and deaths were recorded in carefully preserved church records dating back to the Reformation. I walked the fields of the Schmidt family farm, held in the family name for three hundred years. I met distant cousins and found pictures of myself as a child in boxes of letters and cards sent by my grandparents years ago. I felt an intense desire to know as much as I could about these ancestors. That journey is over, and I live with insights that are to this day deeply significant in my self-understanding.

This book is really about a parallel journey, one shared by members of the R.E.A. over the past seventy-five years. The R.E.A. is like a professional family of origin. There are forefathers and foremothers, rituals and traditions. There are myths, symbols, and family legends imprinted on the profession to this day. Family artifacts and documents legitimate the heirs of that family story.

I believe this story reveals a concern from beginning to end. It is a concern over the signs and symbols which made possible the shared experience of the R.E.A. community. The association never completely resolved its own Babel, but the efforts at resolution are both noteworthy and significant. While it was surely easier to profess a modified vision of a religious democracy in the first decade of the twentieth century than in the eighth, it is still profoundly moving to reflect on the struggle for continuity of vision and purpose during the intervening seven decades. This book argues that the R.E.A. family of origin had some clearly defined signs and symbols. What the association sought was surely a "great community." Though that same task, caring about a public paideia, is despairingly more difficult today, its importance is, I believe, even more profound. It is my hope that clarity about the vision and the signs and symbols inherent in the R.E.A. might become part of the leaven for renewal and recreation. End of preface. The celebration is to follow.

* * * * * *

I have had companions in my search for origins. There was a good deal of familial advice and a supportive but critical network of professional siblings. I happily acknowledge some of those colleagues and friends. Robert Lynn, vice president for religion of Lilly Endowment, Inc., read the manuscript in all revisions and gave generously of his time and historical insight. Philip Phenix, professor emeritus of religion and education at Teachers College, Columbia University, provided early support and encouragement through the entire project. William Kennedy, professor of religious education, Union Seminary, commented extensively on the manuscript. Randolph Crump Miller, emeritus Horace Bushnell Professor of Christian Nurture, Yale Divinity School, offered advice and assistance and negotiated the publication of the manuscript in his capacity as acting general secretary of the R.E.A. Other professional colleagues read the manuscript at various levels of completion: Boardman W. Kathan, general secretary of the R.E.A. from 1970 to 1982; Jack L. Seymour, Scarrit College; Dorothy Furnish, Garrett Evangelical Theological Seminary; Mark Schwehn, University of Chicago; and James Wind, assistant pastor of Grace Lutheran Church, River Forest, Illinois. I owe a special word of appreciation to Herman Wornom, past general secretary of the R.E.A. for extensive interview time and special assistance in the latter chapters of the book. Finally several colleagues at Mundelein College, Chicago, made helpful suggestions: Ann Ida Gannon; Nicholas A. Patricca; Mary Donahey; and Clarisse Croteau-Chonka. Rose Phoenix, proofread each revision and patiently edited the final copy. While these persons gave advice and suggestions, I bear full responsibility for the final manuscript.

STEPHEN A. SCHMIDT
Mundelein College, 1983

Notes

1. John Dewey, *The Public and Its Problems* (Chicago: Sage Books, The Swallow Press, Inc., 1927), p. 142.

2. Evelyn Underhill, *Worship* (New York: Harper & Brothers Publishers, 1936), pp. 120–137.

3. R. G. Collingwood, *The Idea of History* (New York: Oxford University Press, 1956), p. 10.

Introduction

> We need to define religious education in such a way that it shall not mean sectarianism or sentimentalism, but a kind of culture which is indispensable to the normal man. . . . We need to make it clear that religion is as broad as life itself, and that life without religion is impossible.
>
> Frank Knight Sanders
> President's Annual Address
> Official Bulletin #3 R.E.A., May, 1904

This book is an intellectual history of the Religious Education Association from its origin, in 1903, to 1970. In one sense the story is broader than the institutional history of the R.E.A. It is a story about the movement, religious education, the spiritual or religious counterpart to progressive education. The book seeks to understand the relationship among the ideas of that movement, to explain how key ideas changed over time and how these intellectual developments relate to the internal struggle of the R.E.A. as well as to the larger contours of the twentieth-century American life. After describing the association's early period of heroic dreams and triumphant visions, the book traces the development of the R.E.A. through lean years of retrenchment and financial uncertainty into its later period of growth as a healthy professional gathering.

This story is not without surprises and dramatic contrasts. It is an account of great achievements and significant failures. It is not only a story of heroes who seem larger than life, as William Rainey Harper or George Albert Coe often seemed to appear to the R.E.A. faithful. It is also a story about administrative managers, quiet effective general secretaries, or assertive, arrogant leaders, who each gave passionately of their several talents. It is a plot that includes mischief and meanness, professional jealousies, and hidden motivations. It is a tale of glory days

5

and times of melancholy. Above all, it is finally a very human story about real people seeking to make this society and this pluralism of religion and churches into some kind of noble "kingdom of God."

This central religious ideal gave the R.E.A. a lasting sense of continuity and purpose during seven decades of dramatic social and intellectual changes. In the midst of sweeping modifications of human understandings there remained a basic core of agreement and continuity among the values of the principal mentors of the R.E.A. The ideals of William Rainey Harper's notion of democratic religion, George Albert Coe's "democracy of God," Harrison Elliott's "group process," and Randolph Crump Miller's "language of relationship" were each metaphors of similar understandings. The thread of continuity that held these thematic elements together was the conviction that all education, including religious education, was a matter of public pedagogy. The dominant values of that paradigm were these: truth, including religious truth, is enhanced by scientific method; religion is the essence of democratic life; God is the name for the experience of love and intimate affirmation; and the way to the divine is through social processes of human interaction.

While there was a central core of agreement and continuity among these principal leaders of the R.E.A., there was also a good deal of modification of those ideals over time. The ideal of democracy as the main symbol of God's activity certainly changed over the years. The social ideals moved toward a more narrow and parochial understanding of the place where God is to be experienced. There was a shift from viewing the larger culture as the primary arena of God's activity to a more institutionalized and ecclesiastical understanding that viewed the primary place of God's activity as the domain of the church. But whatever the degree of shifting provincialism, the central idea remained one of a concern about democratic relationships and human experiences as the primary method and arena of Christian nurture.

Throughout the history of the R.E.A. there has always been a small dedicated band of hopeful companions who sought to maintain this public religious ideal (paideia), even while they were themselves transformed by it. While interested in public religious education, they sought to keep faith with modernity while maintaining continuity with the ancient vision of a Judeo-Christian hope of a kingdom of Yahweh, a reign of love and justice in the midst of North Americans. This grand purpose energized the R.E.A. founders and continued to inspire their followers, those women and men whom today we casually designate as religious educators. This book is accordingly the story of the founding ideas of the R.E.A. and of the key persons who kept those beliefs alive even as they went about modifying them. Though the R.E.A. always encompassed diversity among individual members, the leadership of the association found consensus around these progressive democratic religious convictions. Discontinuities were evident in changes of emphasis, domestication of ideas, and movements of focus from public religious education to church or ecclesiastical religious education.

*   *   *

The themes of the chapters correspond to the historical periods of the tenures of the general secretaries. Although this structure is arbitrary, it did seem the most historically desirable way to organize the material. Each era of time began with a new agenda, and each period of time ended with reassessments by the association. And for better or worse this association, perhaps more than others similar in design or interest, seemed to succeed or fail in relationship to the success or failure of the general secretary. So the chapter periods are not organized according to equal time frames; rather, they reflect a reasonable way to manage the material, primarily because the organization also seemed to measure its days by these periods of leadership.

Chapter I attempts to introduce the reader to the argument of the book and provides some modest background material to help in understanding the context of the beginning of the R.E.A. Chapter II, 1903–1923, follows the development of the progressive democratic vision of the early founders of the association. It covers the first two decades of the association under its first permanent general secretary, Henry Cope. Chapter III, 1923–1935, sketches the ''glory days'' of the religious education movement (the expansion of religious education in seminary and university), as well as the triumphalism of the association and its ''imperial'' general secretary, Joseph Artman. This period ended in disappointment and despair. Caught in the financial difficulties of the 1930s, the association came closer to failure than at any other time in its history. Chapter IV, 1935–1952, outlines a period of outmoded ideas and leadership. It is the most pathetic part of the story. It is also a chapter about a small group of faithfuls who voluntarily kept the association alive without any paid general secretary and with a very limited office staff. Chapter V, 1952–1970, concludes this book with the story of the rebirth of success and high expectations. The vision of the founders becomes parochialized but never abandoned. The story ends with the general secretary's retirement. A final epilogue raises new challenges and recurrent questions for the future, based on the R.E.A. traditions of the past.

No attempt has been made to continue the history through the 1970s to the present though there was great temptation to do so. The decision to conclude the story at 1970 was made in light of these considerations. There was little possibility for historical distance, since most of the leadership of the present R.E.A. are very much alive and involved in the ongoing story of the association. With the resignation of the executive secretary, Boardman W. Kathan in the fall of 1982, the association will again be nudged to reexamine its goals and future directions. Immediate assessments of the Kathan administration will surely be part of that internal reevaluation. Historical judgments about those years, however, must wait for another time and another historian.

Since so many of the past themes continue to engage the R.E.A., there is little doubt but that the association will continue to struggle with historical continuities and current changes. This research might help the association confront the present with recurrent questions from the past, as well as provide additional evidence that the struggle for continuity is indeed worthwhile. Historians ought not make predictions about the future. What one can do is highlight areas of concern which, if not understood and solved, may continue to haunt the present as well as the future. I believe that the R.E.A. will be around for decades to come and that its future story will continue to be as fascinating as its past.

There are other limitations to this historical interpretation which the reader deserves to know. There is a certain unevenness about the primary data which supports the conclusions drawn throughout this work. That difficulty reflects the condition and availability of the sources. While there are more than twenty file drawers of primary data in the R.E.A. archives from the period of 1950 to 1970, there is less than a single file case of primary papers from the entire earlier period. Thus I was forced to turn to sources outside the institutional records. This has had the advantage of broadening the story, as well as the possible disadvantage of telling a story more inclusive than the single perspective of the association. Since my own interest lay in the larger task, I have not found the imbalance of institutional data to be a hindrance to my work. And though the story is not the history of the entire religious education movement, it is surely a story related to that larger context.

The reader should also know that, although the book was commissioned by the R.E.A., there was never any effort on the part of any R.E.A. executive or member to influence my interpretation. I was given complete access to all of the documents of the association and full encouragement to structure the story according to my own inclinations. That freedom is reflected in the book's lack of evangelical defense of the association. It is also revealed in my struggle to arrive at balanced judgments as nearly as possible reflecting the true history of a very complex and unpredictable story.

I want to acknowledge the historical rootedness of these events and struggles. Racism, sexism, bigotry, and other oppressions are always wrong in any historical period. These negative values are surely criticized in this story. I hope they are also understood within the context of the historical times. While I have tried not to make anachronistic judgments, I have on the other hand not excused the ideas or the authors for their judgments just because they resided in a particular circumstance or time. It is necessary that the contemporary historian attempts empathetic understanding. It is not, however, essential that our interpretation create some kind of deterministic apology for the sins of the fathers and mothers. Claiming "period" limitations is no excuse for human oppression. It never was, and it will not be for us in our own time. To acknowledge the problems of the past is one way to relativize our own sense of self-righteousness.

* * *

History of necessity involves interpretation. I have consciously chosen to be candid about my viewpoint throughout the book. My story may occasionally lack detached scientific objectivity. It is, however, the only story I can tell. It fits the data insofar as I have been able to discover. Other stories are possible, and this book is an invitation to other storytellers. The past continues to elicit our creative energies as we seek to understand our present and prepare for our futures.

Chapter I

A Public Paideia

It is the misinterpretation of the Bible that furnishes the occasion of all skepticism. The friends of the Bible have been its worst enemies. A faith in the Bible constructed upon a scientific basis will be acceptable to everyone who will take the pains to look into it.[1]

The Biblical World, Vol. III, 1894
"Editorial," Editor: William Rainey Harper

When William Rainey Harper addressed the first convention of the Religious Education Association in 1903, his words summed up the progressive hope of the times. His proposal to initiate a new national organization in behalf of "religious and moral instruction" was based solidly upon his conviction that significant progress was possible "in light of scientific investigations." The application of science to the world of religion, education, biblical studies, and "the development of the individual and of society" were part of the creedal convictions of late nineteenth-century religious progressives. Though there were problems to be solved, the task was manageable and hopeful. Caught in the euphoric possibilities of creating a new "righteous America," Harper sketched a future with ample opportunity for all. "There is work in these lines of investigation, real definite, scientific investigation to occupy the time of thousands of men and women if they will undertake it."[2]

A World Come of Age:
The New Science

Harper was an advocate of the new sciences, and these convictions affected his work most intimately in the arena of biblical studies. Harper, trained as a Hebraist, had spent the majority of his adult life concerned with developing an agreeable scientific partnership between biblical criticism and traditional Christian understandings and pieties. When one reviews Harper's *Biblical World* during the decade of the 1890s, one cannot escape his firm belief that the sciences were a great boon to the study and interpretation of Scripture. Harper's editorials and articles provide clear insight into his devotion to the scientific method and to his assertion that the sciences were indeed God's gracious gift to create a better world.

For Harper there was no essential clash between the scientific and the religious task in terms of biblical scholarship. In 1893 Harper would argue that "successful Bible study" required both "investigation and insight." To study the Scriptures properly one must investigate "geography, politics, military operation, schools of thought" as one would study any other type of historical literature. Yet at the same time, one must accompany such tasks with "spiritual sympathy and insight which enable the student to see the great spiritual truths which lie behind and within the facts."[3] Harper was willing to acknowledge the possible dangers of scientific criticism in the world of biblical scholarship, but he knew as well the greater problem of building faith upon subjective speculation without the critique of modern science. Harper's succinct prose revealed his "conservative compromise." "Biblical criticism belongs essentially to the Christian man."[4]

Harper was interested not only in the sciences of biblical historical or literary criticism. In 1895 the *Biblical World* editorialized about the potential dangers and possible values of the new developing science of sociology. The convictions of that editorial could almost be interpreted as a forerunner of George Albert Coe's later theory of a social strategy for religious education. Harper believed that Christian truth "is of necessity a social force." The need, however, according to the editorial, was to relate the Christian influence "more avowedly and more scientifically." The sociologist served to temper the evangelical Christian. Sociology, according to Harper, was "a sober and persistent attempt to discover the laws underlying the association of men as a step in human progress." The problems of society, the "concentration of labor and capital, the maintenance of industrial peace, the settlement of industrial war, the duties of social classes to each other," all these came under the purview of the sociologist.

Harper argued as well against the possible misuses of sociology in the task of relating Christian values to the larger society. The sociologist "is too often quite as ignorant of exegetical processes as is many a new-fledged reformer of economics and social science." The danger of simple sociological application of Christian principles to social ills was connected with an "uncritical" approach to Scripture. Harper called rather for a "biblical sociology that shall do for systematic sociology what Biblical theology is doing for dogmatic theology." Harper advocated a public dialogue between the principles of authentic Christian teaching and the sociological findings of current social theory.

The article rejected an optimistic "trust to evolution" as a corrective of social ills; rather, it advocated Christian progress through the transformation of the individual and the authentic application of the social teachings of the Gospel. It is important to understand how Harper saw positive values in the new sciences rather than threats to the Christian tradition. Sociology could assist in the application of the Gospel to the real world by providing a scientific exegesis of society that would be combined with an equally important understanding of authentic biblical social values, which could only be achieved by scientific scriptural exegesis. Harper understood the limits and possibilities of the sciences.[5]

By 1904 sociologist Max Weber would publish his classic study of the relationships between religion and society. His *Protestant Ethic and the Spirit of Capitalism* revealed how productive the sociological analysis of religion might become. Weber convincingly argued that the development of modern capitalism had historic roots in the Protestant work ethic.[6] Harper had anticipated the future, that time when every aspect of the scientific enterprise would be brought to bear on the study of religion.

Harper's vision expanded with each new scientific development. His *Biblical World* informed the public and celebrated each new possibility. In October, 1900, Harper wrote about a "new phase in the study of religion." He explained to his readers that the new science of comparative religion had produced significant positive results. "We are already deriving much knowledge which helps forward a better understanding of religion." By the study of other world religions one could highlight the distinctiveness and similarities of Christianity in relationship to other religions.

Harper was excited about the potential of that new science which he felt promised to grow with great rapidity and strength. He even made this prediction: "This inductive study of religious experience which is now beginning and of which so much will be heard within the next twenty years promises new insight into the religious quest." He looked to a future when this science would provide a better understanding of religion. He speculated that the coming century was "entitled to a type or types of religious experience quite its own and comfortable to the character and humanity of our time."[7]

Harper mentioned three of his contemporaries as representatives of pioneer work in this field: Edwin D. Starbuck, Stanford University, author of *The Psychology of Religion,* George Albert Coe, Northwestern University, author of *The Spiritual Life,* and Frank Stephen Granger, Nottingham, England, author of *The Soul of a Christian.* One choice was especially interesting in view of the fact that Coe would become the most significant intellectual mentor of the R.E.A. during the first two or three decades of the organization's history.

Coe's book, *The Spiritual Life,* revealed the outlines of that new science, as well as shed light upon his perception of the opportunities of science toward the future study of religion in the United States. Coe accepted the "empirical method" as the modern approach to the study of spiritual realities. He credited this new discipline to the early work of President G. Stanley Hall of Clark University and several of his pupils, especially E. D. Starbuck. Their work utilized the questionnaire method, and Coe hastened to add that such data gathered by empirical means could not be refuted by any appeal to Scripture. He understood Scripture, as did Harper, to be about "instruction in righteousness, not science."[8]

Coe called for a pastoral care which would "become an art" in relying not only upon the scriptural or doctrinal traditions but also upon the insights of contemporary psychological knowledge. Perceiving the difference between the mental activities of a child and those of the mature adult, he defined the guidelines for later developmental theory.[9] He was able to chart the ages of religious awakenings and he viewed adolescence as the age most agreeable to religious development. One should introduce religious instruction "at just the point where the child's mind has a natural instinct for it."[10]

Coe even hinted at the possibility for sequential moral development. While describing teenaged religious thinking, Coe pointed out that "morality is as yet abstract and lacking content." Coe could not have known that the agenda for decades of religious education research would revolve around that question of moral development. Yet in his early work one sees the basic outlines for the future of religious developmental theory, character development, and moral education.

Coe had shown the way toward future psychological research in the area of religion. He did not seek to deny the reality of religion, even the esoteric experience of faith healing of Christian Science. He was, rather, interested in descriptions of the phenomena. One can hardly subscribe to all of his findings in light of future developments. He used the paradigms and knowledge of his time,[11] as indicated in these words about women and men. "Two of the best established general differences between the male and the female mind are these," Coe stated.

"First the female mind tends more than the male to feeling; and second it is more suggestible."[12] Coe was captive to the conventional wisdom of his day, but he was also open to new data and, as we shall see, he spent his life in behalf of broadening religious tolerance and scientific objectivity for both women and men.

Harper and Coe saw the world of the sciences and the methods of empirical research as the key to the future.[13] Harper called for "conservative progressivism," and Coe appealed to the art of the scientific enterprise. Each in his own way was a forerunner of the new age. Each was optimistic in his hope for a modern world, a religious world where mystery and magic gave way to the rational and understandable world of scientific knowledge. Research would shed light upon the religious life and usher in a new age of religious transformations. This new knowledge would enrich the American democratic vision, a dream not unrelated to the ancient hope of the "kingdom of God."

Coe's and Starbuck's work in the "science of religion" was overshadowed by the work of Harvard psychologist, William James. James was invited to deliver the Gifford Lectures at the University of Edinburgh in 1901. Those lectures were published in 1902 under the title *The Varieties of Religious Experience.*[14] When James journeyed to Edinburgh, he went home, intellectually speaking, to the country where the empirical method was first affirmed. He went with a sense of scholarly obligation. He opened his lectures by paying tribute to the traditions of empirical science and acknowledging his indebtedness. James was nonjudgmental about the nature or the truthfulness of the religious experience. Rather he was interested in establishing the empirical criterion for the study of religion. "God is real since he produces real effects," wrote James.[15]

Two observations seem appropriate. First, the fact that James went *to* Edinburgh seemed to symbolize the intellectual continuity of Scottish empiricism and modern American scientific thought. He came to Edinburgh *from* America, suggesting the emerging dominance of the scientific enterprise in the new world. The Americans had come of age, so to speak, and the Edinburgh invitation seemed to underline that intellectual reality. Finally, he came to lecture *about* religion.

Modern science would now stand over against religion in a new relationship, in the posture of judgment and scientific criticism. Harper and Coe understood that relationship and, rather than being threatened by the new sciences, they would achieve working alliances with the world of modernity and the subject of religion. Historical criticism, sociology, psychology, and educational theory were all companions in the new world they sought to bring into being.

They had ample companions, a host of educators both public and religious who shared their hopes and dreams. The education of the public was a major enterprise at the turn of the century. That task, shared by the American family, public schools, Sunday Schools, churches, charitable agencies, and the university, was in the midst of transition. Education moved from private familial settings to public schools, from religious agencies to secular spaces, the laboratory and the city. Teaching, once the domain of religious volunteers, became the responsibility of professional pedagogues. Public education in one form or another was the religion of late nineteenth-century Americans. Harper and Coe shared in the leadership of that transformation. Their agendas matched the times. They were intellectual participants in the last decade of the nineteenth century, so succinctly described by Henry Steele Commager as a decade in which ''the new America came in as on flood tide.''[16] That sentiment was certainly true about the challenges and changes in the concerns of religious persons who were interested in education.

The Public's Education:
Secular and Sacred

By the turn of the century the general contours of American public education (schooling) were fairly well established. Horace Mann's common school reforms had become national practice. Schools were, for the most part, supported by local taxes, controlled by local school boards, and protected by state legislation which joined compulsory attendance to the ideal of free public schooling for all. The struggle for tax-supported religious schools had failed. American elementary schooling had become separated (technically) from ecclesiastical controls and placed firmly in the hands of the state and local community. Sectarian religious values might produce a brief experiment of Presbyterian schools, a modest Lutheran system of schools, or a major network of Catholic parochial schools, but the dominant mode of American education was public, nonsectarian (but generally Protestant), universal, free, and common for all Americans.

George Albert Coe correctly described American schooling at the turn of the century. In 1902 Coe published *The Religion of a Mature Mind,* an early sketch of his future strategy for religious education in the twentieth century. The book was eloquent in its praise of the sciences. It was a convincing argument for the positive value of modern science in behalf of mature religion. In a particularly insightful chapter, ''Salvation by Education,'' Coe was able to capture the mood and commitment of the progressive Christian educator of that period. Coe argued against the grain, in behalf of a synthesis of both the sacred and the secular. Coe wanted to collapse the dialectic between the sacred and secular and move toward a merging of the two categories which he viewed as complementary rather than antithetical.[17]

Coe rejoiced that schooling had "won freedom from ecclesiastical control." He was right. When late nineteenth-century Protestantism opted for public taxation, public local controls, and public access for all children to public supported schools, it gave up significant authority in determining the goals and religious values of the public schooling of American youngsters. Coe understood that compromise. "Modern education," Coe wrote, "is in a sense distinctly secular. It has become an institution of civil government."[18]

There were at least two possible responses to that new reality. Catholics and some Lutherans and a few Jews chose to build their own schools. John Lancaster Spalding, bishop of Peoria and an advocate of public schooling, had no argument with those developments. "Our theological differences make it impossible to introduce the teaching of any religious creed into the public school," he said. He went on, "I take the system as it is, that is, as a system of secular education."[19] Spalding did not count on public education to teach religion. Catholics would be responsible for the spiritual nurture of their own.

Missouri Synod Lutherans were more skeptical. As early as 1870 one district of that church body adopted formal resolutions regarding public schooling. The synod described public schools as agencies of "natural religion," as opposed to a religion which could point to the Gospel or other salvific revealed themes of the Scriptures. Public schools had, these Lutherans felt, an obligation to teach public morality. The resolutions encouraged the "reading of the Bible" in state schools, and urged Lutherans everywhere to "strive that the Bible is not banned from public schools." But the Lutherans were more negative in their assessment of the dangers of public schooling. Public schools sometimes instilled "spiritual poison," they stated, and textbooks often contained "the leaven of false doctrine." All these threats led the convention to encourage "orthodox congregations" to build their own parish schools.[20]

Coe's response was radically different from either Catholics or Lutherans. Secular education, according to Coe, was only secular when contrasting "the school of today with the church of yesterday." When compared with "progressive Christianity," the secularism of public education was to be encouraged rather than denigrated. Coe saw secularization as a virtue of the very same kind of attitude that "Jesus exhibits when, by living a human life, he shows us what God is.'' Coe accepted the secular evolution of American culture as the possibility ''that the Christian life is to be an incarnation, a realization of divine purpose, presence, and communion in our everyday occupations.'' Coe viewed public schooling as ''religious and secular.'' For Coe, all of life was naturally religious: ''Thus the field of the divine life in us is simply our life in its totality.''

Coe's theological bench mark was his view of ''divine immanence,'' the idea that God was to be met in all things, religious and secular. Indeed, Coe advocated that moral training was a necessary aspect of public schooling. He even speculated about the idea that true religion might one day be taught in public schools. ''Let this movement go a little further and who knows but that reverence toward God, as well as kindness to animals, goodwill toward men, will be inculcated in the schools.''

In language reminiscent of Paul Tillich's later theology, Coe posited the essence of God in the depths of human experience. He believed that ''the immanent God is the deepest fact of man's mind,'' and ''progress in the theory of mental development will sooner or later compel recognition of the religious phase as a necessary part of general education.''[21]

Until such a time, the church's task in religious education was to lead in the principles of the best of ''general pedagogy'' which were coexistent with ''religious nurture.''

> It (the church) proposes to utilize, in the interest of religion, the information that general psychology yields concerning the structure of the mind, the information that biology, physiology, and child study can garner with respect to the laws of child development and all the principles and methods that the history and philosophy of education have stamped with approval.[22]

Unquestionably the single most important formal nonfamilial religious nurturing agency for American Protestants in the last decade of the nineteenth century was the American Sunday School. The Sunday Schools had become ''the nursery of the church.''[23] And that agency hardly conformed to the modern scientific ideals of Coe's vision. The fascinating history of the American Sunday School has already been told in detail, and that story need not be retold here. Whatever else the Sunday School was, it became by the twentieth century primarily an agency of lay piety. Taught almost entirely by lay volunteers, it represented a parallel church institution to the public school. Sunday Schools were agencies of simple faith. Still unprofessionalized, they often appeared to intellectuals and trained clergy as misguided agencies of prescientific pedagogy and unsophisticated simplistic theology.[24]

The general curriculum of the late nineteenth-century Sunday School was almost entirely biblical. With the adoption of the "International Uniform" lessons (1872), the Sunday School chose a conservative Bible curriculum uncluttered by the innovations or interruptions of contemporary biblical scholarship, or the emerging new science of educational methods. The common curriculum of thousands of Protestant Sunday Schools formed a Sunday School ritualized creed similar to the routine liturgy of Catholics or high liturgical Protestants.

If the curriculum was dull, doctrinaire, and lifeless, the music of the Sunday School was not. During the 1880s and 1890s, Protestants incorporated countless happy "soft" faith songs for children. From "sunbeams to spirituals," the songs found their focus in simple biblical faith. The bottom line was clear. "Jesus loves me, this I know; for the Bible tells me so."[25]

Proud of its prescientific piety, suspicious of biblical criticism, Sunday Schools at the turn of the century were transitional agencies between the secure world of uncritical biblical certitude and the new world of modern science, professionalism, and progressive educational theory. Future conflict was inevitable.

Not all Protestants agreed, however, that the Sunday School was a lost cause. Coe and Harper represented a growing group of modern intellectuals who wished to reform the Sunday School while not losing the faith of the past. Those persons were involved in the formation of the R.E.A. Their options were alive to the new world, and their passion devoted to their religious convictions, that faith and modernity might join in the transformation of the American dream. How was one to nurture authentic Christian faith in the midst of a rapidly changing intellectual milieu? Was it possible to be faithful to the central tenets of Christian tradition and yet open to the possibilities of modern science? How could one transform the agencies of the past without threatening the constituents? The initial invitation to form some cooperative of interested persons into some new "national Bible school organization" contained all these crucial questions raised by the circumstances of the times. And though the immediate concern which gave rise to the formation of the R.E.A. was the inadequacy of the American Sunday School, the larger agenda of modernity lay behind the immediate Sunday School problem.

In the promotional material to form a new society, Harper clearly indicated that the precipitant issue was the fact that the International Sunday School Association "manifested an unwillingness to lead in the improvement of the Sunday School." But he went far beyond the narrow question of improvement of the Sunday Schools. The problem lay as well in the "divorcement of religious and moral instruction from the other branches of education," a separation that was "producing serious results."[26] Harper's colleague, Clyde Weber Votaw, followed Harper's letter with a second letter of encouragement. He noted at least three disciplines which offered hope for the future of "religious and moral instruction, education, psychology, and biblical studies."[27]

When that first R.E.A. convention finally met, none other than John Dewey, the father of progressive education, added his words of encouragement to the task. He called for a developmental view of the nature of faith in growing children. Using biblical language, Dewey appealed to his audience to consider these new paradigms of education as a "return to the idea of Jesus, of the successive stages through which the seed passes into the blade and then into ripened grain." He shared Harper's and Coe's vision. If this new organization would spend its energies on scientific research and its relationship to the nurturing process, then "it would mark the dawn of a new day in religious education."[28] The formation of the R.E.A. was a dramatic effort to ensure that first sunrise.

Notes for Chapter I

1. *The Biblical World,* Vol. III (Chicago: University of Chicago Press, 1894), "Editorial," p. 3, ed. William Rainey Harper.

2. William Rainey Harper, "The Scope and Purpose of the New Organization," *Proceedings of the First Annual Convention of the Religious Education Association* (Chicago: R.E.A. Office, 1903), pp. 237–238.

3. *The Biblical World,* Vol. II (Chicago: University of Chicago Press, 1893), "Editorial," p. 3, ed. William Rainey Harper.

4. *The Biblical World,* Vol. II, "Editorial," p. 86.

5. *The Biblical World,* Vol. V (Chicago: The University of Chicago Press, 1895), "Editorial," pp. 1–6, ed. William Rainey Harper.

6. Max Weber, *The Protestant Ethic and the Spirit of Capitalism,* trans. Talcott Parsons (New York: Charles Scribner & Sons, 1958, originally published in 1904), pp. 121ff.

7. *The Biblical World,* Vol. XVI (Chicago: The University of Chicago Press, 1900), "Editorial," pp. 243–247, ed. William Rainey Harper.

8. George A. Coe, *The Spiritual Life* (New York: Eaton & Mains, 1900), pp. 12–15.

9. Ibid., pp. 29–55.

10. Ibid., p. 61.

11. Ibid., p. 207. Coe's discussion of the "four temperaments" was part of the conventional wisdom of his age, but clearly reveals as well the historical limits of Coe's insights.

12. Ibid., pp. 236–243.

13. Harper's dedication to the sciences is vividly demonstrated by the choice of the faculty he assembled at the University of Chicago. He was able to "raid" major

universities for the best of their scholars. He decimated the new science faculty of Clark University, hiring no less than fifteen of George Stanley Hall's esteemed colleagues. For a more complete story of Harper's faculty choices see Richard J. Storr's *Harper's University, The Beginnings* (Chicago: The University of Chicago Press, 1966), pp. 65–86 and Thomas Wakefield Goodspeed's *A History of The University of Chicago* (Chicago: The University of Chicago Press, 1916), pp. 189–217.

14. William James, *The Varieties of Religious Experience, A Study in Human Nature* (New York: The New American Library, 1958, first published in 1902).

15. Ibid., p. 389.

16. Henry Steele Commager, *The American Mind,* as quoted in Lawrence A. Cremin's *The Transformation of the School, Progressivism in American Education, 1876–1957* (New York: Alfred A. Knopf, 1962), p. 90.

17. George A. Coe, *The Religion of A Mature Mind* (New York: Fleming H. Revell Co., 1902), pp. 47ff.

18. Ibid., p. 299.

19. John Lancaster Spalding, *Means and Ends of Education* (Chicago: A. C. McClurg & Co., 1895), p. 140. (One should note that Spalding's view was atypical among Catholic leadership.)

20. Missouri Synod, Lutheran Church, Western District, *Proceedings,* 1870, pp. 73–76. Cited in Carl S. Meyer's *Moving Frontiers* (St. Louis: Concordia Publishing House, 1964), pp. 210–212.

21. Coe, *The Religion of A Mature Mind,* pp. 298–304.

22. Ibid., p. 304.

23. Anne M. Boylan, "The Nursery of the Church: Evangelical Protestant Sunday Schools, 1820–1880" (Ph.D. dissertation, University of Wisconsin, 1973), p. 2.

24. See the recently reissued volume by Robert W. Lynn and Elliott Wright, *The Big Little School: 200 Years of the Sunday School* (Birmingham, Ala.: Religious Education Press and Abingdon, 1980); see also Robert Lynn, *Protestant Strategies in Education* (New York: Association Press, 1964) and William Bean Kennedy, *The Shaping of Protestant Education: An Interpretation of the Sunday School and the Development of Protestant Educational Strategy in the United States, 1789–1860* (New York: Association Press, 1966). See selected bibliography in Kennedy's book, pp. 91–93. Also Jack Seymour, *From Sunday School to Church School* (Washington D.C.: University Press of America Inc., 1982).

25. Lynn and Wright, *The Big Little School,* pp. 68–88. The earliest reference I have found to the song, "Jesus Loves Me," is in Theodore E. Perkins, Philip Phillips, and Sylvester Main, *Hallowed Songs* (New York: Carlton & Porter, 1865), p. 103. The song occurs regularly in most Sunday School hymnals by 1900.

26. Letter from William Rainey Harper to possible cosigners for an invitation to call for a national Bible school organization, October 3, 1902, (New Haven, Conn., Religious Education Association Files). Hereafter referred to as REAF.

27. Letter from C. W. Votaw to "the signies [sic] of the call," Nov. 14, 1902, REAF.

28. John Dewey, "Religious Education as Conditioned by Modern Psychology and Pedagogy," in *Proceedings of the First Annual Convention, The Religious Education Association* (Chicago: R.E.A. Office, 1903), pp. 62, 64.

Chapter II

Building the Democracy of God
1903–1923

> I use the term "democracy of God" in place of the "kingdom of God," not because I desire to substitute a new social principle for that which Jesus taught, but because the idea of democracy is essential to full appreciation of his teaching.[1]
>
> George Albert Coe, 1917

The principal architects of the Religious Education Association during the first twenty years of its existence were William Rainey Harper, George Albert Coe, and Henry Cope. The R.E.A. movement was a kindred spirit to the progressive education phenomenon, yet it remained distanced from public education by its specific Christian religious orientation. Postured in a prophetic style, that R.E.A. viewpoint is best understood as a religious commitment to a radical democratic pedagogy (a public paideia). The birthcord, "democratic Christianity," links Harper to Coe and Coe to Cope. Created in their image, the association grew bold, assertive, optimistic, critical, and self-righteous.

By 1923 the R.E.A. reached the end of its adolescence. The early cast of its formative years was to remain the essential mark of its character throughout its adult life. It would always remain bound, for good or ill, with the burden of religious democracy. It was not only an ideal of noble, human persuasion, but a specific kind of democratic viewpoint, a conviction that one's democratic ideals and values were of God. The task of building the "democracy of God" (the kingdom of God) was wholeheartedly assumed by the R.E.A. These early decades portray that incredible idealistic and sometimes arrogant pursuit.

William Rainey Harper:
A Man for a Season

William Rainey Harper was probably not a man for all seasons. His life was tragically short, ending as it did in 1906 when Harper was in the prime of life. He died at age forty-nine. By then there were symptoms of uneasiness among his most intimate circle of companions and in the most cherished institution of his professional career, the University of Chicago. Had Harper lived and continued his expansionistic policies, the university would surely have been in serious financial crisis. As it was, his death was followed by a period of retrenchment and conservative fiscal management which may indeed have saved Harper's historical image.[2]

But if Harper was not a man for all seasons, he was certainly a man for a season, his own special period of influence. Every ounce of his energy seemed perfectly matched for the times in which he worked. He was a living metaphor of those times. In retrospect it almost seemed as though there were a subconscious time clock ticking out his limits, as though he were racing against his own time and his own destiny.

Consider the chronology of his brief professional career. He completed the doctor of philosophy degree at Yale University in 1875 at the age of nineteen. That same year he became principal of Masonic College in Macon, Tennessee. In 1876 he served as tutor at Granville Academy. In 1879 he became professor of Hebrew at Morgan Park Seminary in Chicago where, by 1881, he had not only completed two years of teaching, but had earned the bachelor of divinity degree as well. He returned to Yale in 1886 to accept a position as professor of Hebrew languages, but not before he had founded the American Institute of Sacred Literature (A.I.S.L.). In addition to his regular duties at Yale, he lectured annually at Chautauqua and became director of the summer program there. In 1891 he became president of the future University of Chicago where he ended his career some fifteen years later. During his lifetime he published thirty-six books and more than sixty articles and essays.

He was thus a man for a season, a season when industry was a virtue and work a redeeming quality. He was a man for the times, endowed with a Baptist conscience, an industrialist's expansive outlook, and a work ethic which could serve to illustrate Max Weber's later contention that hard work and Calvinism were intimately related. Harper was the embodiment of that ethic.

His serious scholarship was committed to biblical and linguistic work. Author of several commentaries and study manuals of the Old

Testament, Harper remained a careful (conservative) craftsman of moderate, critical practices of the most acceptable scriptural scholarship of his time. His exegesis was based on solid linguistic and textual work. His conclusions were measured and careful.

Somehow, he was able to manage a satisfactory accommodation to scholarly apparatus and yet remain a servant of a conservative church body. He was attacked on a number of occasions for his biblical "liberalism" and in at least one instance faltered with self-doubt as he debated his own worthiness as a representative of the conservative Baptist tradition in relationship to the question of his potential leadership as future president of the proposed Baptist University of Chicago. Yet these self-criticisms appear to have been stations on the way toward a difficult decision, almost excuses for turning away from destiny. After he made his decision to accept the presidency of the university, his doubts appeared resolved until a final, more personal, crisis at the time of his approaching death.[3]

His hermeneutical style was subjective and faith-filled. He knew that one's viewpoint of Scripture determined how one saw, read, and heard. He approached the Bible as a believing Christian and never seemed shaken by new critical insights. He put aside any personal doubts and questions and held them secondary to the pursuit of truth. He was a modern in every sense of that term as he used all the scientific tools available, not to threaten or intimidate the faithful, but to serve as a serious negotiator between modernity and the faithful tradition.

In a small incident recorded in a letter to a Mr. Fraser (a lay person in Alberta, Canada), Harper reveals both his exegetical principle and pastoral concern. His letter is obviously written in response to a crisis in personal faith for some unlettered, anxious Christian. Harper indicated that he was always happy to respond to an inquiring mind. In general, he assured the farmer that the Old Testament records were truthful and indeed established by modern scholarship. There were, however, instances where the Old Testament was at "variance" with reliable information derived from other sources. He counseled his friend that these difficulties ought not trouble him, for the Scriptures were never meant to be modern historical accounts. Harper noted that the main purpose of the Old Testament was to sketch the development of the religion or theology of Israel throughout its long history. Facts were not of themselves valuable, but served rather to point to the religious values which served for the "edification of the nation." In a homey analogy, Harper compared the Old Testament Scriptures to a contemporary preacher. The sermon might contain scientific inaccuracies, even mistakes, "from the point of view of a man who is well posted in science," yet the truth of the homily remains the religious message the preacher is conveying. "In this same way the vital truth of the Old Testament stands even if many dates and figures were to be shown to be inaccurate." Harper ends the letter by encouraging the farmer to continue his reading and makes suggestions for reading material. He wishes him "success in your efforts to know the truth and live up to it."[4]

Harper's careful scholarship and popularization of Old Testament research is widely acknowledged. He founded the *Biblical World,* a journal for biblical research. He formed the American Institute for Sacred Literature, an early American correspondence-school form of popular higher education for adults, and he later consolidated the A.I.S.L. leadership into a "Council of Seventy," a support group of elite biblical researchers from across the United States, to continue that effort. Harper was able to recruit the most able minds in support of his pursuits. The membership list of the "Council of Seventy" reads like a Who's Who list of biblical experts of the period. Old Testament scholars, Charles R. Brown, Augustus Carrier, Owen Gates, Charles Kent, Frank Sanders, and Herbert Willett joined New Testament biblical experts like Edward Bosworth, Ernest Burton, Doremis Hayes, James Riggs, William Stevens, and George Goodspeed, in addition to a host of other significant academics sharing in a common goal, to support modern biblical scholarship.

Harper served as one of the nation's celebrated lecturers in his capacity as Bible instructor at Chautauqua and elsewhere in the liberal Protestant world. His style was modest, prosaic, and even pedantic. Yet the thoroughness of his method and the exactness of his content served his students and hearers well. He was a popular teacher and lecturer, even though his manner and style was staid and sometimes dull.[5]

But Harper's unique pedagogical charisma sprang from his desire to extend intellectual matters to common persons, to the unlettered public. He was the progressive personified if one accepts Lawrence Cremin's cryptic definition of progressive as "the radical faith that culture can be democratized without being vulgarized."[6] He would popularize the study of Hebrew among hundreds of Americans, an unlikely prospect at best. By 1895 his adult education program, A.I.S.L., enrolled more than 8000 persons in the correspondence study of Scripture, summer school, and extension services. Through the efforts of the A.I.S.L., Harper promoted summer school, not only as an educational innovation, but as an effective use of free time for lay persons who would study Hebrew and related biblical subjects. Here was democratization with a radical twist. Harper believed and practiced his ideal to educate an entire mass culture with integrity and lack of compromise. There were no prerequisites except for the keen desire to learn and the agreement to practice rigid discipline of time and energy. Students had to devote total energy to the language, putting aside all outside interests and diversions.[7]

Harper's vision for the university included such progressive insight. What was really new about the University of Chicago was that democratized value. Other universities had pioneered in graduate education. Johns Hopkins was well established before Harper's "great university" was even an idea in his mind. Other universities accented research, some provided extension services, still others had experimented with quarter systems and summer schools.

But Harper's vision went beyond these existing patterns. He proposed a regular summer school session, an effort to utilize learning styles that he knew a great deal about through his contact with Chautauqua and his earlier summer schools. He sought to initiate an extension service from the beginning of the university and managed to transfer all the work of the independent A.I.S.L. to the university by 1905. He even tried to incorporate the Chautauqua Reading Circle as part of the extension department. His proposal for a University Press was not a new idea. Yet what that press became in terms of publishing materials for popular consumption was a new idea. Harper's publishing company translated the highest knowledge to the most common person. In cooperation with the divinity school Harper organized the publication of a sophisticated series of religious books for Sunday Schools and church schools for that period. The *Constructive Bible Studies* series remains the best testimony to the accomplishment of the ideal that scientific research and Christian faith could be usefully joined in the nurturing process of the young. And these publications for Sunday School were produced by the University Press, a clear instance of Harper's progressive spirit.

There was no special educational creativity about the texts; rather they provided discriminate use of biblical research to assist young Christians in the pursuit of a valid faith for the twentieth century. Harper's biblical colleagues did not surrender to the social sciences but used all the useful insights of the new sciences in the study of biblical writings. The series is a tribute to the creative use of the university in behalf of popular public education. It served to illustrate Harper's key idea that the university was a service institution for the larger culture, and, in this case, the Christian faith.

Following a well-established principle of American higher education, Harper used theological metaphor to depict the task of the university.[8] When he wrote of the mission of the university, he used the threefold categories of Old Testament literature: prophetic, priestly, and sage or wisdom literature. He had no difficulty identifying the university as prophet, priest, and sage. The university was prophet in behalf of democratic idealism, called to speak out against social abuses and in behalf of justice. As priest, the university served as mediator between persons and individual interests separating social groups. As sage, the university exercised its major task of verification or seeking truth. The University of Chicago's role was defined in behalf of these noble, scriptural ideals. The university should serve as guardian and advocate the democratic, religious principles—the university was Messiah!

One can question whether Harper's university achieved those ideals. Many of the critics of his day felt it did not. One can also raise specific questions about Harper's handling of academic freedom and the relationship of Harper's actions to his democratic rhetoric.[9] But it is my belief that, in general, Harper did sustain those high biblical self-chosen values. His rhetoric may have been awkward, enthusiastic, and sometimes exalted. His actions, however, were a constant second witness. Harper's extension school, his University Press, his A.I.S.L., his Sunday School teaching at Hyde Park Baptist Church, and his intense work with Chautauqua all underlined his democratic spirit, evangelical to a fault. He was a man living out a vision of a religious democracy.

His most careful expressions about the university's mission occur in an essay titled "The University and Democracy," written in 1899. One reads a mature and seasoned academic warrior at the height of his career, still eloquent in his defense of the university and its role in American life. He wrote:

> It is the university that, as the center of thought, is to maintain for democracy the unity so essential for its success. The university is the prophetic school out of which come the teachers who are to lead democracy in the true path. It is the university that fights the battles of democracy, its war cry being: "Come let us reason together." It is the university that in these latter days goes forth with buoyant spirit to comfort and give help to those who are downcast, taking up its dwelling in the very midst of squalor and distress. It is the university that, with impartial judgment, condemns in democracy the spirit of corruption which now and again lifts up the head and brings scandal upon democracy's fair name.[10]

Harper's enthusiasm was both catching and caricatured. The university was referred to as "Harper's Bazaar." Walter Metzger wrote of Harper's university and called it "Rockefeller's Eden in Chicago," and Lawrence Veysey commented cryptically on Harper's giftedness though lack of intellectual maturity: "Here surely was charisma without ideology.'' I disagree with Veysey and view Harper as the absolute ideologue. His writing, research, administrative style, personal life, and consistent actions embody the democratic ideal, perhaps with messianic overtones, but certainly never without cause and vision.[11]

Harper's democratic ideology was best articulated in a series of essays contained in *The Trend in Higher Education in America,* published in 1905, and in a compilation of student addresses, *Religion and the Higher Life* (1904). Both books, written near the end of his life, poignantly summarize a lifelong ideal, that democracy represented a high expression of the truest religious experience.

Illustrative of that value and representative of Harper's broad educational perspective was an essay written about the relationship of the seminary to the larger society. Entitled ''Civic Relationship of Seminary,'' it appealed to the metaphor of baptism as symbolic of the new life necessary for the seminary. ''The seminaries must receive a new baptism, this time a baptism of the spirit of democracy which I make bold to say is one expression of the Holy Spirit itself.''[12] The entire curriculum of the seminary was to be democratized.

In another significant essay (possibly the best theological curriculum reform piece of that period), ''Shall the Theological Curriculum Be Modified and How?'' Harper revealed the transforming role of his democratic spirit-filled ideal in America. He noted the narrowness of the seminary curriculum. He criticized the current seminary practices with candor:

1. Present seminary education highlighted preaching but was too narrowly defined for other ministries.
2. Seminary education tended to promote a ''narrow and exclusive spirit.''
3. Seminaries allowed preaching too early in the seminary experience.
4. Financial (paternal) support of ministerial students produced students who revealed an ''utter lack of independence.'' These would be antithetical to the democratic spirit.[13]

Specific curricular weaknesses were revealed:

1. Too little science was taught in the seminary curriculum. (This was a recurring theme with Harper.)
2. No instruction in modern psychology was offered. (Harper's appeal here is parallel to the same concern that initiated the R.E.A.)
3. Bible teaching was not thorough. It often accented language competence rather than knowledge of biblical content and history.
4. The compulsory teaching of Hebrew tended to prove ''wasteful, inju-

rious, and in most cases distasteful.'' (This criticism, in light of Harper's own specialty, is reflective of his genuine objectivity about his perception of needs and goals.)

5. English literature was lacking in seminary education. (Harper believed literature to be pregnant with theological insight.)

6. The English language requirements were inadequate and related directly to poor preaching and ministerial ineptitude.[14]

Harper's correctives were new in seminary theory. They were innovative yet conservative in their democratic intent. What Harper proposed would tend to individualize the seminary curriculum. Scholarly students would pursue languages, whereas others training for congregational work would receive fewer language requirements and more opportunity to ''cultivate the talent with which he has been endowed.''[15] Harper called for multiple ministries, redefining the ministry to include options such as teaching, administration, college academic careers, music, and medical missionary work. Harper advocated a broad definition of the word ''ministry'' and encouraged specialization in the profession similar to other related professions: medicine, law, or teaching.[16]

President Harper was not one to turn away from problems. His messianic vision of the university as prophet, priest, and sage served his entire life as a vision for problem solving.[17] The university would function in the educational enterprise and the entire culture as God's instrument of salvation. The redemption which Harper had in mind was a transformation of America into the ideal religious democracy.

Harper's usual staid prose (Goodspeed believed that Harper was incapable of rhetoric) extended beyond limits when he wrote of such dreams. In rare moments of literary excess, Harper's vision was clearly and distinctively Christian. He sounded almost Baptist, and though he did not refer to specific Christological categories often, he did finally rest his theology of democracy in the Christ event, in the historical story of Jesus. In one revealing excerpt, Harper wrote: ''In Christ the Son we are accustomed to say, and we believe, that God the Father revealed himself. But it is also true that in him for the first time ideal man and ideal humanity were revealed, and that discovery . . . is only gradually coming to us in these centuries of Christian progress.''[18]

One can hardly miss the optimism as well as the possibility. Such a vision of Jesus as the ideal human expression of God's creation led even Harper to overstatement. As democracy took hold of a people, as it purified a culture by the specific freedom of education, intelligence would nurture culture and America would become the setting of the new age of God's democratic revelation. Democracy, science, and education would join the historic promise of Christianity in purifying a people into the "righteous empire."

Democracy itself had little to do with religion as the practice of dogma or ecclesiastical practices. It rather had to do with the "undisturbed exercise of religious liberty." Where education has done its work, there religious life can be lived in freedom and righteousness. The great civilizations of Babylon, Syria, and Great Britain were dead or dying, but according to Harper the new promise of God's blessings and revelations rested with America, specifically because of the blessings of democracy and the exercise of modern science.[19]

Such a vision was broader than the hallowed halls of the university. Harper's dream went beyond the agencies of formal schooling. Harper's view of the educational community included a vast panorama of agencies, institutions, and cultural influences. He conceived of education as the collection of social services and events that form a people. He included the family, church, school, marketplace, newspapers, and libraries in his educational ecology.[20] His university was but the peak of a large pyramid of educational influences.

Harper extended his own educational service in characteristic fashion. As chairman of the Chicago School Commission, he influenced future years of public education in that city. The committee recommendations were not accepted until years later, but there is little doubt that the essential nonpolitical emphasis of the report was a far cry from the usual educational policy and practice in Chicago public school matters.[21]

So it was entirely in character that Harper became the active catalyst in the formation of the R.E.A. It is my opinion that had he lived the R.E.A. might have been tied organically to the university and become a popular extension program of the university, for the idea and the function was so in keeping with his vision of the service of the university to the larger society.

Founding of the Religious Education Association

Morton G. White, in his insightful study of modernity, *Social Thought in America: The Revolt Against Formalism,* noted that the early American liberal was "haunted by a fear of being remote." In describing William James and John Dewey, White wrote: "Dewey, like James before him, wanted to drag the loftiest of all disciplines down to earth."[22] Such a comment vividly described Harper's efforts to popularize Bible study, religion, science, and the pursuit of the democratic ideal. The genesis of the R.E.A. is firmly grounded in such a democratic tradition.

The R.E.A. was an intimate part of Harper's popularization effort. It grew naturally out of his concern for making scholarly biblical research available to the common person, especially to Sunday School teachers. It was a natural companion agency to Chautauqua, and it expanded Harper's preachments to a new constituency, to those interested in the educational activity of the church. The R.E.A., or some similar institution, was in the mind of Harper at least ten years before he was able to sell the idea to the council of the A.I.S.L. Harper was not to be discouraged—his dream did not die. It waited for the opportunity. That opportunity would grow out of conflicts over curriculum concerns for the American Sunday School movement. Those issues evolved in the last quarter of the nineteenth century, between the leadership of the International Sunday School Association and Harper's A.I.S.L. Council of Seventy.

The International Sunday School Association (I.S.S.A.) decided in 1872 to adopt the principle of uniform lessons. The notion that a single lesson should be taught at all age levels across the country was powerful enough to last more than five decades as the prevailing Protestant curricular ideal for American Sunday Schools.

Two decades later, Harper initiated a letter, dated November 3, 1893, to leading Sunday School people across the country. In this letter he proposed adoption of a modified "Blakeslee" series (a new, graded biblical Sunday School series). Harper urged the formation of a new committee called the "American Bible School Committee," appointed by the A.I.S.L. After considerable discussion among the A.I.S.L. leadership, Harper's suggestion was dropped and the matter of Sunday School concerns moved, for the moment, to the background of the association.[23]

In February of 1894 the Sunday School issues again surfaced at A.I.S.L. meetings. This time the International Sunday School Association (I.S.S.A.) Committee invited the institute to send representation to Philadelphia in March to present suggestions to the International Committee. The institute responded by sending Frank Sanders (Harper's aide-de-camp) to represent its position to the committee. In Harper's words, he was instructed to advocate "the planning of a system of lessons such that the pupil who pursued it will gain a comprehensive and connected knowledge of biblical teaching and history."[24]

The institute's position was clear. Biblical material was to be taught sequentially and chronologically. Related historical material was to be part of that teaching. Though there was no specific mention of "graded" lessons, materials were suggested that would be designed for advanced classes. Furthermore, the institute suggested that the International Committee appoint an advisory committee consisting of specialists in Old and New Testament studies. The I.S.S.A. committee rejected the recommendation and proceeded to continue the unified lesson pattern with little modification.

In 1897 the matter was again raised by the Council of Seventy. This time Harper had additional support. The last agenda item taken up by the council was the matter of the Sunday School. How could the A.I.S.L. aid the Sunday School? Harper was supported by his colleague Ernest E. Burton, who advocated graded courses and special training for Sunday School teachers. The council invited Rev. W. F. McMillan of the Congregational Sunday School and Publishing Society, to report to the council. He lobbied for the "home study department," a strategy for in-service education for teachers. Finally, the president of the council was authorized to appoint a committee to analyze the current Sunday School material. They were instructed to report at the next meeting.[25]

Though the committee did report to the Council of Seventy in 1898, little attention was given to the matter again until the summer of 1902. Then the council senate sent an invitation to members to consider "the advisability of undertaking at this time a new movement toward an improved Sunday School curriculum for America."[26] That meeting could hardly be called the beginning of a grand movement. Seven members attended and only three were senate members, not enough for a quorum.

The next meeting was held October 13, 1902. Sixteen members were present; obviously interest was revitalized. In the absence of President Barrows, who had died in June, Harper chaired the meeting. He presented the results of his first promotional letter, and in a spirit of unified support the senate decided to form a new organization. Again one saw Harper turning a near defeat (apathy in the council and the A.I.S.L.) into a new and larger vision. Harper risked his overextended energy in behalf of his lifelong goal, the building of a religious democracy to transform society.[27]

Harper's concerns and priorities were articulated in the official "Call for a Convention to Effect a National Organization for the Improvement of Religious and Moral Education Through the Sunday School and Other Agencies." That document listed four reasons for the formation of an association which became the R.E.A. First, the "call" noted that the present practices in religious and moral instruction were inadequate and not correlated with "other instruction in history, literature, and the sciences." Second, the Sunday School was in need of serious revision. Graded lessons were needed which would sequence the material to the "stages of the mental, moral, and spiritual growth of the individual." Third, the other agencies of religious education, the home, the day school, and other agencies of education all needed assistance in the "right education" (current modern methods and recent psychological insights and materials which were based upon the new sciences and biblical scholarship). Fourth, all these improvements could best be achieved with the support of a national organization which would be aimed single-mindedly to this purpose. The call sought to institutionalize concerns for biblical scholarship, the new sciences and new educational insights both in learning theory and developmental tasks. Here was a broad-based concern for the religious and moral education of all persons in many agencies.[28]

The first draft of that call was mailed "confidentially" to selected leaders across the country soliciting their support as cosigners. Harper's flair for public relations was evident, and he had waited too long for this moment to risk failure. He would make every effort to generate excitement and anticipation in order to secure general support for his movement. He was successful. His first response was signed by more than two hundred persons. The following is a small sample of the colleagues Harper solicited: Charles R. Brown, Newton Theological Institute; Thomas C. Hall, Union Theological Seminary; Henry Churchill King, Oberlin College; E. C. Moore, Harvard Divinity School; E. D. Starbuck, Stanford University; L. Wilbur, General Secretary of the Chicago YMCA; E. J. Jones, Northwestern University; Francis Brown, Union Theological Seminary; George Albert Coe, Northwestern University; Sam Dutton, Teachers College, Columbia University; F. M. McMurray, Teachers College, Columbia University; J. B. Angell, University of Michigan; Charles A. Young, *Christian Century;* Nicholas M. Butler, Columbia University; Andrew Draper, University of Illinois; Charles Hall, Union Theological Seminary; G. Stanley Hall, Clark University.[29]

"Movement" was the best way to describe this time and this effort,[30] and "call" was the correct word for the vision. Here was an opportunity to respond to destiny, to a divine call to change the moral and religious climate of an entire nation. This vision required an organizational structure vast and complex enough to enfold the movement. The model was taken from the structure of the National Education Association. The Council of Seventy patterned the R.E.A. after the N.E.A. so that the "new organization might consist of a large and indeed practically unlimited number of persons engaged in all kinds of religious and moral education.''[31] Though there are no data to indicate any major joint policy, the concerns and interests of the two organizations often coincided. However, the R.E.A. was never able to recruit a large number of public school persons, even though a great deal of public school concern was exercised by the early R.E.A.[32]

Evidence indicated that the Council of Seventy cautiously sought a middle path to solicit the largest national support and alienate the fewest possible members. The ''Official Documents #1 and #2'' went to great lengths to explain that this new movement was not in opposition to previous religious education efforts. The appeal went to all agencies of religious nurture, and a special invitation was extended to the membership of the Y.M.C.A. and the International Sunday School Association. Invitations were mailed to the churches of many Protestant denominations, to Sunday School teachers, and to university and college leaders. There was to be a ''comprehensive scope'' to the organization. The initial fourteen areas of interest (each was to become a section of the R.E.A.) were so inclusive that no one could claim any sort of provincialism. Suggested areas included:

1) Universities and colleges	8) Sunday Schools
2) Theological seminaries	9) Young peoples' societies
3) Secondary public schools	10) Home
4) Elementary public schools	11) Libraries
5) Private schools	12) The press
6) Teacher training	13) Art and music
7) Churches and pastors	14) Y.M.C.A. and Y.W.C.A.[33]

There was no evidence in the formation of the movement that it planned to serve a broad ecumenical purpose except among Protestants. All of the signers were mainline Protestants. One cannot prove on the basis of the present data that any Catholic or Jew (two were listed as members)[34] was in attendance at that first convention in February (1903). (However, by 1904 one Catholic and six Jewish members are listed as members of the R.E.A.) The Council of Seventy remained entirely Protestant throughout its history, even though there was an invitation to Bishop Spalding to explore his interest in joining the group. Apparently he declined the invitation, since his name does not appear in any of the records as a member.[35]

Clearly any Jewish representation would have conflicted with the avowed Christian perspective of the proposed organization. The council's specifically Christian intent was the vision of its leader, Harper, as well as its own. In its invitation summary, the council wrote: ''It is a normal, timely, and vital step in the development of our Christian civilization.''[36] The young R.E.A. was Protestant liberal Christian!

So it was that in February of 1903 the first convention of the ''National Organization for the Improvement of Religious and Moral Education Through the Sunday School and Other Agencies'' met to form what would later become the R.E.A. Registrations numbered 407. They came from twenty-three states and Canada and represented forty university and college presidents, as well as pastors, Sunday School teachers, and youth directors. The opening session was crowded with an attendance of over 3000. The largest representation included pastors, followed by university personnel. In its origin the R.E.A. represented the highest levels of responsible, liberal American Protestant leadership.

President James Angell of Michigan presided at the opening ceremonies. Frank Knight Sanders was elected president. Addresses were given by Coe, Dewey, Stewart, Sanders, Mathews, and Harper, in the absence of scheduled speaker Nicholas Murray Butler. The days of the convention were filled with dreams and progressive rhetoric, all preserved in the 422 pages of proceedings.

The association published twelve pages of newspaper reports, two of which catch the flavor of those enthusiastic days. The *Christian Century* wrote in praise of the meeting. The *Century* called the meeting ''one of the greatest and most significant religious conventions of modern times.'' The journal went on to commend the convention and paid the R.E.A. a well-earned compliment. ''The whole convention was characterized by a constructive conservatism.''[37] The *Century* had captured the image that the association had sought to project; progressive, yet conservative about values and objectives.

The Boston Evening Transcript was even more lavish in its praise. It noted that the convention was successful beyond the dreams of the planners. Specifically, the meeting did not lead to ''the expected antagonism to the International System of Sunday School Lessons.'' The R.E.A. did not plan on publishing any courses or authorizing any new Sunday School materials. Rather, *The Transcript* reported that the R.E.A. would not duplicate any other agencies of religious education, nor trespass into their established fields of responsibility. The report ended with good wishes. ''Success then to the R.E.A.''[38] The R.E.A. steered clear of narrow parochial concerns and by such discretion was able, initially, to garner broad support.

Harper's vision materialized. And he might have felt deep contentment as he read the *Proceedings* of that first convention. His view was shared; there were companions, qualified and compatible. The future was in good hands. Future leadership had emerged, for one cannot read

Coe's convention essay, "Religious Education as a Part of General Education," without sensing his unity of vision with Harper. Harper did not know in those heady days of February that this convention would be the first and last that he would attend. He did not know of his impending death. Nor could he have known that the man who envisioned the dream with him would become the single most important mentor of the religious education movement.

Coe's address to that first R.E.A. convention contained most of the major motifs of his later social theory of religious education. Coe believed that education was ethical because "the child's nature is ethical." Christian education is Christian because we are created "in his own image and likeness." Coe agreed with the early church father (he did not identify the source) who wrote: "The soul is naturally Christian." According to Coe, God does not engage the child outside the experience of daily life. Coe held no transcendent viewpoint unrelated to the earthiness of human exchange. Religion matures from within, "in the normal unfolding of a child's soul." Religion was the natural arena of daily life. The "spirit of religion must be infused into the whole educational organism." Public education, according to Coe, had separated itself from religion as "from the vine of which it is a branch." Finally, Coe sought a unified approach to education. He envisioned the church, the home, and the public school as intimate partners in the educational enterprise. Coe wrote: "We must never regard either the home or church as normally successful until it is no longer the exception but the rule for children to grow up Christian and never to know themselves as being otherwise."[39] (Coe used Horace Bushnell's cryptic phrase as his own.)

George Albert Coe:
Mentor of a Movement

Although Harper was never able to attend another R.E.A. convention, his influence on the R.E.A. extended until the time of his death and beyond. By 1904 he knew his health was in serious trouble. Just days before his first exploratory surgery, Harper wrote to Frank Sanders, president of the R.E.A., and mentioned his concern for the future of the organization. Harper's appeal was meant to give direction to the organization for another year, and though Harper's great vision was that of a Christian democracy, his personal style of leadership sometimes bordered on authoritarian. Not only did he suggest a successor to Sanders, but he also outlined a strategy to assure his election. His method, of necessity, hardly matched his democratic idealism. Harper wrote: "The important thing I wish to say is that Charles Cuthbert Hall (president of the Union Theological Seminary, New York) is the man of all men for the presidency next year. Please do not allow him to say no. Appoint your committee on nominations with this one thing in mind and pledge the chairman of the committee beforehand so that there can be no question."[40]

A year later when Harper's condition had deteriorated considerably and his "execution" (Harper's metaphor) by cancer was certain, he wrote a second letter in behalf of the future of the R.E.A. This letter was not about a single-year presidency, but was a kind of commission for life. Harper was not to leave destiny to chance. In a brief letter to Coe, thanking him for his support and help, and revealing that he knew his future was limited, he ended a letter of appreciation with this prophetic sentence: "Hoping that you will stand by the R.E.A. to death, I remain. . . ."[41]

In those few words Harper passed the mantle of leadership on to Coe. His wish and trust was not to be broken. Coe continued throughout his life to be the dominant intellectual influence on the R.E.A. until his own death some forty years later. Harper's vision was in safekeeping; Coe would assure continuity of purpose and ideals.

Forty years later, writing as honorary president of the R.E.A., Coe was able to reflect on that continuity of ideal. His remarks were instructive: "I think of the Association, first of all, as a religious fellowship. . . . These were strong men and women, resolutely responding to what they believed to be a call from on high. . . . The religious education movement . . . has been working all along upon the central issue of the present moment—the issue of democracy."[42]

Coe's intellectual leadership in the R.E.A. movement was an earned position. He dominated the religious education world until his retirement, and even then he continued to write. His relationship to the R.E.A. was that of prophet as he challenged the organization to be true to the ideals of its formation.

Coe's theology was always left of mainline Christian Protestantism, but never without continuity. In 1897 he wrote an essay on religious experience and the scientific movement. He appealed for an end to science and religion debates, articulating his position that Christian faith is faith in Jesus and that such Christological commitment was not antithetical to science. "Jesus, himself, enters scientific theology through the door of experience."[43]

That style of Christianity was woven throughout his writings. More than thirty years later, Coe wrote his popular book, *What Is Christian*

Education? and though it was true that Christology had become less important in his thought the key argument of that book was consistent with his earlier view. Christian education was the experience of Jesus incarnate in others or it was not Christian at all. Coe's Christology moved from the historical Jesus to the incarnate experience of Jesus in the life of all Christians. His classic definition of Christian education summarized that point: "It is the systematic, critical examination and reconstruction of relations between persons, guided by Jesus' assumption that persons are of infinite worth, and by the hypothesis of the existence of God, the great Valuer of Persons."[44] Unless there were living epistles there could be no living Christology.

Coe's major theoretical positions related to religious education were contained in his most significant book, *A Social Theory of Religious Education*, published in 1917. The argument of that book was the logical consequence of his core persuasion that Christianity was learned in experience or it was not valid. Coe asserted that religious education was a social phenomenon. He had a social view of sin and a social view of redemption. The key theological idea was incarnational.[45] Healing, hope, growth, and Christian life all happen in the presence of incarnational love. The death/resurrection experience was not one of story, but of lived reality.[46] Coe saw more clearly than did individualistic Protestantism that the genesis of sin was both genetic and social. He understood the struggle and demonic force of social sin; the need for conversion was not merely personal, but essentially social. The cure of the sinful condition was social correction, so that habits, rituals, and selfish instincts were not reinforced but corrected.[47] Coe's treatise on social theories of religious education finally concluded that "the educator in all education is society."[48] If there was to be a future, that future rested in the transformation of society into what Coe coined as "the democracy of God."[49]

Coe understood the social problems of his day and remained a radical social critic throughout his career. His criticism of social structures developed during the first World War, and it is to his credit that such a critique continued after 1920 and into the 1940s. There would be no accommodation to neo-orthodoxy. His prophetic word would be in behalf of a purified democratic ideal, experientially verifiable.

In 1924 Coe wrote about the "sickness of society," and he was most direct in his criticism of capitalism as an economic system and as the extension of a corrupt industrial system.[50] One might conclude that Coe veered toward socialism. I believe that his criticism continued to represent a radical democratic viewpoint.[51]

In summary, Coe's "democracy of God" ideal was about a cultural transformation. He may be accused of elevated democratic idealism. On occasion that criticism is just. He may be faulted for being too visionary. But in balance, it is remarkable to note his profound, consistent faith in the transforming power of society by the democratic spirit, a spirit which he interpreted as the highest expression of Christian faith. The spirit was none other than the spirit of Jesus (a most conservative viewpoint).

Coe cannot be accused of being visionary and deluded on the issue of evil. He understood evil and its social implications better than did his progressive education companions. His genius, I believe, was the ability to use the democratic tradition to criticize the practice of democracy in real life. His "democracy of God" operated as an ideal by which to measure present practice and hold hope for the future.

The R.E.A. embodied his closest supporters. They institutionalized his beliefs. He never forgot their support and common loyalty. Writing in 1944, he paid tribute to that intimate relationship: "To me it seems that the only unqualifiedly religious way to deal with religion in the public schools or anywhere else is the unafraid democratic way. Toward this position I think the R.E.A. slowly and hesitantly has been tending."[52]

Henry Cope:
The Rhetoric of a "Holy Crusade"

If George Albert Coe was the intellectual mentor and Harper the founding patriarch of the religious education movement, then Henry Cope was surely the leader of the volunteer trained and untrained recruits in the army of new religious educators. While lacking the academic sophistication and disciplined thoughtfulness of Coe and Harper, Cope managed to compensate with boundless energy, dedication to the cause, and dogged hard work.

Cope was not really chosen for the job of executive secretary of the R.E.A.; he volunteered for the position. He made himself invaluable in the daily operation of the organization. He first came to Chicago to accept employment with a publishing company, but ended up procuring a position as secretary to the president of the Chicago telephone company. He attended the first R.E.A. convention and was a charter member. The R.E.A. tried twice to hire an executive secretary. After two years of unfortunate administrative leadership and two resignations of national secretaries, Cope accepted the position of assistant secretary until a more suitable man of "national reputation" could be found. By

1907 the R.E.A. gave up on that search and appointed Cope as general secretary, a position he held until his death in 1923.[53] He was well suited for his managerial position, as Coe would note in words of gratitude after Cope's death. Coe caught the essence of his leadership: "He fitted his job, he fitted us; he fitted the times and emergencies that they brought."[54]

Emergencies were not uncommon to the fledgling R.E.A. The most serious initial emergency was the matter of finances. Before his death Harper had tried valiantly to eradicate the indebtedness of the organization. His last efforts related to the R.E.A. were devoted to raising funds to match the movement's expenditures. Harper's vision always surpassed his realistic fiscal planning, and the R.E.A. was no exception to that rule. What Harper had plotted on paper had become an expensive reality.[55]

After one year in office, Dr. Ira Landrith resigned his office as general secretary of R.E.A. because of inadequate finances. A second general secretary, Clifford W. Barnes, resigned a year later for the same reason. When Cope took office as interim secretary, in 1906, the organization was almost $8000 in debt. Cope reduced this to $3449 by 1907.[56] In 1909 the indebtedness was completely erased, and by 1912 Cope was able to report a balanced budget with a surplus of $66. Cope often tried to move toward a fiscally responsible position, encouraging new membership and advocating the necessity of ongoing endowment.[57] He was never successful in accumulating any significant surplus and died without securing a strong financial structure for the organization. The fault lay in the board rather than in his own planning and leadership. The organization simply allowed one person to expend himself in its behalf without reasonable compensation. Cope never received the fiscal support he requested and needed.[58]

The larger, ongoing emergency was one of inadequate staff and difficult administrative structure. Cope was responsible for all administrative detail. In addition to editing the journal, planning conventions, recruiting for new chapters, and handling public relations, he represented the organization at conferences and national conventions. His annual reports (published in *Religious Education*) reflect an incredible amount of office work and travel responsibility.

In his first year of service Cope traveled over 11,000 miles in behalf of the R.E.A. In his fifteenth annual report to the convention, he indicated that he had delivered more than 233 public addresses in the past year, and traveled more than 52,000 miles; his office had processed more than 227,000 pieces of material, answered more than 10,000 letters, and had been in contact with over 200,000 persons during the course of the year.[59] Such involvement could only be called a crusade.

Cope once complained that some people thought of the R.E.A. as a "one person organization." As one reads the annual reports of his work, it is easy to see how that impression was created. He became the symbol and living metaphor of the R.E.A. The compliments paid to Cope in memorial were earned expressions of gratitude and corporate guilt. The organization had profited from his unusual dedication and expressed its debt after his death more eloquently than before.[60] One could hardly criticize Cope for his industry, dedicated loyalty, managerial effectiveness, administrative competence, and overall excellent service to the R.E.A.

On the other hand, when one turns to Cope's intellectual leadership a different judgment is necessary. Cope's popularization and translation of the ideal were sometimes unworthy of the tradition. Cope acknowledged his debt to Dewey and Coe. Most of Cope's more than fifteen books have many references to Coe's work. His imaging of his mentor was sometimes blurry and skewed, and his writing often went beyond the bounds of Coe's usual, careful prose. Cope wrote: "(The Sunday School) . . . does exist in the highest sense to save the world through the children, to save the world from sectional hatred, to save it from feud, from suicidal rivalries, from selfishness that breeds conflict, from low aims, from the loss of its soul."[61] His rhetoric knew no limits: "We are saved by our shortcomings and our struggles. From Valley Forge to the Panama Canal is one eloquent chapter of splendid moral achievement under the curriculum of a nation's birth throes."[62]

Cope was also the master of cliche. He wrote: "working with God is the only way of walking with God." "Helpfulness is half of happiness." "Inspiration ought to lead to perspiration." "Do not try to mend a watch with a steam shovel." Throughout his books, articles, and reports to the R.E.A., one finds repeated instances of this folksy habit.

Cope's democratic values sometimes appeared inconsistent, even in his own writing. This tendency to advocate a democratic process, yet illustrate with one's own prose a different value, is characteristic of a blind spot in Cope's thinking. In several of his books, one gains the impression that he had a deep concern for the religious nurture of boys. His concern rarely extended to the education of girls. The most obvious instance occurs in *Efficiency in the Sunday School*.[63] Cope devotes more than twenty pages to the question of educating boys. He follows with two brief paragraphs on "the girls." His attitude toward women was obviously biased (though perhaps not more than his contemporaries). The sexism revealed in Cope's patronizing values could have done nothing to affirm women in the organization or in the profession of religious education.

Cope's books advanced no new ideas. Though they varied in style and content, they all reflected the general ideas of Coe and other religious educators of that period rather than new concepts of his own. He overstated the case for social education. He was not careful in his criticism of American education, and he often went beyond the limits of reasonable argument and cautious language.

Ten years after the formation of the R.E.A., he wrote: "If ever the history of the R.E.A. is written adequately, it will tell not alone of organizational conferences, methods, and materials, but of a new spirit, a truly holy crusade."[64] Cope could be judged more positively on his organizational conferences and his popularization of methods and materials than on his "holy crusade." He served well the former intents; he did not serve the cause of religious education well if he is to be judged by his educational theory and the articulation of those ideas.

The First Twenty Years:
Utopian Vision and Earthly Reality

Patricia Graham, in her *Progressive Education: From Arcady to Academe,* cites Stanwood Cobb, major organizer of the Progressive Education Association, as saying: "The new education was twenty years old in 1919, the year the P.E.A. was founded."[65] In a sense the P.E.A. came after the fact. Such was not the case in the formation of the R.E.A.

While it may be true that the R.E.A. was not dramatically effective in modifying public education in America, or even in seriously affecting that major school movement, it is unquestionably true that the R.E.A. was most instrumental in promoting the progressive vision among the churches, Sunday Schools, and related Christian associations. If, as Lawrence Cremin suggests in *The Transformation of the School,* progressive education was the "educational phase of American Progressivism writ large,"[66] then it is equally true that the R.E.A. embodied the religious aspect of the progressive vision. And it is also true, as Cremin suggests, that "the public school has never functioned alone or in isolation . . . it has functioned as part of a configuration of education that has included families, churches, and Sunday Schools, all committed to similar or complementary values."[67] The R.E.A. was specifically committed to the task of that kind of support system, valiantly trying to create a cooperative relationship between churches, Sunday Schools, families, and the best of the new education in conjunction with the public school system in its own progressive period.

The first twenty years of the journal, *Religious Education,* leaves dramatic testimony to that vision. Year after year, the journal raised the question of religion and moral values in relationship to public education. More than eighty articles were published on this subject before 1920. Uneven in style and content, they form a sketch of R.E.A.'s democratic vision, clear yet always in danger of vulgarization and overstatement. A certain Charles Williams wrote in support of patriotism as the major instrument of moral education. "The greatest moral discovery of modern times is the realization of the close connection between national welfare and individual righteousness."[68] Edwin Starbuck offered more cautious, reasoned advice: "The most direct way of approach to the larger life of humanity and God is through the positive expression of the social relations in school life. The school must become more like a family and less like a machine or an army."[69]

The R.E.A. published an entire issue on the question of moral education in public schools. In February, 1911, a symposium revolved around this issue. George Strayer, Teachers College, Columbia University, had the lead article, "The Legal Aspects of Moral Education," and Samuel Dutton, also of Teachers College, closed the symposium with an appeal that argued for lived religion in public schools which he believed to be equally effective in moral development as the practice of moral preachments or dogmatic recitations.[70]

Institutionally, the R.E.A. had its most direct relationship with public school theory and practice through a long and regular dialogue with the N.E.A. From 1903 until the mid-teens the R.E.A. scheduled regular conferences in conjunction with the N.E.A. Special leaders of the R.E.A. were regular participants in the N.E.A. and occasionally presented papers within both organizations. Mutual support emerged around the issue of moral education in the schools; joint committees were suggested; regular N.E.A. publicity appeared in the R.E.A. journal and shared programs became regular practice.

These relationships never produced combined institutional statements, but the data suggest a sustained relationship between the members of the R.E.A. and the N.E.A. One is hard-pressed to document specific results of this interaction. It seems obvious, however, that the concerns and goals of each organization were for a time related to a view of a more educated public around the ideal of democracy.[71]

It is not true that the major emphasis of the R.E.A. had to do with public education, at least not public schooling. Rather, the R.E.A. was primarily concerned about religious education specifically as it related to the Sunday School, the church, and other related religious organizations. The journal was the educational tool for promoting the major ideals of that movement: the utilization of contemporary scientific method in religious instruction, the practice of critical biblical scholarship, and the overarching social viewpoint about a public pedagogy (George Albert Coe's "democracy of God" in various guises). As one reads those volumes, one is struck with the variations of that ideal as it became the popular jargon of the emerging new profession. Cremin's warning words about popularizers fits the R.E.A. dilemma: "The popularizer seeks pungency and simplicity; the slogan soon replaces the extended discussion."[72]

The early R.E.A. journals were burdened with such simplification. A certain John H. T. Main wrote: "What is modern man. . . . He believes in One God—the God of science, of history, of social progress, of religion. He believes that God has put his spirit into all life and into his own heart as well."[73] A second author would speak of the possibility of "civic righteousness" as a product of the democratic "gospel of the kingdom." As the American churches would combine efforts to bring about that reality, the "vision of the last of the apostles of the City of God coming down out of the heaven from God, prepared as the earthly bride of the heavenly bridegroom" would become realized.[74] Theodore Soares imaged the R.E.A. as an association filled with religious fervor so passionate that it would recapture the "power of the old revival." The R.E.A. would form partnership with "this great modern scientific age." All this energy would result in cooperation of those who, filled with goodwill, join together "to see the kingdom of God come with power."[75] One can hardly miss the obeisance to science and the optimistic conviction that a new day was coming, a messianic end-time when the fulfillment of God's democracy might become the reality of American daily life. How reminiscent of Harper's dream, and yet how hopeful an attitude for the future.

Regardless of how exalted the leaders' rhetoric, their democratic vision faltered at critical junctures in the R.E.A.'s institutional practices. There was no serious attempt through the first two decades to enlist the growing Catholic Christian population of religious educators. Apart from a single article and a few "news notes" the journal was solidly liberal Protestant until after 1920. The democracy of God was not yet wide enough for Catholics, and there was little interest on the part of Catholics to be included. (Catholics had their own educational agenda, the development of Catholic parochial schools.) Though some were invited, they chose not to attend. Jewish minorities were accepted earlier, judging from Jewish contributions to the journal. During the first twenty years there was a series of articles written by Jewish authors about Jewish educational life and values. My impression is that this phenomenon reflected the R.E.A.'s perception of the dogmatic character of the Catholic tradition, while it viewed the Jewish tradition as nonconfessional. The R.E.A.'s democratic ideals could not (in this period) include doctrinal traditions. Fundamentalists and Catholics were outside the fold of the democratic fellowship. And although the R.E.A. continued to support the ideal that it espoused "no one religious viewpoint," it did in fact exclude an important segment of the American religious experience, perhaps to its own later detriment.[76]

Blacks were also among the minorities that seemed to escape the evangelical gospel of God's democracy. The journal, always reflective of the times during this period, published little about blacks, and what was published speaks best for itself.[77] Samuel Mitchell, president of the University of South Carolina, wrote in 1909: "It takes a long time to rear a race. It was so with the Saxon. . . . Moreover, we know how toilsome since that time has been every step in the slow upward climb of the Saxon endowed so rightly as he is with political capacity and moral responsiveness."

Mitchell noted that the "American Negro" had gone through four stages of development; "savagery in Africa, slavery in this country, a decade of political power during Reconstruction, and now the beginning of the long, slow process of training him for the duties of citizenship in a democracy." He raised this question: "Is the Negro a sick man or a child?" Mitchell's answer was to suggest the latter. The Negro was not a sick man but was rather the product of a race that was in the process of maturity. Slavery "was only one stage in a chronic racial situation." The Negro problem was one of, "How can you best rear a race?"[78]

In an article reminiscent of the founder of Tuskegee Institute, G. Lake Imes, also of Tuskegee, argued a position in keeping with his training. He wrote supporting the role of the rural farm-preacher and called for practical rather than theological training: "That part of the preacher's training that might be called purely religious would have a practical rather than a theological aspect; that is, it would fit him to understand and teach life rather than theology, and such a life as country people must grapple with. Theology does not go far in the country."[79]

In that same volume Wilbur P. Thirkield, president of Howard University, argued for "Negro" Sunday Schools. He ended his essay with these words: "The basis for effective work through the Sunday School is found in what Stanley Hall and others have emphasized—the genius which the Negro has for religion. No race surpasses the Negro in religious endowment."[80] The best expression of the needs of Negroes was written by Thirkield in 1911. In dealing with the question of higher education, he argued that Negroes are to be treated like other human beings; there was a militancy to his prose: "The Negro is a man. Therefore, educate him as a man. Do not force education upon him. Do not veneer him. Simply open the door to highest opportunity in the intellectual life. Let him have a man's chance."

He appealed to the notion that blacks would best be educated by their own. He advocated the DuBois thesis of the "talented tenth," and he urged education of an elite Negro class who in turn could save the race. He understood the difficulties of blacks in white America.

Thirkield called for a "trained and consecrated ministry." And he noted that one of the more serious problems of the Negro community was the inability of the race "to hold the progressive, aspiring Negroes of the rising generation to the church." He referred to Booker T. Washington's observation that "too large a percentage" of those ministers "are not fitted morally or intellectually for that office."

Thirkield was a realist and a gradualist. He knew the struggle ahead: "Let us not forget that it is only generations of discipline and patient education of the people . . . that will lift the masses into the larger and higher fellowship of the intellectual life." He saw the struggle as more difficult than that of educating one person. "While we may educate the individual in a few years, the intellectual and moral equipment of a race is a question of generations, and it may be of centuries."[81]

Women, on the other hand, received little attention in the journal during this period. There are only a dozen articles that relate at all to women during the first twenty-year period, none substantial. It is clear that at this stage in the professional development of women interested in religious education there was little concern, at least on the part of the R.E.A. Women were simply not significant. They may be assistants to pastors, and they need to know religion because they nurture children (an allusion to mothering), but they were not to be active or vocal in this profession or this organization. The R.E.A. was captive to the contours of the conventional wisdom of the times.

By 1920 there were token women on the council, surely a minority membership in comparison with the number of male colleagues. Though they were to become the majority membership in the profession, they were largely absent in the formative years of the religious education movement. During the twenties their positions in the organization changed, though, as we will see in later chapters, their status as women continued to define their role and future in the R.E.A.[82]

Membership throughout this period remained relatively constant; there were about two thousand members during the first ten years and about three thousand during the next ten, largely due to the efforts of Cope and his persistent recruitment program. Concern for membership was high during this period because membership fees were the major financial support system of the organization. They were in every sense the lifeline of the organization.

Several factors contributed to the modest membership. The most important was a development which really occurred outside the organization itself. In 1903 there were three or four major agencies of religious education among mainline Protestants: Y.M.C.A., Y.W.C.A., the International Sunday School Association, and the R.E.A. By 1923 these groups had been joined by more than twenty additional organizations, denominational agencies, and special-interest groups. Mainline Protestants joined together in forming the International Council of Religious Education (1922). Despite the presence of the I.C.R.E., denominational concerns led to separate agencies and related organizations within each denomination. Though not reported in the journal, there were additional fundamentalist groups and a large, growing Catholic educational enterprise. The Catholics formed their own style of N.E.A. in 1904, calling the organization the National Catholic Educational Association (N.C.E.A.). The point is clear: the proliferation of other organizations diminished the national appeal of the R.E.A.[83]

A second factor, probably equally important, was the decision on the part of the R.E.A. not to become the serious professional association for the emerging religious education professional. Though the R.E.A. was supportive and encouraging in the formation of a small professional association, there was no effort to provide a serious professional home within the R.E.A. itself. The diverse membership of the association prevented it from becoming a viable "union" for the emerging profession. In retrospect this judgment on the part of the R.E.A. assured its continued modest existence. While professional groups organized throughout America and unionization in industry flourished, the R.E.A. was not to provide a serious support system for its own. While claiming to be responsible for a totally new profession, the R.E.A. gradually turned its back on its offspring and in so doing assured a limited professional membership among a rapidly growing number of professionals.[84]

Perhaps the most significant factor in the stunted growth of the organization was the R.E.A.'s dogged commitment to a "classless ideal"[85] at a time when the several publics of the R.E.A. were seeking professional identity, intellectual stimulation, and practical advice. As one reads from those first twenty years of the journal, one cannot but be impressed with the unevenness of the content and style of the articles. Topics ranged from simple pedantic to rhetorical and inspirational to scholarly and academic. Research focused on important issues. Theological education was of key concern to a select few. There were even occasional political statements during and before the World War I period.

It is not surprising that there was no focus. For the R.E.A. had decided to serve everyone interested in religion and education from the untrained volunteer Sunday School teacher to the university professor to the harried parish preacher. The journal attempted to address the needs of all these.

The council of the R.E.A., the essential policy makers and unofficial inner circle, was composed almost entirely of professional educators and university or college personnel. This was obviously the small inner circle, the new experts who charted the leadership and set the themes for conferences and the journal. At one level the organization was a collection of college and university professors, captive to what a latter-day historian, Burton Bledstein, calls *The Culture of Professionalism* yet avowedly supportive of a broader egalitarian vision.[86]

But there was another R.E.A., that of the regular membership, the silent readers and those who attended the conventions. These lay folk— Sunday School teachers, pastors, youth directors, and new fledgling religious education professionals—all could take the R.E.A. at its word, that it was a movement of simplicity, nonacademic and nonphilosophical. Their interests were the Sunday School, parish, youth groups, worship life in the church, etc. Their focus was practical. The journal had become almost schizophrenic, offering two faces, one practical and the other scholarly and complex.

It is my firm conviction that the democratic ideal, while visionary and exemplary, was unworkable, institutionally, over the long term. The divergent interests and needs of the membership were too diverse. So as other agencies and associations came into being to fill those needs, membership in the R.E.A. never grew to the expectations of the organization. The departmental structure never evolved successfully to serve the pluralistic membership of the association.

Yet during this period, the R.E.A. never backed away from its populist perspective. The attempt would be made. All were welcome, especially all who accepted the ideal of the kingdom of God come alive through the messianic age of religious education. Such an effort produced the R.E.A. and sustained membership of disciples who adhered to the ideal carefully articulated by Coe and so misappropriated by others.

Though he denied it, and though the R.E.A. council rejected the notion, Henry Cope was, during these early decades, the public image of the Religious Education Association. And if that is true, then it follows that the essential image of the association was eclectic, popular, practical, liberal, and increasingly professionalized. The democratic ideals were relativized and the new image was less true to the original and more vulnerable to misunderstanding and cliche. Such was the state of affairs in 1923 when Henry Cope died. The R.E.A. was forced suddenly to reevaluate, a decision long overdue!

Notes for Chapter II

1. George Albert Coe, *A Social Theory of Religious Education* (New York: Charles Scribner's Sons, 1917), p. 54.

2. Richard J. Storr, *Harper's University, The Beginnings* (Chicago: University of Chicago Press, 1966), p. 368. Storr writes cryptically: "What might have been a disastrous explosion failed to occur, possibly because of Harper's illness." Harry Pratt Judson, second president of the university "liquidated" many of Harper's experiments and probably saved the university from serious disaster (pp. 369–370).

3. Ibid., pp. 369–370.

4. Letter, W. R. Harper to M. J. Fraser, March 24, 1905, (University of Chicago Archives), Harper Letter File. Hereafter (U.C.A.)

5. Lawrence R. Veysey, *The Emergence of the American University* (Chicago: University of Chicago Press, 1965), p. 370.

6. Lawrence A. Cremin, *The Transformation of the School: Progressivism in American Education* (New York: Alfred A. Knopf, 1962), p. ix.

7. A.I.S.L. Statistical Statement, October, 1895, U.C.A. One hundred fifty students were enrolled in Hebrew classes, fifty in New Testament Greek, forty in English Bible, five hundred in Bible Students Reading Guild, four thousand in the outlined Bible Club course, and four thousand in summer school. For summary of A.I.S.L. enrollments, finances, and expenditures, see Kenneth Nathaniel Beck, "The American Institute of Sacred Literature: A Historical Analysis of an Adult Education Institution" (unpublished Ph.D. dissertation, University of Chicago, 1968), pp. 280–300.

8. See George H. Williams's *Wilderness and Paradise in Christian Thought* (New York: Harper and Brothers, 1962), pp. 211–245, for historical background on the use of theological ideas to support the idea of the university. Harper's vision of the university as prophet, priest, and sage parallels earlier usage of theological themes, "Wilderness and Paradise," and the tripartite Christological "prophet, priest, king" imagery involving early Harvard University. Harper uses neither of those themes but modified the idea in keeping with his own literary interests in Old Testament typologies. There was something less sectarian about Harper's notions than the earlier Christological type, but the same intention was present. Harper used scriptural imagery to undergird the authority and prestige of the modern university.

9. Veysey, *The Emergence of the American University*, p. 369. Veysey's summary statement catches the balanced view: "To such a man the whole question of academic freedom, with its egalitarian overtones, would ring strangely, and yet after a few false starts he learned to live with the idea surprisingly well." For a more detailed analysis of Harper's "prophet, priest, sage" imagery of the university see Storr, *Harper's University*, pp. 193–209. Also see William Rainey Harper, *The Trend in Higher Education in America* (Chicago: University of Chicago Press, 1905), pp. 20–33.

10. Harper, *The Trend in Higher Education*, p. 19.

11. Veysey, *The Emergence of the American University*, p. 368. Also see Walter P. Metzger, *Academic Freedom in the Age of the University* (New York: Columbia University Press, 1955), p. 150. A less critical, even laudatory, view of Harper is found in Thomas Wakefield Goodspeed, *William Rainey Harper, First President of the University of Chicago* (Chicago: University of Chicago Press, 1928) and in his more balanced interpretation found in *A History of the University of Chicago Founded by John D. Rockefeller: The First Quarter-Century* (Chicago: University of Chicago Press, 1916). Goodspeed is admittedly a close friend of Harper and a long associate of the university.

12. Harper, *The Trend in Higher Education*, p. 232.

13. Ibid., pp. 242–245.

14. Ibid., pp. 245–251.

15. Ibid., p. 252.

16. Ibid., p. 256.

17. Ibid., p. 12. "The university is the Messiah of the democracy, its to-be-expected deliverer."

18. William Rainey Harper, *Religion and the Higher Life: Talks to Students* (Chicago: University of Chicago Press, 1904), p. 176.

19. Harper, *The Trend in Higher Education*, pp. 10–11 and Harper, *Religion and the Higher Life*, p. 175.

20. Harper, *The Trend in Higher Education*, pp. 36–43. Harper distinguished between popular education and formal education. Formal education was schooling, while popular education involved a broad collection of educational influences. He mentioned newspapers, books and literature, reading circles, Lyceum Lecture courses, Chautauqua assemblies, programs of the Y.M.C.A., Sunday Schools, etc. Here was no narrow progressivism, but a vision of the impact of culture upon the formative child and adult. Harper's vision was progressive in the broadest sense. He seemed to illustrate Cremin's view that progressivism was not "narrowly practical." See Cremin, *The Transformation of the School*, p. ix. Later progressivism tended to narrow its concerns to the agency of the public school and deserved the criticism against the educational nonsense known as the "child-centered school." See Patricia Albjerg Graham, *Progressive Education: From Arcady to Academe, A History of the Progressive Education Association* (New York: Teachers College Press, 1967), p. 46.

21. *Report of the Educational Commission of the City of Chicago* (Chicago: Lakeside Press, 1898). This book contains recommendations of the Harper Commission for the city of Chicago. The major recommendations sought to depoliticize the school system by placing responsibility for the schools on an appointed board of eleven members. These recommendations were finally adopted in 1921.

22. Morton G. White, *Social Thought in America: The Revolt Against Formalism* (New York: Viking Press, 1952), p. 1283.

23. Beck, "The American Institute," p. 121.

24. Ibid., p. 121.

25. A.I.S.L. papers, U.C.A., A.I.S.L. File.

26. A.I.S.L., Minutes of Meeting, August 20, 1902, U.C.A., A.I.S.L. File.

27. A.I.S.L., Minutes of Meeting, October 13, 1902, U.C.A., A.I.S.L. File.

28. "A Call for a Convention to Effect a National Organization for the Improvement of Religious and Moral Education Through the Sunday School and Other Agencies," R.E.A.F., New Haven, Connecticut.

29. (Confidential) "First Draft of a List of Signers of the Call," 1903, R.E.A.F., New Haven, Connecticut.

30. "The Council of Seventy," reprinted from *The Biblical World,* January, 1903, R.E.A.F., New Haven, Connecticut.

31. "Official Document #2: Program for the Convention," reprinted from *The Biblical World,* February, 1903, pp. 15–16, R.E.A.F., New Haven, Connecticut.

32. Orville L. Davis, "A History of the Religious Education Association," *Religious Education* XLIV (January–February, 1949). Davis speaks of the "connection with the National Education Association" (p. 42). The R.E.A. did hold some regular meetings with the N.E.A. beginning in Los Angeles, California, July 8–12, 1907. This meeting was well attended and received good press. See *Religious Education* II (August, 1907), p. 120.

33. "Official Document #2," p. 16. This multi-departmental structure never succeeded, except on paper. By the mid-1920s, only the departments of the Sunday School and the council remained viable.

34. The *Proceedings* of the first convention lists two Jewish members, Rabbi Joseph Silverman (New York) and Rabbi Abram Simon (Omaha, Nebraska). Silverman was a Reform Jew and is cited as one of the early advocates of Sunday morning services for American Jews. See Sidney L. Regner "The Rise and Decline of the Sunday Service: An Instructive Episode in the History of Reform Judaism," *Journal of Reform Judaism* (Fall, 1980, Vol. XXVII #4) ed. Bernard Martin (New York Central Conference of American Rabbis).

35. Letter, Harper to Spalding, April 19, 1892, U.C.A., Harper Letter File.

36. "Official Document #2" p. 10.

37. Reprint from *Christian Century* in "The Religious Education Association" (Chicago: R.E.A., 1903), pp. 38–39 (public relations promotional bulletin).

38. Ibid., p. 40.

39. George Albert Coe, "Religious Education as a Part of General Education," in *Proceedings of the First Annual Convention,* Chicago, February 10–12, 1903, pp. 48–52.

40. Letter, Harper to Frank Sanders, February 27, 1904, U.C.A., Harper Letter File.

41. Letter, Harper to Coe, February 21, 1905, U.C.A., Harper Letter File.

42. George Albert Coe, "The Religious Education Movement in Retrospect," *Religious Education* XXXIX (July–August, 1944), pp. 220, 223.

43. George Albert Coe, *Religious Experience and the Scientific Movement* (1897) p. 6 (no publisher given). Perhaps the clearest Christological statement of the "early" Coe was his presentation "The Content of the Gospel Message to Men of Today" at the Fourth Convention of the R.E.A. See *The Materials of Religious Education* (Chicago R.E.A., 1907), pp. 173–179. Coe wrote: "The Gospel is not a printed word or a proposition of thought or even a code of conduct; it is Jesus himself, in whom the Word is made flesh," p. 174.

44. George Albert Coe, *What Is Christian Education?* (New York: Charles Scribner's Sons, 1929), p. 296.

45. George Albert Coe, *A Social Theory of Religious Education* (New York: Charles Scribner's Sons, 1917), p. 113.

46. Ibid., p. 93.

47. Ibid., pp. 164–183. "Sin, then, is rooted in instinct, confirmedly habit, and propagated by informal social education," p. 168.

48. Ibid., p. 15.

49. Ibid., pp. 54, 67, 225.

50. George Albert Coe, *Law and Freedom in the School* (Chicago: University of Chicago Press, 1924), pp. 112–117. Coe's suggestions are balanced and reasonable.

His key argument is that schools must deal with the "darker as well as the brighter side of our economic life."

51. Ibid., p. 129. Coe posits the radical democratic vision against the sick society: "As the faithful minister of religion endeavors to obey God rather than men, so the real educator, enduring (if need be) as seeing the invisible, leads forward into freedom a society that is fettered by selfishness and by institutionalized timidities. He leads society into freedom by leading children into it and this he does by giving them practice in it."

52. Coe, "The Religious Education Movement," p. 224.

53. For an optimistic appraisal of Henry Cope, see Dorothy Jean Furnish, "Pioneers of Religious Education: Henry F. Cope, General Secretary, 1906–1923," *Religious Education* LXXIII (September–October, 1978), pp. S16–S24. Furnish is evangelical in her praise of Cope; however, she only devotes two paragraphs to an analysis of his writing. Cope receives high praise from Orville L. Davis in "A History of the Religious Education Association," *Religious Education* XLIV (January–February, 1949), pp. 7–8. Also see the memorial issue of *Religious Education* XVIII (October, 1923). In this issue more than fifty R.E.A. members eulogize Henry Cope.

54. George Albert Coe, "Mr. Cope's Unique Contribution to Our Generation," *Religious Education* XVIII (October, 1923), p. 267.

55. Letters: Harper to Burton, February 17, 1905; Harper to Ryerson, February 2, 1905; L. Miesser to Harper, July 20, 1905; Miesser to Harper, October 4, 1905; Harper to Charles Hall, February 7, 1905; Harper to Coe, November 9, 1904; Harper to Sanders, November 1, 1905, U.C.A., Harper Letter File.

56. See Cope's report in *Religious Education* II (April, 1907), p. 34.

57. See Cope's secretary report in *Religious Education* VI (April, 1911), p. 125.

58. Theodore Gerald Soares, "History of the Religious Education Association," *Religious Education* XXIII (September, 1928), p. 626. This history is a direct, non-evangelical appraisal of the first twenty-five years of the R.E.A. He indicated the heavy responsibility placed on the executive secretary and the general lack of financial support during his tenure.

59. Henry Cope, "Annual Report," *Religious Education* XV (August, 1920), p. 217.

60. *Religious Education* XVIII (October, 1923). This memorial issue is devoted to memorials for Henry Cope. The underlying guilt is reflected in the poignant words of Coe: "Hence it is that we took him for granted, as though he belonged to the nature of things and was not subject to weariness and frailty of body," p. 267.

61. Henry Frederick Cope, *The School in the Modern Church* (New York: George H. Doran Co., 1919), p. 42.

62. Henry Frederick Cope, *Education for Democracy* (New York: The Macmillan Company, 1920), p. 74. This is perhaps Cope's most poorly written book. It is filled with cliches, generalizations, and rhetorical excesses.

63. Henry Frederick Cope, *Efficiency in the Sunday School* (New York: Hodder & Stoughton, 1912), pp. 118ff. See also Henry Frederick Cope, *Religious Education in the Church* (New York: Charles Scribner's Sons, 1918), p. 179 and Henry Frederick Cope, *Religious Education in the Family* (Chicago: University of Chicago Press, 1915), pp. 173ff.

64. Henry Frederick Cope, *Ten Years' Progress in Religious Education* (Chicago: Religious Education Association, 1913), p. 5.

65. Graham, *Progressive Education*, p. 21.

66. Cremin, *Transformation of the School*, p. viii.

67. Lawrence A. Cremin, *Public Education* (New York: Basic Books, Inc., 1976), p. 58.

68. Charles W. Williams, "Patriotism as an Instrument for Moral Education in the Public Schools," *Religious Education* II (June, 1907), p. 60.

69. Edwin Diller Starbuck, "Moral and Religious Education—Sociological Aspect," *Religious Education* III (February, 1909), p. 217.

70. *Religious Education* V (February, 1911), pp. 599–732. This symposium included authors W. C. Bagley, University of Illinois; Clarence F. Carroll, superintendent of schools, Rochester, New York; Frank Chapman Sharp, University of Wisconsin; Harrold Johnson, London; and others. The quality of the articles is exceptional, well-defined, and representative of viewpoints at the time. Throughout this twenty-year period, there are numerous instances of this kind of scholarly enterprise. This particular issue of the journal would rank among the best of its time. Such was not the case of many other issues which reflected unevenness and lack of cohesion in content and theme.

71. Illustrations of this unified effort and mutual support can be seen in the R.E.A. presidential report given by Bishop William Fraser McDowell in April 1906. Fraser talks about cooperation with other existing organizations and then proceeds to cite "other institutions (which) have made most encouraging declarations which are in line with our policy." He quotes from declarations adopted in the July N.E.A. meeting of that year, an appeal to the higher aims of public schools: ". . . how to live righteously, healthily, and happily." *Religious Education* I (April, 1906), pp. 7–9.

72. Cremin, *Transformation of the School*, p. 271.

73. John H. T. Main, "The Modern Man and Religious Education," *Religious Education* IV (December, 1909), p. 479.

74. Graham Taylor, "Church and Civic Education: Community Activities as a Means of Education in Civic Righteousness," *Religious Education* V (October, 1910), pp. 385–390.

75. Theodore Gerald Soares, "Federation for Religious Leadership," *Religious Education* VIII (April, 1913), p. 11.

76. Jewish members are listed as early as 1903. See *Religious Education Proceedings, 1903.* Articles written by Jewish authors appear regularly in every volume after 1911. The first article by a Catholic appears in 1905, while the earliest article written by a Lutheran (one of three before 1920) appears in 1915. At least one person recognized the R.E.A.'s liberal problem and wrote this striking paragraph (1914): "One of the results of this is that men are not only becoming impatient of dogma, but of all exact and firmly held intellectual beliefs. Loose and emotional sentimentalism is welcomed as a relief from exact statement and clear thinking. Now this is not the proper remedy. Never did a situation need clearer thinking and more courageous facing of the fact than today. We can never save the day by indirection. Has Roman Catholicism a good case, it should be heard. It is a shame that Protestants are so often content with antiquated caricatures of Rome. Men like Leo XIII and Cardinal Newman were no fools. We need clear and able defense of historic Protestantism with its claims for an infallible Bible, instead of an infallible Pope. We need sane and nonhysterical treatments of the New Protestantism which has risen since the days of Hume and Kant." See Thomas C. Hall, "Religious Inspiration and Religious Dogma in Civic Progress," *Religious Education* IX (February, 1914), p. 5.

77. See President Henry S. Pritchett, "The Ethical Education of Public Opinion," *Proceedings,* 1905, pp. 47–52, and William E. B. DuBois' discussion of that essay on pp. 53–54.

Before 1909 only one black man addressed the association. William E. B. DuBois responded with a brief two-page discussion to a presentation titled "The Ethical Education of Public Opinion," part of the public address at the third convention of the R.E.A. DuBois wrote:

"In a world of men, even of differing and different men, we cannot, on account of cowardice, treat any of these men as less than men: we cannot slink back of Darwinism to discover excuses, or whiten our lies by laying them on the Lord." He continued: "To induce, then, in men a consciousness of the humanity of all men . . . is not merely to lay down a pious postulate, but it is the active and animate heart-to-heart knowledge of your neighbors . . . that is what will build a new humanity."

It is unfortunate that DuBois was not the major presenter; his message was so eloquently clear in contrast to the bland generalizations of Henry Pritchett in his major presentation. The next articles written by blacks were all after 1909, written by lesser known personages and of a different quality from DuBois' brief response.

78. Samuel C. Mitchell, "Religious Education and Racial Adjustment," *Religious Education* IV (October, 1909), p. 317.

79. G. Lake Imes, "The Negro Minister and Country Life," *Religious Education* VII (June, 1912), p. 174.

80. Wilbur P. Thirkield, "Negro Sunday Schools: A Plan for Constructive Sunday-School Work Among the Colored People," *Religious Education* VII (October, 1912), p. 450.

81. Wilbur P. Thirkield, "The Higher Education of the Negro," *Religious Education VI* (December, 1911), pp. 420–423.

82. Minutes of the Religious Education Association Council, 1909–1919, R.E.A.F., New Haven, Connecticut. Though the data are sparse, the few minutes in existence indicate the dominance of the male members of the council. All dialogue, motions, and decisions were made by male participants. One gains the impression that the women members were silent observers. In the memorial issue of *Religious Education,* dedicated to Henry Cope, there are forty-nine tributes written by men, two by women.

83. Cope lists more than twenty new organizations formed in the movement by 1923. See Cope's last report in *Religious Education* XVIII (October 1923), p. 315. In that same issue, Soares candidly confesses: "There are, undoubtedly, too many coordinating agencies in the field" (p. 322).

84. This development is really part of the decade of the twenties. For a full discussion of this issue, see Dorothy Jean Furnish, *D.R.E./D.C.E.—The History of a Profession* (Nashville, Tenn.: Christian Educators Fellowship, The United Methodist Church, 1976), pp. 25–33. Probably the best written article Henry Cope wrote in the Journal dealt with the question of professionalism of the religious educator. Had the association followed his plans, the history of the R.E.A. might have been far different. See Henry F. Cope, "The Professional Organization of Workers in Religious Education," *Religious Education* XXI (June, 1921), pp. 162–167.

85. By "classless ideal" I mean the egalitarian notion that the R.E.A. existed for all segments of concerned persons interested in religious education. In one sense the R.E.A. was strictly middle class or higher. Never in its history did the R.E.A. appeal to significant minorities. Blacks were never numerically important.

The major denominations largely represented by the R.E.A. were mainline upper-middle-class white Americans. The professional professorial leadership of the association guaranteed its upper-class caste and apart from the leftist leanings of an aging

George Albert Coe, the R.E.A. remained solidly disassociated from the cause of the poor, disenfranchised, or lower-class Protestant fundamentalist.

86. Burton J. Bledstein, *The Culture of Professionalism: The Middle Class and the Development of Higher Education in America* (New York: W. W. Norton & Company, 1976).

Chapter III

Religious Triumphalism:
Building the "Imperial" Organization
1923–1935

> The growth of the association the past several years has been phe-
> nomenal, and I am firmly of the conviction that within the next few
> years the R.E.A. will be one of the most strategic of all movements
> in America, and will occupy the imperial position conceived for it
> by the early founders of the Association.[1]

Joseph M. Artman
R.E.A. General Secretary, 1929

When Henry Cope died in 1923 he left the R.E.A. with a dramatic
leadership void. His personal embodiment of the movement no longer
could provide unity and focus or an ongoing recruitment of new membership. A new coalition was needed. The drama of serious reevaluation
focused on the heart of the organization, its reason for being. Deciding
in characteristic democratic fashion, the R.E.A. commissioned a full-
scale research procedure to evaluate the past efforts of the organization
and make recommendations for its future.

Leadership in the R.E.A. continued to be assumed by important
academic professionals. These professors of religious education dominated the literature of the field. Schools of religious education developed in several universities and seminaries. Religious education became
a profitable enterprise for major universities, and those schools became
identified with particular theorists and "schools of thought." The
R.E.A. story is linked to these institutions and their religious education
faculties, all key figures in the association.

The field of religious education grew rapidly. The R.E.A. recommit-
ted itself to the pursuit of modern science with even more optimism than

56

in previous decades. Theology and biblical exegesis received less attention. Educational method, behaviorism, and "character" formation
became the focus of major interest. Gradually those perspectives replaced the more social-political pedagogical idealism of earlier leaders.
Process and method dominated the field, rather than concern for the
larger question of a public paideia, or a more social theory of religious
education.

But it was finally outside events and internal mismanagement which
tempered the imperial expansive vision. The economic crash of the
thirties with its succeeding years of financial hardship plagued the organization. By 1935 the imperial secretary of the association, Joseph M.
Artman, was forced to resign, leaving the R.E.A. deeply in debt to
outside creditors, but also in debt to the general secretary, for the credit
line he had extended to the association. Triumphant dreams were in
disarray, and once again the association was forced into new directions
and revised purposes.

Reevaluating and Setting Priorities

In one of the more perceptive and critical addresses delivered by an
R.E.A. president, Arthur Cushman McGiffert, president of Union Theological Seminary and the R.E.A. (1921), set the tone for future religious education efforts in the third decade of the association. Lacking
the usual triumphant rhetoric of R.E.A. leadership, McGiffert sketched
the serious dilemma of church education and suggested realistic directions for future guidelines that seemed to lay claim to the most characteristic elements of early R.E.A. democratic Christianity. His essay was
delivered at the seventeenth annual convention of the R.E.A. and reprinted as the opening article in Volume XVI of the journal (1921).

McGiffert was a liberal realist. His argument began with a review of
two books, *The Army and Religion* and *Religion Among American
Men*.[2] Both books highlighted the "lamentable ignorance" of young
soldiers toward classical Christianity. Not only were young American
and British soldiers ignorant of Christianity, they were unaffected by its
influence, or as McGiffert concluded: The Christian church achieved a
significant failure in its effort to educate a young Christian generation.

McGiffert's analysis proceeded along these lines. The primary educational mistake of Christian Protestants was as old as the Reformation
itself. When the Catholic church (equated with Catholic culture) was
abandoned by the sixteenth-century reformers, no adequate systematic
structure of teaching and life developed to fill the vacuum. Scholasti-

cism as a system of thought and life regulated the daily routine and behavior of all pre-Reformation Catholicism. Protestantism never developed a sufficient alternative system either ethically, ritually, ecclesiastically, or culturally.

Instead, Protestants tended toward schism and developing denominationalism. Multiple biblical interpretations replaced a single unified body of theological opinion. Though Protestantism seemed to agree on the infallibility of the Bible, there was little unity of interpretation or little agreement on worship rituals. McGiffert noted that the sectarian self-centeredness of American Protestantism was a serious offense to young American servicemen and their attitudes toward the church.

A second failure was the inability of Protestant evangelicalism to develop a serious ethic related to the realities of human behavior. Protestant evangelicals tended toward inspiration rather than education or systematic Christian formation. Revivalism and conversion were ill-equipped to provide a generation of young Americans with significant answers to questions of meaning or morality. Christianity was unrealistic and unrelated to the hard and serious questions of the real world. "One of the most frequently repeated criticisms, according to the British and American reports, has to do with just that matter, that the church is repeating ancient formulas which have little or no applicability to the life of today and are consequently quite incomprehensible to the mass of men."[3]

McGiffert placed blame for these failures squarely at the feet of church educators. He deplored the fact that democratic methodology, while practiced in modern, secular education, seemed not to have affected the church. Instead he criticized the church for remaining in an age of "pedagogical autocracy," still appealing to the authority of tradition or historical dogmatic formulations, but unable to be open to the pursuit of truth and the possibility of new theological formulations.

He called for more theology rather than theological abandonment by the church and by religious education. But he opted for a theology free of the pressure of infallibility and open to evaluation by the "persuasiveness of its own appeal." He urged a theology detached from specific economic or social dogmatism. Such a theology would emerge through the democratic interaction of serious theological research and absolute commitment to scholarly criticism. He was of course advocating the same high ideals of the early R.E.A. patriarchs, Harper and Coe.

His essay was a reminder of the best of the heritage of the R.E.A. He was advocating the development of a Christian educative environment related to human life. He was urging a reinterpretation of Christianity based on research and criticism. And he was calling for a democratic educational method where the outcome desired was discovery rather than a reconfirmation of some ideal dogmatic history. He urged a religious education that one might rightly call Christian realism.

McGiffert was aware that dogmatic theology was unimportant to persons outside the arena of church professionals. The "average" person was interested in questions of spiritual life, of personal issues related to one's real being. Indeed the major question was one of belief: "The possibility of believing in God at all in such a world." In the real world, the "modern materialistic mechanistic age," theology had better address the real issues of human existence, rather than the interesting but unimportant questions of sophisticated theological debate.[4]

Here was a realism interested in life and death questions. Here was a theological agenda that urged examination of the most critical aspects of human existence. Here was a summons to a liberalism open to serious question and unfettered dialogue, yet committed to the essence of the Christian affirmation of the Gospel. In McGiffert's own words, his appeal meant "to trust Christian truth enough to let it make its way as any other truth must make its way, not by pressure of infallibility but by the persuasiveness of its own appeal."[5]

Had his agenda been taken seriously the next fifteen years of religious education might have witnessed the most thoughtful revision of Protestantism and the most genuine kind of ecumenism. However, such developments were not to occur. Other forces within the organization, more individualized, more de-Christianized, more humanized, would lead the R.E.A. into privatized research and ultimately toward a neo-Christian humanism.

While President McGiffert initiated the 1920s with presidential criticism, the organization accelerated its own scientific reevaluation after the untimely death of its first executive secretary, Henry Cope, in 1923. Obvious changes were almost immediate. The council (an R.E.A. version of Harper's Council of Seventy) was eliminated because of constant and growing complaint about selective elitism. A more democratic election process was begun for the election of the executive board to replace the council as the main administrative body to operate the organization between conventions. These changes probably would have happened even if Cope had lived on and served as executive secretary. His death simply hastened the process of self-evaluation and change of structures to appease the most overt criticism of the organization—that it was run by a small clique.

After Cope's death, interim measures were enacted to maintain the organization until a full reevaluation could be completed. George A. Coe served as consulting editor of the journal, and as one might imagine, both the quantity and the quality of articles improved. An assistant general secretary, Laird T. Hites, was hired on an interim basis to replace Cope until the board could determine future directions.

Internal Evaluation

The most useful and long-range decision made by the association was to commission an outside evaluation of the R.E.A. by an impartial research association known as the Institute of Social and Religious Research. Those investigations took place during 1925 and 1926 and were completed in February of 1926. The report was published in a special document, ''Report of an Investigation of the Religious Education Association.'' Of more interest is the unpublished report which remains in the files of the R.E.A.[6] The document is revealing both in its candid criticism of the R.E.A. and in its apparent objective summary. The published report does not contain the criticisms of the association, only the recommendations and suggestions. The published version does however indicate that the complete file was available to membership, upon request, at the 1926 convention.

The purpose of the study was to review the activities of the R.E.A. in an effort to ''discover whether these are being duplicated by other agencies in order to help the association determine whether or not it should continue, and to make suggestions, in view of past activities, as to its future organization, field function, and relationships.''[7]

The first section consisted of a straightforward summary of the history of the R.E.A. including lists of committee members, pages of financial statistics, and general objective review of the tasks and goals of the R.E.A. The data regarding members are the only compilation preserved to date and contain interesting details. According to the statistics, ''the records include three Catholics and eighteen Jews, but again this report should be regarded as of questionable value. A canvass at this point is highly desirable.'' The uncertainty of the data existed ''for the obvious reason that the association purposely ignored these cleavages (denominational membership) as far as possible.''[8]

In describing the journal a number of fascinating observations are in order. A list of contributors indicates that George A. Coe submitted by far the most articles to the journal, thirty-six in all, nine more than the second most prolific writer, Henry Cope. On the other hand, John Dewey, Washington Gladden, and Walter Raushenbusch each are listed as contributing only one article during those first twenty-three years.[9]

Equally interesting is the description of the Title Classification of the highly touted R.E.A. library, consisting at the time of 2785 volumes. One quickly gains a general impression of the interest and preoccupation of the association. Those statistics indicate the following:

Number of Books	Titles of Classifications[10]
34	Bible
28	Religion and Philosophy
21	Christianity
195	Education
218	Psychology
3	Press
51	Pedagogy and Methods
64	Ethics
155	Social (Crime, Amusements, Civics, Health)
255	Home and Family
190	Churches
198	Youth
860	Sunday School (Textbooks, etc.)
297	Public schools (Texts on Morals)
71	Universities and Colleges
5	Theological Seminaries
30	Vocational Industrial
43	Art and Music
3	Libraries
62	Christian Associations
2	Organizations Similar to the Y.M.C.A.

Two observations are striking. Though the original major interest of Harper and his associates was surely biblical studies, the library collection failed to reflect that continued interest. On the other hand, though the R.E.A. consistently advocated a broader basis of interest than Sunday Schools, the library holdings reflected an obvious abundance of Sunday School materials.

Two other points are important. The first is a comment regarding the journal, cryptically descriptive and from my own viewpoint an accurate evaluation:

The magazine has no consistent policy in the organization of its content. It is not topical (as for instance the *Annals of the Academy of Political Science*) or organized departmentally (as the *American Journal of Sociology* or *Social Forces*). The appearance of the *Journal of Religious Education* (Rafferty, editor) may make it possible for the magazine *Religious Education* to take on a more distinctive character.[11]

Second, the R.E.A. (until this date) had attempted to do too much and lost leadership by attempting to serve too broad a constituency. The report highlighted the problem. The R.E.A. conventions were neither professional nor scholarly, nor even popular gatherings to serve the unlettered church layperson. The report indicated that conventions had been least successful for the latter group, "(not) providing for several thousand people who are not able to participate in discussions except as they are intimately related to their limited experience and more specific needs." The conventions seemed unlikely to meet the expectations of any of the groups, the scholars, professionals, or volunteer lay religious educators.[12]

Part II was by far the most fascinating section of the entire investigation. The material contained candid evaluations by friends and open criticism by those hostile to the R.E.A. The responses were grouped into three categories dealing with functions of the R.E.A., criticisms, and suggestions about which groups the R.E.A. could best serve in the future.

In the report it was evident that all respondents quoted regarding the purpose of the R.E.A. noted the distinctive aspect of "fellowship" as a central function of the R.E.A. No criticism was offered in this segment of the report. Best summarized, this section affirmed "the idea that the association has a fellowship very much worthwhile."[13]

The critical responses might be divided into two categories. The first related to the party line of the R.E.A., and the second, considered by the report as more significant, had to do with the lack of scholarly seriousness of the association, related to its attempt to serve all levels of religious education, from the uninformed to the university specialists. Both criticisms are worth examining.

This section began with extensive quotations from Walter S. Athearn, a respected and reasonable member of the R.E.A. and noted author of that period. He was also an advocate of the day school movement. (Day schools were not parochial schools, rather sessions held during the day after public school.) Athearn could not be classified as an enemy of the R.E.A., but he certainly was a disenchanted companion. Athearn caustically criticized narrowness of viewpoint specifically dominated by George A. Coe. He wrote: "It [R.E.A.] has failed to be free, its controlling group being of one color and belonging to one school. It represents Columbia and Chicago, especially George Albert Coe. . . .

The Movement is too behavioristic in psychology, too deterministic in philosophy and too nonpersonal in its theology."[14]

Others, though less personal in their attacks, agreed with Athearn. Edmund Davison Soper of Duke University wrote critically of its future: "Religion is too thin in the R.E.A. group." And Bishop Hughes noted that the R.E.A. had no room for honest conservatives who were trying to "think their way through."

The report did not assess these criticisms. Thus, although the most profound critique was contained among those responses, it never emerged in the report summary. In denying the conservative, the honest dissenter, the more theologically minded, the R.E.A. cut off the very debate which would have been so essential to a truly open forum. Yet as the twenties and thirties unfolded, Athearn's basic criticism did ring true, though it was more prophetic and predictive than analytical of the period in which he wrote.

A second major area of criticism opened with the inclusion of a long letter from Edwin D. Starbuck, professor of philosophy at the University of Iowa. Starbuck had dropped his affiliation with the R.E.A. only after careful consideration and years of frustrating leadership as secretary of the Department of Universities and Colleges. His letter underlined the difficulty of the scholar and intellectual in achieving dialogue within the context of the R.E.A. He noted that the organization appealed to those "wholesomely interested" in religious education but not really involved in pursuing scholarly investigation. As leader of the Department of Universities and Colleges, he described his frustration in leading scholarly work in that area. "I had to fight constantly to keep people of the Y.M.C.A. type and the students who were simply interested in bibliographical interpretations from capturing the meetings."[15]

So the organization seemed caught in its own historical dilemma. How could it serve a diverse membership with varying interests and levels of educational competence without becoming either a gathering of professionally elite or more pluralistic, appealing to religious education volunteers as well as church professionals.

The early attempts to provide departments of interest had not worked successfully except in the case of the Council of Religious Education (sixty members elected by the board of directors). That effort at maintaining a special self-perpetuating elite leadership had led to charges of special privilege and authoritarianism, as well as narrowness of viewpoint.

The journal's editorial policy remained unresolved; it continued to be open to all sorts of articles from serious to practical to mundane. Attempts to revise the conventions into discussion sessions had not, according to the report, received general acceptance. The library which Coe believed "should in time become one of the greatest research libraries of the country" was inadequately housed, inaccessible to a large percentage of membership, and, as indicated earlier, certainly not uniform or comprehensive in significant areas of religious education concerns (especially theology and biblical studies).

Most of the criticisms could be summarized by noting the paradoxical assumption of the association, that democratic inclusiveness could sustain intellectual and scholarly excellence. The 1925 investigation attempted to address that question and the recommendations reflect a decision to maintain that historical quest. Problems and inherent difficulties would reemerge, but the ideal was not to be abandoned.

Recommendations advised continuation of the R.E.A. without any significant change in membership. No effort was made in the report to resolve the lay-professional dilemma. The suggestions simply advised the continuation of the past, with its failures, successes, frustrations, and democratic potential. Forces to move the R.E.A. to a "learned" society failed and democratic idealism prevailed.

The report advised modification in certain policies and practices. Membership fees were to be raised. The staff was to be enlarged to include a full-time secretary and an editorial secretary responsible for all publications.

The journal was advised to coordinate policy with the new *International Journal of Religious Education (I.J.R.E.)*. The report suggested that *Religious Education* might become the more scholarly and research-oriented while the *I.J.R.E.* would represent the practical and methodological.

Conventions received considerable attention. Convention planning must be more thorough with specific attention given to adult learning. Conventions were to be held in conjunction with other learned societies thus enhancing the scholarly appeal and enriching the R.E.A. constituency while not tampering with the decision to remain an open non-scholarly independent gathering of any and all religious educators.

A significant recommendation established a committee on research designed to promote and seek financial support for important religious education research. Though the R.E.A. would not directly undertake research (clearly consistent with early practice), its role would be that of support and promotion.

The report proposed further study of the role of the R.E.A. in relationship to other similar organizations. It modestly suggested that far more research and time needed to be spent on this question. Duplication and the emergence of many related "learned societies" meant that the R.E.A. needed to spend more time determining exactly which role it might play in the future.

Final recommendations simply affirmed the new constitutional changes already adopted which had democratized the organization with the development of the board of directors instead of the council, thus insuring the idea that the leadership of the R.E.A. would truly be representative of its membership and not just a select inner circle.[16]

Results

The association essentially maintained its historical character. It was liberal, white, Protestant. It consisted of left-of-center religious educators who were tolerant of liberal excesses but intolerant of dogmatism and conservative authoritarianism.

Some changes were easy. The staff recommendations were almost immediately followed, and within the next few years, the R.E.A. office consisted of four full-time workers—a general secretary, editorial secretary, higher education specialist, and assistant secretary.

No conclusive judgments can be made in regard to the recommendation to coordinate editorial policy between *Religious Education* and *I.J.R.E.* No primary data conclusively document the fact that any meetings between the editors of the new *I.J.R.E.* and *Religious Education* did in fact happen. Yet as one compares these two journals, it seems apparent that such coordination did take place. (The offices were in close proximity in Chicago.) The journals did not duplicate efforts as indicated by style, organization of topics, and public editorial policy.

The *I.J.R.E.* published its first issue in October of 1924. Representing "thirty-five Evangelical Communions and fifty-six State and Provincial Councils,"[17] the journal was geared to Sunday School workers and other primarily nonprofessional types as well as professional religious educators and pastors. The appeal went out to all groups, but the material was much like that of earlier Sunday School journals. As one reviews those early volumes, one finds many R.E.A. leaders writing brief articles for the new journal. Betts, McKibben, Bower, Richardson, Winchester, Vieth, Elliott, Artman, Hartshorne, Chave, and Coe were all contributors in the first two volumes. The style and focus of the *I.J.R.E.* was distinctly different from the R.E.A.'s own *Religious Education*. Articles were brief, one or two pages. Advertisements filled the issues, and readers were encouraged to purchase all sorts of Sunday School and church paraphernalia.

The I.C.R.E.'s journal could not afford to offend its diverse public, so the majority of the content was inspirational, not scholarly. Specifically Protestant-Christian, the new journal contained no material written by Jewish or Catholic religious educators. If there was an early concern by the R.E.A. about overlap of content or style, it was probably unnecessary. *Religious Education* became increasingly scholarly, technical, and scientifically oriented while the *I.J.R.E.* remained the Sunday School teacher's manual, complete with Christmas programs, poems by Edgar Guest, and regular post mortem "Sunday School sayings of Marion Lawrence," long-time leader of the American Sunday School movement. Since the new journal was supported by so many denominations, special care was exercised to dilute controversial material and attempts were made to represent the wide spectrum of evangelical Protestantism.

The new journal was an outgrowth of the new International Council of Religious Education, a major successful Protestant ecumenical effort of that decade. The history of that development is fairly told in a balanced interpretation, *Protestantism Faces Its Educational Task Together,* by William Clayton Bower and Percy Roy Hayward.[18] Long years were spent in building this coalition; once conceived, every effort was made to sustain its success and build its future.

The *I.J.R.E.* was the natural child of the two earlier magazines: the *Sunday School Worker* and the *Church School.* It was therefore in the vulnerable position of representing a wide spectrum of theological opinions while remaining committed to the basic theology of the new council. One perceives a distinctly conservative Christocentric position. *Religious Education,* on the other hand, was more experimental and seemed to have been given free rein to develop into a first-class scholarly journal without any serious competition.

Conventions would continue as in the past. Planning was more careful, staff more abundant, and finances more available—for a time. In this period the R.E.A. never drew the large numbers that attended the early conventions of the association. It could not match the successful annual conventions of the International Council where thousands attended regularly (more than 7000 in 1926). As one compares agenda and reads presentations made at the two related organizations' conventions, it is clear that the R.E.A., though never acknowledging the fact, was by far the more professional and scholarly of the two groups. Moreover, the R.E.A. was broadly religious rather than specifically Christian in perspective.

Research became an important concern for the R.E.A. during this period. The association successfully supported and encouraged serious research in *Religious Education,* regularly publishing results and new doctoral research on an annual basis.

Finally, the association remained financially independent and maintained a profile separate from all other associations, either churchly or academic. Determined not to become either popular or professional, the R.E.A. continued its faltering path toward a decade of major success, destined to end again in crisis some ten years later. The R.E.A. would remain a fellowship of those committed to the task of changing the world by professionalizing the task of religious education.

Religious education might not change the world. It did however change the universities. Religious education programs became important departments in major universities and the literature of religious education grew with the new discipline. Leaders of the R.E.A. represented the first generation of professionals committed to building a new profession, that of religious education. Their productivity was impressive and the quality of their work, though uneven, represented a serious intellectual effort to build a body of disciplined research and theory to nurture the new profession and the growing numbers of religious educators.

Professionalizing Religious Education: Educating the Educators

One of the marks of any recognized profession is a body of literature that serves as a standard and rule (paradigm) for the practitioners of the field. Members of the R.E.A. were the major authors of that growing body of literature which would serve as the accepted professional guidelines for the practice of religious education. Though the R.E.A. did not set about a major publication effort (with the exception of the regular journal *Religious Education*), many significant leaders of the R.E.A. were at the same time the professional mentors of the emerging new discipline. The R.E.A. served as neutral ground, as a space where the new insights could be debated and encouraged. As a haven for liberal progressives, the R.E.A. gave collegial support to those whose careers were to lead a new profession into maturity.

In 1903 there was no professional literature of religious education. There was no common word with which to image the phenomenon. There were Sunday School manuals and volumes of helpful Bible commentaries to assist in teaching the Bible, but there was no literature of religious education. By 1923 that literature had grown into a voluminous body of material ranging from a great deal of progressive conventional wisdom to mature, thoughtful theories of public nurture. The first generation of literary leaders were almost without exception members of the R.E.A. They were the theorists, experimenters, innovators. They were also the elite group of professors who dominated the developing field of religious education in the seminary and university.

The three major concentrations of religious education literary activity corresponded to the three major centers of educational activity of that period: Chicago, represented by the University of Chicago, Northwestern University, and Garrett Biblical Institute; New York, represented by Teachers College, Columbia University and Union Theological Seminary; and New England, dominated by the intellectual centers of Yale University and Boston University. Each school was usually associated with a major theorist and together these academics molded the literature of religious education for the next three decades.

In 1930 Paul Vieth, then executive director of curriculum development of the *I.C.R.E.,* published the most important book of his career: *Objectives in Religious Education.* In attempting to select the major theorists in religious education at that time, he submitted a questionnaire to two hundred thirteen professors of religious education throughout the United States. Eighty-four persons responded to his inquiry and nominated the top ten most significant authors of that period. They were the following:

Joseph M. Artman, R.E.A. Executive Secretary

Walter Scott Athearn, Dean of the School of Religious Education, Boston University

George Herbert Betts, Northwestern University

William Clayton Bower, University of Chicago

George A. Coe, Columbia University (in retirement)

Henry F. Cope (deceased), first General Secretary of the R.E.A.

Hugh Hartshorne, Yale University

Norman Egbert Richardson, Northwestern University

Theodore Gerald Soares, University of Chicago

Luther Allan Weigle, Yale University[19]

In addition to these names it is useful in retrospect to add several others whose contributions during the twenties and thirties equalled those listed by Vieth. In the Chicago cluster, three significant contributors must be added. Shailer Mathews, dean of the Divinity School at the University of Chicago, continued until the end of his career to lead the Chicago school, especially as religious education related to the critical area of biblical studies. The University of Chicago's style of liberal modernism was not yet divorced from those biblical moorings. Ernest Chave was added to the staff at the University of Chicago in 1928 completing a faculty that felt secure in its leadership role in religious education. In 1928 Dean Mathews would write: "We have what is coming to be regarded, as it undoubtedly is, the best department of religious education in the United States."[20] And one could hardly omit the name of Frank McKibben of Garrett/Northwestern who served for years as a moderate influence on the Chicago scene.

Though it is true that George Albert Coe dominated the Columbia/Union religious education community from 1909–1927, four additional first generation religious educators completed that constellation and provided leadership in the Coe tradition during the twenties and thirties. Those persons were Harrison Elliott, disciple and heir-apparent to Coe, Goodwin Watson, Columbia-appointed professor of religion after declining the offer to become general secretary of the R.E.A. after Cope's death, and two women, early pioneers in religious education. They were Sophia Fahs, director of the Union School of Religion and instructor at Union Seminary, and Adelaide Case, professor of religious education at Teachers College, Columbia University. The productive Teachers College/Union Seminary connection dominated the liberal religious education scene, particularly during Coe's tenure and long after his retirement.

Though it is probably risky and impossible to describe with accuracy a school of thought associated with each major center of study, one can make some basic generalizations about the work of each institution and the significant features of their key contributions.

Boston School of Religious Education

Walter Athearn, dean of the Boston School of Religious Education and Social Science, promoted church day-school efforts during the twenties and thirties. As founder of the Boston School of Religious Education and the Malden Plan, Athearn expanded his theory to encompass the entire national system of public and church education in an effort to build a new Protestant strategy of religious education. His model was derived from his own pioneering work in Malden, Massachusetts. The central ideal was to organize religious education in every community throughout the nation into a system of religious instruction which would parallel the public school system and equal that system in excellence, facilities, faculties, and modern methodology, as well as modern material.

Such a system would include four elements:

1. A system of schools of religion for people of all ages;
2. A system of leadership training;
3. A system of administration and supervision; and
4. A system of professional agencies to guarantee the academic freedom of the schools and the professional growth of teachers and administrators.[21]

In a book entitled *A National System of Education* (1920), Athearn outlined a comprehensive proposal to redesign all of American education. His proposals, were they to have been successful, would have changed the basic character of American education. And for a period of time during the twenties, the "day school" (released time) movement did flourish in many communities. City systems existed in Gary, Indiana; Evanston and Oak Park, Illinois; Pittsburgh, Pennsylvania; Birmingham, Alabama; Austin, Texas; and scores of other communities throughout the country.[22]

Athearn's forte was administrative theory. His books included specific designs for churches and schools plus details about the organization of physical facilities.[23] He provided exacting instructions for curriculum design with special attention to the curriculum for training professional leaders in religious education. He tested his theory in his own Boston School of Religious Education and Social Service. He modeled this educational program around professional goals rather than the customary academic four-year college or typical Ph.D. programs.[24] Athearn was severely critical of the R.E.A. and its single-minded theoretical position of Coe. Yet, as one reads carefully his extensive publications of design and theory, one is drawn to the conclusion that inadvertently Athearn, perhaps more clearly than any other colleague, understood and implemented Coe's notions about a public democratic pedagogy; he had created a functional design for Coe's esoteric "democracy of God."

In his volume *Religious Education and American Democracy* (1917), Athearn's community system of religious education effectively demonstrates what a "democracy of God" might look like. His description and safeguards are reasonable and thorough. Consider these guidelines. Each community would be responsible for the election of a board of directors. The selection would be representative of all elements in the community. Such a system would be free from ecclesiastical control. Safeguards would be built into the design to prevent commercial control, and a strong appeal was made in behalf of academic freedom. Religious educators would determine the limits of their curricula and methodology. The board of directors would be elected in a manner similar to the election of school boards.

The least detailed and most unrealistic part of his design had to do with the financial basis for such a program. Athearn turned to goodwill, endowments, church contributions, and voluntary fees plus modest tuition charges. This fiscal program proved most difficult to manage as the day school movement grew. No system of taxation ever emerged; no community support base similar to the public school tax base ever began. As the prosperous days of the 1920s turned to lean depression years, the movement lost momentum—not because of theory, but because of fiscal instability.[25]

Apart from Athearn's unrealistic economic projections, he tended toward yet another optimistic excess. He believed in the messianic character of religious education. He lacked Coe's realism about evil and was euphoric about the potential of religious education to save the world. As medical science had removed yellow fever so the "science of religious education can as effectively eliminate dishonesty, lying, cruelty, and other vices." Athearn's national system of education was designed to accomplish that goal.[26]

The Chicago Scene

In contrast to the Boston School of Religious Education and Social Services, the Chicago arena is more difficult to characterize. Centered at the University of Chicago and Northwestern University/Garrett Biblical Institute (Garrett-Evangelical Theological Seminary) in Evanston, complemented by the R.E.A. central promotional office, Chicago dominated the literature of religious education during the early 1920s. The reasons are not difficult to understand. Chicago had been the center of the origin of the religious education movement in the formative days of the R.E.A. Coe and Harper significantly influenced the profession, both organizationally and professionally. By the middle 1920s the University of Chicago Divinity School was considered to be among the most esteemed of the modernist centers of theological education. Built initially by Harper and presided over by Harper's close friend, Shailer Mathews, the Chicago school had a solid reputation in the modernist camp early in the twentieth century.

If the University of Chicago was the prominent center of liberal Protestant modernism, Northwestern University could claim to be the most popular center of religious education training. In an annual report submitted by the education department to the university president, Walter Dill Scott, in 1923, the following figures indicated the high interest and success in the religious education program of the university. Registered students in the religious education classes were the largest number in these related courses.[27]

	1919–1920	1920–1921	1921–1922	1922–1923	1923–1924
Biblical Literature	166	165	136	207	270
History of Religion	31	113	135	120	105
Religious Education	201	356	274	347	336

Religious education became part of the School of Education at Northwestern. It was located in the Divinity School of the University of Chicago. These placements are reflected in the literature from both schools. Northwestern was more representative of educational concerns, and the University of Chicago was more characterized by biblical and theological considerations.

The University of Chicago

A contemporary University of Chicago theologian, David Tracy, in his recent *Blessed Rage for Order, the New Pluralism in Theology,* succinctly defines modernism as follows: "The liberal and modernist theologian accepts the distinctively modern commitment to values of free and open inquiry, autonomous judgment, critical investigation on all claims to scientific, historical, philosophical, and religious truth."[28] That Shailer Mathews was central to that movement is clear from Sidney Mead's cryptic description of Mathews as "the oustanding modernist."[29] Mathews' own productivity undeniably gained him—and the Chicago school—that distinction.

In a series of books published between 1910 and 1934, Mathews articulated the parameters of Christian modernism. Claiming that modernism is neither theology nor denominational bias, Mathews stated: "It is the use of methods of modern science to find, state, and use the permanent and central values of inherited orthodoxy in meeting the needs of the modern world." According to Mathews, the modernist movement was "a phase of the scientific struggle for freedom in thought and belief." Modernists were "Christians who accept the result of scientific research as data with which to think religiously." They "adopt the methods of historical and literary science in the study of the Bible and religion." They were committed to "help men meet social as well as individual needs." They were optimistic Christians who believed "that the spiritual and moral needs of the world can be met because they are intellectually convinced that Christian attitudes and faiths are consistent with other realities." But Mathews insisted that the modernist was specifically Christian. "That is, they accept Jesus Christ as the revelation of a Savior God." And in summary he stated: "In brief then, the use of scientific historical, social method in understanding and applying evangelical Christianity to the needs of living persons is modernism."[30]

Those sentiments dominated the thinking of the University of Chicago school of religious education in the early years. The *Constructive Series* initiated by the Harper/Mathews/Burton partnership was built on these convictions. The religious education literature produced by the central figures of the University of Chicago continued those essential beliefs, though gradually they moved from Christian ideology to humanistic pluralism.

Theodore Soares, William Clayton Bower, and Ernest Chave continued the modernist tradition with special application to the arena of religious education. Though trained in educational theory rather than theology (as Mathews' and Harper's training had been), they extended the modernist position into the field of religious education.

Theodore Soares outlined this position in a volume entitled simply *Religious Education,* published by the University of Chicago Press in 1928. All the elements of Mathews' description were present in Soares' argument. He rejected any "natural depravity," opting instead for a scientific viewpoint that the essential nature of a person was to be defined "sociologically and biologically." Morality was not an inherent value, it was a matter of social process. In agreement with Coe's viewpoint about democratic religion, Soares called for a social theology built around an ideal community which lived out its beliefs. In the tradition of Harper and Mathews, Soares was dedicated to finding God in the social process. Even as late as 1928 he wrote with optimism about "rebuilding a world that has been sorely shaken."[31]

A spiritual depression in the middle 1920s, so convincingly described by Robert Handy in *A Christian America: Protestant Hopes and Historical Realities,*[32] failed to dampen the enthusiasm of the University of

Chicago religious educators. While it might be generally true that the 1920s represented difficult days for liberal Protestantism, those effects were not felt until the 1930s in the field of Protestant religious education. The 1920s were days of profound optimism among the Chicago leaders of religious education. The profession was only beginning, schools of religious education were filled with students, and the publication of literature was highly successful.

Ernest Chave, writing in 1931 about the *Supervision of Religious Education,* described that optimism. "There is no need of a pessimistic attitude or feeling of inevitability when one witnesses the multiplied shortcomings of religious education. Things can be changed, and supervision offers one of the most fruitful ways of effecting change."[33] While the book was a serious description of supervision techniques, the underlying presupposition was an enduring optimism that God is "at the heart of the universe" to be discovered and worshiped by the process of social involvement. Chave's own definition of religious education is reminiscent of that of the founder of the R.E.A. Such sentiments were in direct continuity with Harper's religious democracy. Chave wrote:

> By religious education we mean the development of the ideas and habits that are of the highest social character. We mean a growth in a vital conception of God, an increasing valuation of life itself, and an enlarging capacity and responsibility for all social relationships. It involves the study of the best religious experiences and traditions of the race, including a particular study of the records in the Bible, with the current beliefs and practices of religion in the world today. It also means helping each person to get a working philosophy of life, and to put into practice the ideals inspired by an evolving religious experience.[34]

Perhaps the most significant religious educator at the University of Chicago was William Clayton Bower. Bower's influence extended beyond 1935, and two of his most significant books were written after that date. These were *The Living Bible* (1936) and *Christ and Christian Education* (1943). His best known work was published in 1925, *Curriculum of Religious Education.* Bower wrote the book before coming to the University of Chicago, while still on the faculty of the College of Bible in Lexington, Kentucky. The book was a careful statement of the best of current progressive curriculum theory of that period. Bower was committed to an experimental view. "Curriculum is experience under intelligent and purposeful control." He was in agreement with a social view of education similar to Dewey's viewpoint expressed in *Democracy and Education.* Bower was also directly aligned with the liberalism of his day. Christianity was the exercise of social experience. Its outcome was to hasten the kingdom of God. He wrote: "Without neglecting persons or groups, it must seek in the end to build a Christian society that rests upon shared Christian ideals and purposes. Only so can the kingdom of God, in which persons are all the while finding a rich and abundant life, be realized."[35]

Bower's influence expanded with his appointment to the University of Chicago faculty. His published books and articles were balanced, thoughtful assessments of the best progressive educational theories of his time. Not given to rhetorical excess, his work was compelling and intellectually satisfying. Deeply committed to the scientific enterprise, he maintained an equally responsible allegiance to historical Christianity. He viewed *The Living Bible* (1936) as his major contribution. The book was a conscious effort to save the Scriptures in a manner congruent with the best of scientific evidence while avoiding the impact of neo-orthodoxy. Bower's writing is an example of the best of the modernist tradition: "In a prescientific period, Christian theology thought of our world as static, and therefore it thought of creation as having been accomplished through fiat. Modern science, however, has demonstrated that our universe is a process, continuing through vast extensions of time." Bower continued: "As a result of the same process, the modern Christian has come to think of creation as still in process, with unimaginable possibilities still in store for the human race."[36]

The University of Chicago religious educators would not limit educational theory to schooling, but would accent the broader dimension of education, maintaining a cultural understanding of the social task of education and an awareness of the multitude of agencies and influences which form children. The University of Chicago theorists were the natural heirs of the Harper tradition, and from my viewpoint, kept that tradition alive well into the 1930s. No better summary of that understanding could be made than Bower's own words about the scope of the educational enterprise. "The education of the child is by no means confined to the conscious efforts of the formal school, whether public or religious, or of the home, however deeply concerned it may be with the normal development of the child. Every thing that enters, even in the remotest way, into the life of the child educates—the atmosphere of the home, the news of the daily press, the advertisements on the way to and from school, the informal face-to-face groups that form and dissolve on the street, the moves, the subtle 'atmosphere' of the community."[37]

The University of Chicago department of religious education operated as a liberal group of colleagues, neither narrow in their religious viewpoint nor limited in their professional relationships with other Chicago academicians. The collegiality had long extended from Hyde Park to Evanston where professional companionships were formed. Relations between these two departments had a long history of harmony dating back to the time when Coe (Northwestern) and associates initially formed the R.E.A. Shailer Mathews was open in his admiration of the Northwestern/Garrett efforts in progressive education.[38] And the two schools of religious education maintained close relationships through their local R.E.A. contacts as well as by their prolific publication schedule.

Northwestern/Garrett

Three names dominated the literature of these institutions: Norman E. Richardson, Frank McKibben, and George Herbert Betts. Their work dealt mostly with religious education method and early research rather than with theological distinctiveness or serious biblical criticism. The major Northwestern/Garrett influence had to do with educational issues and administrative practices. Since both schools were supported directly by Methodist constituencies, the theological demeanor of the practitioners tended toward a more conservative and Christocentric model of concern than did their neighbors to the south at the University of Chicago. The school of religious education remained closely aligned with the latest public school research and literature. It is interesting and probably understandable that one of the major voices of criticism of religious education in that period published his public critique of liberal religious education one year after he left Northwestern to become a professor of religious education at Presbyterian Theological Seminary in Chicago.

That person was Norman Richardson. His early works, *The Church at Play* (1922) and *The Religious Education of Adolescents* (1913), were not particularly distinctive or creative statements of research or intellectual prose. They were summaries of current theory in the field of education at the time they were written. They were pedantic in style and certainly noncontroversial in tone and content. They had to do with practical matters of child development and principles of recreational leadership as applied to the church.[39]

Richardson's book, *The Christ of the Classroom: How to Teach Evangelical Christianity,* rejected the liberal religious education movement associated with the R.E.A. and the University of Chicago. The basic lines of Richardson's argument follows:[40] Religious education ought to be centered around the person and teaching of Jesus. The early chapters attempted to develop a religious education method after the practices of Jesus, the master teacher. Calling for an evangelical religious education, Richardson reminded his readers that religious education needed to address the learner as sinner and teach conversion. He called for biblical content and clear Christian objectives, namely the rehearsal of the events of Jesus's life, death, and resurrection as means toward changing behavior. Again the style of these chapters tended toward a proof-text method.

The best argued viewpoint and most satisfying reasoning were contained in the chapter which evaluated the current practices of religious education. Richardson singled out the then president of the R.E.A., William Adams Brown's statement which pleaded for cooperation between the humanist and the theist. Brown's viewpoint seemed to Richardson to be a denial of the Christian perspective.

Richardson claimed that R.E.A. leaders were asking Christians to deny their basic convictions. "Those who cherish a mystical experience of the Holy Spirit which to them is a sacred and mysterious demonstration of God within their own personalities are asked to consider these facts of experience from a naturalistic point of view." All this, according to Richardson, so that they can have fellowship with the "ethical culturalists" and promote religious education thinking which is on an "avowedly secular basis."[41]

He then referred to the 1929 Northwestern conference on the relationships between religion and conduct (the second research conference sponsored by the R.E.A.) and noted the lack of Christian conviction represented by the religious educators in attendance. He hastened to underline their basic timidity by quoting an article by Eustace Haydon (of the University of Chicago) which disparaged the use of the Christian tradition as relevant to contemporary religious education practices.

Then in a sarcastic and bitter attack, he reviewed the coverage by *Religious Education* of John Dewey's book, *The Quest for Certainty*. He pointed out the lack of serious Christian witness by the *Religious Education* reviews; they reflected uncertainty and unfaith. The review, according to Richardson, suggested that "our people would be far better off if there weren't any professors or departments of religious education." Such men (believing Christian professors) were according to the review "a social nuisance in proportion to the genuineness and sincerity of their religion." Richardson chided those "brilliant philosophical" minds who believe that religion is "educed out of empirical experience." In sum, Richardson taunted those who ridicule "a transient brush of a fancied angel's wing." Richardson went with the "angels."[42]

Richardson was not shy about his own Christian convictions or about the genesis of the religious educator's problems. He pointed to the reliance of religious education on secular education theory (certainly on target!) and to the influence of behaviorism and the widespread ''science-mindedness.'' He advocated instead a spiritual religious education, a reliance on religious values and faith concerns rather than scientific verification. He urged a renewal of biblical values and challenged the religious educator with the task of faith. His appeal was conservative and though not totally convincing (for the biblical method seemed imposed and strained), Richardson did in fact point to some significant future dangers in the development of liberal religious education, specifically the absence of theological seriousness and biblical continuity, as well as the pseudo-scientific optimism of overly zealous scientific believers.

Richardson's criticisms paralleled Walter Athearn's (another R.E.A. colleague) views in *The Minister and the Teacher*.[43] In that book, Athearn had leveled his most lucid criticism against the emergence of behaviorism, empiricism, and the inadequacy of the ''project method'' as the single best method for evangelical Christian religious teaching. But Richardson went further than Athearn in a strong objection to Athearn's basic principle of community control of religious education. He called for a renewal of biblical traditions and the vital role of the church as arbiter of the truthfulness of its message.

He claimed that in ''some quarters'' (the R.E.A.) there was a denial of the great ''spiritual affirmations'' and ''the eternal values of the Gospel message.'' Richardson was labeling religious education as essentially non-Christian.[44] Richardson's contribution was significant, in retrospect, though negatively so. There is little evidence that his convictions changed the opinion of his more liberal R.E.A. colleagues. Yet his critique was more prophetic than he or his peers could have known at the time. Later in the decade and into the 1940s, the essentials of his argument would gain support with the advent of neo-orthodoxy. His voice predicted the R.E.A. drift toward humanistic values which were ill-prepared to abate the future realities of financial collapse and the awesome evil of Nazism, along with the major metaphor of sin of the twentieth century—the Holocaust.

Frank McKibben, a student of Richardson and a graduate of Northwestern University, had returned to teach there in the 1920s. He became chairperson of the religious education department in 1930 and joined the faculty at Garrett as the major professor of religious education in 1942. McKibben represented the moderate, informed, committed churchman throughout his career. While accepting the essential progressive educational attitudes of the times, he consistently affirmed the dimension of faith as the central quality of Christian education. His books[45] were always modified with an evangelical sensitivity which made his work theologically noncontroversial and inherently useful to the Methodist community and its educational future. Religious education prospered under his leadership at Northwestern and Garrett, and he framed the tradition that continues until the present at those institutions. Less controversial than Richardson, gentle and thorough in administrative skill, he lived out his professional career leaving a legacy of competence and moderation in the school of religious education at Garrett Seminary.[46]

The third and most significant Northwestern author was George Herbert Betts. His tenure at Northwestern extended from 1919 to 1934. Most of his books were concerned with method rather than religious education theory.[47]

Two books dealt with specific religious education research which Betts conducted while at Northwestern University. The first, *The Beliefs of 700 Ministers and Their Meaning for Religious Education* (1929), described an interesting research project which Betts conducted among the Protestant clergy of the Chicago area. The questionnaire addressed to the more than 1500 clergymen consisted of fifty-six questions related to belief categories, the question of God, the view of Scripture, images of Jesus, and doctrinal concerns related to traditional Christian beliefs. Betts' work is important for it illustrates basic research in behalf of religious education theory.[48]

According to Betts, great diversity of belief existed among all denominations except among Lutherans. He concluded that "no denomination except perhaps the Lutherans has any right to demand that fixed creeds shall be taught the young. For the clergy of any denomination themselves do not subscribe to a common creed beyond belief in the existence of God."[49] Methodists, on the opposite end from the Lutherans, reflected the least unity of belief. Large numbers expressed doubt on traditional questions of the veracity of miracles, the resurrection, scriptural inspiration, and even the dogma of the Trinity. Twenty percent did not accept a Trinitarian view of God.

Theological students responding (200) were even more diverse in their viewpoints and considerably less orthodox. Betts commented: "As compared with the ministers, the beliefs of these students reflect a more distinct drift away from the older or orthodox positions and a tendency to be in accord with the scientific thought of the day." He continued: "Like the ministers, all accept as fact the existence of God. Less than half (44 percent), however, accept the doctrine of the Trinity, against 80 percent of the ministers. Nor do the students believe in an unchangeable God, 44 percent either denying this concept or expressing uncertainty. The Genesis account of Creation is literal fact to only 5 percent of this group while 47 percent of the ministers approve the view.''[50]

Betts made these suggestions. No Protestant denomination except the Lutherans has any right to demand of its religious educators the teaching of specific doctrinal standards, for the clergy themselves do not agree. Some very simple form of creedal statement ought to be developed by all denominations. Such a creed dealing with a few great areas of experience would have general acceptance among major denominations. The Apostles Creed and other traditional creedal statements probably should not be taught nor used in worship, for there is such general disagreement about the tenets of those traditional statements. Since there is such wide diversity of belief among Christian ministers, Betts concluded that no individual or sect ought to enforce on the young particular beliefs, for such data are always a belief and not accessible to any demonstrable proof. Christians should form a commission of scholars to formulate a new creedal statement, growing out of universal human experience, proved knowledge, and reasoned conclusions. Until then, one should accept belief as one instrument in the development of individuals or societies, but not a matter to warrant arrogance or intolerance. Honest agnostic seekers are much preferred to the militant dogmatist who demands acceptance of truth as he believes.[51]

Betts' appeal was an implicit rebuke to the more conservative and fundamentalistic religious communities. His proposals were consistent with the R.E.A. tradition, one should teach only those values that are derived from reasonable human experience. Rather than seeing the data as a manifestation of theological inadequacy or a signpost to a future ''gathering storm''[52] between laypersons and professionals, Betts preferred to accept the wisdom of diversity and skepticism rather than examine its origin or modification.

In 1931 Betts published a second research project titled *The Character Outcomes of Present-Day Religion: 300 Churchmen Judge the Effect of Current Teaching and Preaching*. He addressed two questions to the 1000 persons invited to the 1929 Northwestern Conference on religion and conduct. These questions were:

1. Do our churches today teach and preach a religion that can effectively influence conduct and character?
2. If they do, why is it not working better to that end?[53]

Knowing the results of that conference and having edited the conference papers in a volume titled *Religion and Conduct*,[54] Betts obviously anticipated the outcome of his own research and that bias surely found expression in question two.

Three hundred respondents replied representing these categories of churchmen:[55]

Ministers 63
Directors of religious education 45
Members of overhead organizations (administrators) 55
Professors in colleges and seminaries 96
Laymen active in the church. 41

The results underlined the uncertainty that Richardson was so critical of in his attack on current practices in religious education. Betts' results were as follows in question #1:[56]

	Yes	No	Qualified
Ministers	28%	45%	27%
Directors of religious education	28%	36%	36%
Members of overhead organizations (administrators)	27%	20%	53%
Professors in colleges and seminaries	29%	34%	37%
Laymen active in the church	25%	36%	36%

The findings were not surprising to Betts. He was able to corroborate his own research with that of the Hartshorne-May findings, Hightower's University of Iowa Studies in Character, and Mursell's study related to delinquency and religious knowledge. All these studies produced essentially the same result as summarized by Goodwin Watson in the May 26, 1931, issue of *Christian Century*. "Scientific investigations have revealed beyond any reasonable doubt that people given the religious training now common in homes and churches do not develop characters superior to the ordinary virtues of persons without such training."[57]

Betts had five suggestions to modify those results. The church needs to focus its teaching and preaching on the task of influencing the daily conduct of members. Young Christians are equally important as adult members. The church must be in tune with modern knowledge. The focus of ministry must deal with "character" goals. And finally, churches need to direct their teaching and preaching to real-life questions.[58]

One might argue that Betts himself fell into the trap of advocating moral character change without really defining how those behaviors would be modified. The essential tone of his suggestions was obviously meant to alert the church to the behavioral rather than to the intellectual or sacramental task of nurturing faith.

Betts typified the R.E.A. progressive religious education. He sought to improve religious education by taking seriously the scientific data available and making application to the work of religious instruction. His major contribution was to inform the religious education community of the prevailing theories growing out of psychology and public education theory and adapting those theories to religious education. Never claiming to be a theologian, he sought insight from his own discipline, psychology.

Yale Divinity School

In contrast to the educational accent and social science orientation of Northwestern, the major themes of religious education literature which grew out of Yale's divinity school could be characterized as essentially concerned with a more biblical orientation. The two dominant Yale figures of the 1920s and 1930s were Luther Allan Weigle and Paul Vieth. Both wrote extensively and extended their influence throughout the Protestant world particularly as contributions to the national and world Sunday School movement.

Luther Allan Weigle came to Yale as the Horace Bushnell Professor of Christian Nurture in 1916 and remained there until his retirement in 1949. During that time his students produced a significant amount of research in religious education, published as the "Yale Studies in the History and Theology of Religious Education."[59] Another important contribution remains his successful leadership and guidance toward the publication of the *Revised Standard Version of the Bible.*

His most popular volume, *The Pupil and the Teacher,* was published early in his career (1911), while he was professor of philosophy at the small midwest Carleton College. That single book sold more than a million copies and remains today a marvelous document of readable prose for Sunday School teachers. He managed to introduce the major research and theory of that period in understandable, nontechnical language. The book was a synthesis of religious and education theorists, of psychological and theological opinion, but written with a deep faithfulness to the Christian tradition. While introducing thousands of Protestant Sunday School teachers to modern religious education theory, Weigle was also able to affirm their religious convictions and faith concerns. It is the best of ''mediational'' literature. The same comments might be made of Weigle's *The Training of Children in the Christian Family* (1922), which I view as a twentieth century restatement of Bushnell's *Christian Nurture*.[60]

But Luther Weigle was essentially a theologian and philosopher, and his concerns remained biblical throughout his career. At the end of his professional life (1933) he wrote an essay, "The Religious Education of a Protestant," which was published posthumously in a set of essays entitled *The Glory Days*. The following excerpts illustrate Weigle's theological facility, his deep loyalty to the Christian Gospel, and his ability to expand that vision ecumenically. While remaining moderate in theological perspectives, he was able to assimilate the liberal tradition without abandoning the central message of historical Christianity.

Protestantism according to Weigle was about "democracy in religion." Protestants affirm "the right of individual judgment and the universal priesthood of believers." Protestants are not about monastic cells, celibate vows, or withdrawal from the world. Rather they are concerned with the "common duties and the homely responsibilities of this present world." Salvation "is possible here and now." God's fatherhood is assured "in the life and teaching, the death and resurrection of Jesus Christ." It is because Jesus gives "us a glimpse of ultimate Reality" that we understand the character and disposition of God. Protestantism is not organizational, or concerned primarily about polity; it is rather "a spirit, a way of thinking and living. To realize this gospel in my own life and to equip young people to be its effective ministers is my vocation."[61] Those statements reveal the deep Christology and theological conservatism of Luther Weigle. Though he outgrew his Lutheranism, he never lost the imprint of that tradition.

Paul Vieth came to Yale in 1931, the end of the period under consideration in this chapter. He remained at Yale until 1963, when he retired. The book which was possibly his most influential, *Objectives in Religious Education,* was published in 1930 while he served as an administrator for the I.C.R.E. The book was the published version of his doctoral dissertation written under the guidance of his mentor, Luther Weigle. Vieth's research was based on the theoretical work of the top ten religious educators of the 1920s. Seeking the middle ground, Vieth outlined in seven objectives the major tasks of religious education. Interestingly, the first two objectives dealt with theological questions, the third with character development, and the fourth through seventh with the broader social concerns of the Christian life.[62]

In November, 1979, Randolph Crump Miller, Horace Bushnell Professor of Christian Nurture at Yale University, delivered a brief eulogy at the annual meeting of the Association of Professors and Researchers in Religious Education (A.P.R.R.E.) in Toronto. Referring to his long-time friend and colleague, Paul Vieth, Miller noted that Vieth's *Objectives in Christian Education* remains to date the most satisfying, inclusive statement of objectives in Protestant religious education.[63] I agree with Miller's evaluation.

Vieth's other books of that period, *Teaching for Christian Living* (1929) and *How to Teach in the Church School* (1935), were synthesizing efforts as well. They drew from all the major sources of the movement and were written essentially for the lay volunteer Sunday School teacher. This objective tended to make them unusually readable and satisfying prose, lacking in excessive rhetoric and always seeking moderate positions.[64]

Vieth was in touch with the center of the Christian theological tradition and was equally aware of the more liberal religious education tradition. He managed to wed these two streams in his writing and career, always attempting to relate theology to life and religious concerns to education problems.

His books built bridges from the liberalism of the 1920s to the neo-orthodoxy of the 1940s. While perhaps not as intellectually consistent in theory as George Albert Coe or Shailer Mathews, Vieth tended to reject the extremes and always maintained a close working relationship with institutional Protestantism. This is most evident in his long and involved relationship with the I.C.R.E. I suspect that this association made his work more realistic, less excessive, and as a result, less controversial. While espousing the social dimensions of the religious education tradition, Vieth always maintained an evangelical or theological balance sometimes lacking in the work of the more humanistically inclined of his R.E.A. peers.[65]

Union Seminary/Columbia University

While Yale represented a moderate influence in the development of religious education theory, Union Seminary/Columbia Teachers College probably maintained the most consistent social theory of religious education throughout this period. The constellation of educators surrounding George Albert Coe included Harrison Elliott, Hugh Hartshorne, Adelaide Case, Sophia Fahs, Goodwin Watson, and others. But it was Coe's social theme that dominated the religious education scene throughout this period, and it was his influence that molded his Morningside Heights companions.

Coe served as professor of religious education at Union Seminary from 1909–1922 and at Teachers College from 1922–1928. It was Coe who brought Hugh Hartshorne to Union to serve as director of the Union School of Religion. And it was Coe's deep, personal and social sense of justice that prompted his own resignation from Union in August of 1922 over the issue of tenure for his younger colleague, Hartshorne. Coe lived out his religious education theory, always behaving consistently with his social principles. The series of letters between President McGiffert and Coe, though laden with human misunderstanding and personal bias, clearly indicate that Coe moved to Teachers College simply because he felt that his colleague, Hartshorne, had not received justice at Union. He sacrificed some of his own financial benefits by the move but was not deterred.[66]

Coe was also influential in the selection of his successor at Union, Harrison (Sunny) Elliott. It is my conviction that Harrison Elliott, more than any other author, continued Coe's social theory by developing a specific method consistent with that theory while at the same time seriously limiting the focus of Coe's intention to method, rather than the broader educational matters of theory and philosophy. Elliott carried on in the Coe tradition at Union through the days of neo-orthodoxy until the time of his retirement in 1950. Probably more than any other person, he remained loyal to the social theory of his mentor, and as we shall note, he became a significant defender of the R.E.A. spirit of religious educa- tion with the publication of his most thoughtful book, *Can Religious Education Be Christian?* published in 1940.[67]

Elliott's major effort during the 1920s and 1930s was not, however, a theological defense of religious education theory. Rather, as Philip H. Phenix, of Columbia University, puts it, Elliott had one overwhelming interest and that was "group process."[68] Though that may not be a flattering assessment of Elliott's work, it seems a fair appraisal of his single-minded perspective.

Elliott titled his inaugural address at Union Seminary "The Signifi- cance of Process in the Progress of Christianity." The early outlines of his entire educational quest are contained in that essay delivered in 1925. Elliott criticized any form of indoctrination. He believed that religious education's concern with theology or religious matters was really an appeal to "authority," which developed dependency resting "quietly under the shadow of authority." Elliott advocated a more democratic process "involving the participation of each according to his capacity." His solution to all of religious education's problems was the application of democratic group process. Elliott opted for the experience of Christianity rather than the content of that tradition.[69]

Using psychological theory as his basis for religious education theory, Elliott inadvertently sought a new authority, that of the social scientist. In 1927 he wrote *The Bearing of Psychology Upon Religion,* a slight book which argued the traditional R.E.A. liberal position. Persons are not sinful; rather, the "kind of personality the individual has depends upon the kind of experience he has had." Elliott, still optimistic, could write, "If we would start practicing in groups, small and large, the ideals of Jesus, today we would be able to grow a generation which would not know war, a generation the members of which had developed the Christian characteristics because they had grown in an environment in which these qualities were fundamental in the life of the group."[70]

God was to be met solely in human experience. Elliott wrote, "True confidence, which is faith, grows by practice. Strength comes through endeavor. God is found as individuals find themselves in the great cooperative enterprises for human progress, in comradeships, in the great endeavors of life, in home, school, community, in race relations, political affairs, in international endeavor."[71]

Elliott's early statement of educational theory was titled *The Process of Group Thinking,* published in 1928. Once having made the intellectual equation that religion equals Christianity and Christianity equals democracy, Elliott formed a process to facilitate the democratic theory. Elliott's argument was simple. Group process theory was the basic method for democratic practice. By careful group procedures and skilled group leadership, the democratic ideal might be realized.

Elliott saw the aim of democracy as that of achieving "active participation of every individual." It was a process "all inclusive" and would take "cognizance of the immature child, of the moron, and even the criminal." In group processes persons "come with open mind and with problems." But according to Elliott there were some issues which "are not discussable." (It is not always clear what those issues include.) These values and goals were sometimes thought of as religious; they were sentiments which could be "theistic or nontheistic." For Elliott, it made little difference, for "psychologically the same thing is happening." A group "reached the spiritual plane when it is conducting its discussion in a recognition of and a search to conserve the very highest and best the group knows." Religion was reduced to group consensus.[72]

It was perhaps this kind of excess that would motivate H. Richard Niebuhr's caustic evaluation of that brand of twentieth-century radical liberalism. Niebuhr wrote: "A God without wrath brought men without sin into a kingdom without judgment through the ministrations of a Christ without a Cross."[73] Though perhaps an overstatement, Niebuhr's judgment does ring true as a single-sentence review of Elliott's *Process of Group Thinking.*

In summary, the literature of religious education nurtured by the R.E.A. leadership was generally similar. They read each other, they quoted each other's books, they knew each other, and they met annually at R.E.A. functions to celebrate the developing kingdom of religious education. Surely there were exceptions and even occasional criticisms from within the movement (Athearn and Richardson), but for the most part the literature was singularly uniform. There was a religious conviction about the positive results of modern science and a general capitulation to the social sciences as the new arbiters of truth. There was a deemphasis upon the theological aspect of the process (with notable exceptions, e.g., Shailer Mathews) and a greater emphasis on method, even minor methods. Research became the accepted epistemology, replacing faith or the religious tradition (theology).

The theorists of religious education were supported by their individual professional academic appointments. University and seminary shared the religious education vision. Birthed in an academic setting the R.E.A. continued in close relationship with religious higher education. Religious education departments became profitable, and each school had characteristics generally reflecting the thought of the most significant mentor. Externally the R.E.A. leaders were prospering; internally the association felt the same prosperity.

Internal Affairs:
Successes and Disillusionment

After the sudden death of Henry Cope in 1923, the R.E.A. managed with interim measures until 1926. Theodore Soares, George Albert Coe, Laird T. Hites, D. J. Cowling, along with other members of the board, filled leadership positions until the future of the association could be reevaluated. Coe's influence was most significant as he gave immediate editorial leadership to the journal which improved dramatically in quality and quantity of content. The 1923 volume contained 376 pages. In 1924 the journal increased to 416 pages; in 1925, to 504 pages; in 1926, to 600 pages; and it reached its largest size in 1927, with 1070 pages. The content of the journal reflected Coe's influence as well. Articles were more scholarly, generally scientific, and a larger section of material was devoted to recent research as well as annual reports of research conducted in the religious education centers throughout American higher education.

The selection of a new general secretary was no doubt difficult. A young graduate of Chicago Theological Seminary, Clifford Manshardt, originally stepped in as interim acting secretary. By June of 1925, however, he determined to accept a call into foreign missions in India.

There is only one extant document related to this subject in the R.E.A. archives. In a "Memorandum" to the committee on "Nominations of a General Secretary," dated January 14, 1925, there is evidence that the inner circle was hopeful that Manshardt would stay on. However, the memo makes clear that a New York committee consisting of Coe, Sanders, Elliott, Case, Winchester, and Soares reached a unanimous decision to support Goodwin B. Watson, instructor at Union Seminary. Watson was scheduled to complete his doctorate in the spring of 1925. A second meeting held in Chicago reached unanimous agreement with the New York recommendation. A memorandum noted that, though Watson lacked executive ability, there was agreement about his "technical and public ability." The memorandum signed by Soares ended with a request for a formal vote of recommendation for Watson.[74] There is no information to indicate what the results of that vote might have been. Nor is there any indication that Watson was actually offered the position. There is a brief notice in the June, 1925, issue of *Religious Education* stating that the selection of a new secretary would be postponed until the fall. The August issue of that same year indicated that the R.E.A. budget for 1924–1925 was $15,000. This amount was reduced to $12,940 for the 1925–1926 year. That budget contained only $3000 for an assistant secretary and no money for a general secretary.[75] After the Toronto convention in 1926 the board committed itself to an expanded future. In an upbeat report written by George A. Coe in June, 1926, the selection of Joseph M. Artman, of the University of Chicago, was finally announced.

Coe's report indicates that this choice was difficult to arrange. Artman would not be attracted away from his increasingly influential professorship unless he could be convinced that all parties were supportive of the expanded R.E.A. program. He believed that the key weakness of the R.E.A. needed correction before he would devote his future to that struggle. That malady was the old but recurrent financial problem which again seemed to plague the organization. Artman wanted assurance that the R.E.A. would not repeat its earlier history and attempt a utopian future without funds and commitment to fulfill those visions.

Coe referred to Artman as a "steam engine personality," and if the budget increases of the next few years were any indication of Artman's energy, Coe was certainly correct in his assessment. Artman's initial success was almost miraculous and filled with historical ironies. It was a period which paralleled Harper's early visions and financial limits. And again it was a Rockefeller who came to the rescue.

The board determined to add $15,000 to the budget. But after a meeting with Lucius Teter, a Chicago businessman and a member of the board, the proposed budget of $30,000 was viewed merely as a baseline. Teter aimed for an additional $30,000.[76] Artman was a convincing salesman. Two grants were arranged. The Rockefeller Foundation donated $15,000 over a period of three years, and the Carnegie Corporation contributed $10,000 over a period of two years. Artman accepted the board's offer and assumed the office in October 1926.[77]

Artman was an excellent administrator for good times. Throughout his tenure, his greatest contribution appears to have been in this area. The budgets for the remaining years of the 1920s were impressive indices of Artman's success, and were it not for the Depression there is no reason to believe that his initial imperial hopes might not have been realized. Consider the following figures:

Budget Appropriations by Year[78]

1928	$41,260	1933	$25,000
			(reduced to $13,875)
1929	$50,967	1934	$13,890
1930	unavailable	1935	$15,085
1931	$58,437	1936	$ 4,650
1932	$45,175		

By 1935 Artman's imperial vision left the board in debt more than $24,000, of which $14,000 was owed to the executive secretary, Artman himself. Artman's plans and enthusiasm exceeded his practicality, but it was the economic crash of the 1930s which really devastated the R.E.A. Blinded by the liberal vision of endless possibility, motivated by the passion of seeking the kingdom of God this side of paradise, the imperial vision faltered. Like other forms of triumphalism, the dream collapsed in the presence of real evil. The R.E.A. by 1935 faced financial collapse and loss of members (by 1936 there were fewer than 900 members).[79] The R.E.A. had yet to face the future challenges by the crisis theologians, the American counterpart to European Barthians. The R.E.A. ended a decade of glory days and faced a future of leanness and retrenchment.

Artman's devotion and drive did lead the organization to new heights of success during the first five years of his leadership, but his expectations always exceeded the realities of the tight financial situation of the association. The R.E.A. liberal spirit did not extend to an outpouring of financial backing.[80]

Artman successes are found in these significant developments during his secretariat. New and liberal support was given to the R.E.A. emphasis on research. Annual research conferences were initiated in 1927 and continued for the following years. Those efforts drew together significant researchers of that period and stimulated both support and interest in the scientific application of research to the task of religious education.[81]

In consort with his colleagues, Hites and Coe, Artman turned the journal into an aggressive instrument of intellectual freedom and discussion. The journal improved during this period, reporting research, expanding the book review section, developing an ethical statement on book reviews, and reporting on religious education efforts international in scope. The tone and content of the journal was substantially improved over the previous decade. A new editorial policy was adopted which encouraged significant comment on a variety of issues. Consider the following issues raised in one volume in 1928:

"The Outlawry of War" (Artman, February, 1928)

"The Pope and the Professor" (Rall, March, 1928)

"Character as a Community Responsibility" (Artman and Jacobs, November, 1928)

"Theological Seminaries and Research" (Holt and Starbuck, May, 1928)

"Religion and Politics" (Garrison, December, 1928)

"Three Needs of Religious Education" (Wieman, October, 1928)

Those editorials challenged the legality of war, the infallibility of the pope or biblicistic authority, and the question of social character formation. They advocated greater support for research by seminaries, more church involvement in serious social issues, and the need for clarity of focus among religious educators. The editorials were free expressions of various segments of the R.E.A. movement; they were forthright indicators of significant positions taken by individual leaders within the movement. And even though there was no official imprimatur for these viewpoints, the results were the same. The R.E.A. appeared to affirm significant liberal positions even when those ideas were controversial.

Artman himself never published extensively. He did not dominate the journal or the professional literature as had Henry Cope, who published regularly both in the journal and outside. Artman's keen interest was really left of the R.E.A. center, and he consistently advocated a change in the language as well as the tenor of religious education. As early as 1930 he attempted changing the name of the journal to "Character

Education,'' a change indicative of his more secular intention.[82] Artman's view of character development was heavily rooted in the behavioral sciences, with little interest in the theological or religious values of classical Christianity.

After losing the struggle to change the name of *Religious Education*, Artman set about to sell the idea of publishing two journals. By 1933 he advocated the publication of a new journal companion to *Religious Education* entitled *Character*. The journal was to be a popular presentation of current character education theory and an opportunity to expand the influence of the R.E.A. The board finally approved this action in 1934 and published its first issue of *Character* in October–November, 1934. *Religious Education* was reduced to a quarterly and severely limited in size (eighty pages for the year 1935).

The policy statement of the new journal was clearly a step toward secularizing religious education into a more public, popular movement. ''*Character* will be nonpartisan, noncreedal, nonracial.'' In fact, underlying the new journal was a silent but obvious creedal position. The journal had shifted focus from religion to formation of behavior. The religion of the new journal could best be classified as liberal humanism with a touch of theism. While a decade earlier, George A. Coe advocated a democracy of God, *Character* now advocated a democracy of behavioral accommodation. By 1944 the journal had modified its objectives and produced its own creedal statement:

1. The character of the individual is the product of the total community.
2. Citizenship is the expression of the individual's character in action in and on behalf of the community.
3. Good character is the sole foundation of good citizenship.
4. The citizenship of the individual is the creator of the community.[83]

In cyclical formation, character produces citizenship which in turn produces community, which produces character, etc. A behaviorist paradox is complete: character produces community and community produces character. Religion was lost in the process and the democracy of God became simply good citizenship. The vision of the R.E.A. was lost to the *Character* enthusiasts. Continuity was broken both intellectually and actually in 1935 when Artman left as general secretary. The board assigned the ownership and publication of *Character* to him as well. This was a proper decision in light of the intent and aim of the new journal.

Artman continued as editor of *Character* until 1941. His pilgrimage was the natural extension of his underlying conviction that:

In short, there is a science of character building as well as a technique. The lovers of justice and the genuine humanitarians should thrust aside all their theoretical and doctrinal differences and cooperate harmoniously in the great but neglected field of character building for the ills of the modern world are attributable principally to selfishness, levity, indifference, suspicion, fear, and irrational enmities.[84]

The Character of the Imperial Organization

Generally the movement in the R.E.A. between 1923 and 1935 was away from religion in the direction of character education. Mimicking the public educators and always seeking to be current, the R.E.A. drifted toward secularity. It seems appropriate to end this chapter with a view toward the character of the R.E.A. itself. Did the R.E.A., so intent upon character formation in public education, concern itself with its own character, integrity, and social behavior? So sure that indoctrination and belief structures had little to do with character behavior, was the R.E.A. any better off by its concentration on scientific method, non-creedal affirmations, and liberal generalizations? So committed to the reordering of society by an experiential process, was the behavior of the R.E.A. an example of its own ideals? So dedicated to the democratic process, did it act out those values in its own affairs?

While not attempting any retrospective psychoanalysis of the R.E.A., this summary will attempt, by anecdotal method, to highlight the composite character of the R.E.A. Specifically I will try to evaluate the R.E.A. by its own affirmation that experience is the essential (sole) method for religious education. How did the experience of the R.E.A. measure up in relationship to its principles and its constituents?

In relationship to minorities, the character of the R.E.A. literature and action was inconsistent and unreliable. Consider these examples. After publishing ''Fundamentalism vs. Modernism,'' one of the few articles written by a conservative Christian, the journal saw fit to print a reply in the very next issue. George H. Betts, certainly among the inner circle of R.E.A. protagonists, wrote a caustic and telling rebuke titled ''Give Us the Facts.''[85] Yet in that same volume when two authors published the article ''Church and Sunday School Attendance of Negro Children,'' and arrived at conclusions outlined below, no one within the R.E.A. establishment felt inclined or motivated to respond with corrective. Consider these findings: ''It may be that religion to the Negro is an escape mechanism, a device by means of which he frees himself from environmental inhibitions and feelings of inferiority.'' The authors noted that: "It is possible that the Negro, with his emotional nature, secures so much gratification from church activities in the form of 'emotional glow' that he later feels no need for performing 'good works.'" These conclusions follow: First, "Religious activities probably enable the Negro child to escape consciousness of his inferior social status." Second, "There is no evidence to show that the Negro child's more frequent church attendance results in superior moral conduct." Third, "It is possible that the emotionality manifested by the Negro in his religious activities provides a substitute gratification that takes the place of 'good works.'" All that, and the authors blandly state: "The writers do not attempt to analyze the effect of church-going upon the Negro."[86]

Betts' article, "Give Us the Facts," would surely have been an appropriate response to that kind of data.

Or consider the conclusion of another article on blacks, "Sex Morality Among Negroes," where the key argument was that sexual morality among Negroes is not a product of "sex instinct or African inheritance," but is a matter of "moral order," lack of family cohesion, and "breakdown of the intimacy of a family group." The authors cite case studies of black families that maintained solidarity and produced amazing results: "The sex morality of this family has been for three generations the sex morality of the great American middle class." Finally the authors conclude (without data): "In the city where most primary group relations are dissolved, we find illegitimacy and sex delinquency as indices of this lack of social control."[87] There were no letters of dissent, no articles in defense of a more scientific position. Evidently the constituency and leadership saw no problem in the conclusions, or the conclusions were not as significant as the theological fundamentalist minority position, which incidentally was purely theological and not experiential.

Certainly there were other articles on racial issues which were more reasonable and less prejudicial. The general rhetoric of the R.E.A. was liberal in this regard. Yet it is interesting that it was 1936 before any serious suggestion was made regarding black membership on the board of the association.[88]

The character of the R.E.A. was somewhat more commendable in its relationship to other religious minorities within the association. This period marked a significant increase in ecumenical efforts. Jewish/Protestant/Catholic dialogues regularly appeared in the journal, and that same denominational triad balanced all convention presentations. There was greater interaction with the Jewish community than with the smaller Catholic membership. Historically the organization had closer ties to the Jewish community, and Jewish membership on the board became representative rather than token.[89]

Perhaps the most impressive evidence of this supportive relationship came during the early 1930s. Harold D. Lasswell wrote an insightful analysis of German socialism for the 1934 volume of *Religious Education* sharply critical of Nazism, illustrating that German anti-Semitism had its historical roots in middle-class Christian society.[90] In 1933 the journal called attention to the German persecution of Jews but linked those events to a brief homily about bigotry in the United States.[91] However no voices were raised in support of efforts to assimilate larger numbers of Jewish immigrants. Nor was there any serious attempt to promote public outrage over German atrocities. However, there were many articles and editorials which argued against the war, the draft, and the nationalism developing among United States citizens. The liberal character of the organization was discreet, perhaps not liberal enough as it remained opposed to the war, aghast at atrocities, but never offering proposals for correctives. Even the Jewish membership failed to publish any articles related to the treatment of German Jews. They too seemed more interested in character matters.[92]

The Catholic contribution during this period consisted of increasing numbers of articles explaining the Catholic viewpoint regarding religious education. Membership in the organization remained small, and occasional articles criticized the Catholic position of indoctrination or the papal position of infallibility. Apparently there was a concerned effort made to accommodate the Catholic membership and keep conflict from interfering with cooperation. However, behind the scenes one suspects that there might have been prejudicial difficulties and old, reemerging sentiments. Perhaps the most vivid illustration of this fact is found in a letter from Hugh Hartshorne, president of the R.E.A. from 1935–1939, to Harrison Elliott of Union Seminary. Hartshorne wrote regarding an impending convention.

> As usual the Roman Catholics won't play unless they can have their own way. I don't care personally at all how the matter is decided provided what is done shall be genuinely interreligious. If this is unacceptable to the Roman Catholics then we shall have to choose either to have no religious service or else ignore their views. If hymns are to be used I think the words should be printed and I believe my choice would be acceptable to all groups. Does the use of a psalm in unison constitute formal worship in the eyes of the Catholics? I think such a judgment is carrying things a little too far, and possibly compromise could be reached at that point.[93]

The most impressive treatment of minority matters during this period was the publication of an entire issue devoted to the topic of race. The issue was printed in February, 1931. Articles dealing with Indians, Negroes, Mexicans, Chinese Americans, and Japanese were included. Those articles were serious efforts to purge bigotry and racism in religious education and generally reflected the best of the liberal tradition, calling for understanding and brotherhood.[94]

In balance, the character of the R.E.A. reflected basic inconsistencies in relationship to minorities but tended toward high moral principles. In practice, however, the association sometimes faltered and contradicted those high ideals. The journal and its membership were surely part of the spirit of that period. One ought not to expect insights beyond the times, unless of course an organization claimed such virtues.

The relationship of the R.E.A. to women suffered the same malady. Articles and publications reflected a liberated position toward women, a position possibly far ahead of its time. Yet, curiously, the R.E.A. women members, when given opportunity to set direction and lead the organization, failed impressively as they worked to achieve equality with men.

Lewis Mann, president of the R.E.A., addressed a letter (1935) to Adelaide T. Case of Teachers College. In that letter he asked for specific direction from women members of the association. Case gathered the following women together to consider the request: Edna Acheson, Presbyterian director of religious education; Frances Edwards, National Council of the Episcopal Church; Sophia Fahs, lecturer at Union Seminary and former head of Union School of Religion; Margaret Forsyth, Teachers College; Blanche Nicola, National Missions of the Presbyterian Church; Hazel Orton, Missionary Education Movement; Edna Pyle, general secretary of the Central Branch of the New York Y.W.C.A.; Marie Russ, Y.W.C.A.; Mrs. Rupert Stanley, Friends Society; Grace Wilson, dean of women at Colorado State Teachers College; and Helen Wright, secretary of the Federation of Churches in Toledo, Ohio.

They answered all of Mann's questions about future directions for the R.E.A. Women were not mentioned in any of those answered with the exception of the answer to the sixth question: "In view of the developments in the movement for religious and moral education, what shifts of emphasis, if any, should be made in the objectives and work of the R.E.A.?"

The women responded with these suggestions. They felt it was possible to "secure two people (women) for the salary that is now on the budget for the general secretary." They believed that hiring a woman "was not essential" but perhaps a good idea "because we could proba-

bly secure her for a lower salary than a man of similar qualifications."
The most forthright statement regarding women that the group managed
was the following plea for more women in the leadership of the R.E.A.
"The whole group feels that women should be given a more adequate
place in the leadership of the organization and on the program of its
conventions. There was some criticism at the last convention in this
regard."[95]

Couple those sentiments with the scientific research published in
1926 in the journal and one gains a feeling for the mixed message of the
R.E.A. Kenneth L. Heaton, a director of religious education, wrote that
"it had long been realized by sociologists that the religious life of boys
tends to be somewhat different from that of girls." He believed that men
discharge energy at a higher rate than women, "while woman stores up
energy for her children." He noted that Luther Gulick believed that the
church had not attracted boys because "religion was considered as a
state of being rather than a progression, as anabolic rather than ket-
abolic." Boys of course were interested in the "energetic and enthusiastic." Heaton argued that "the church has not put emphasis upon those
qualities that represent the best and noblest side of young men. . . . The
qualities demanded by her are chiefly anabolic and subjective." These
were of course "feminine not masculine in composition."[96]

Mixed signals probably reflected the ambiguity within the association
itself. As women gained leadership positions in religious education they
assumed a larger role in the life and management of the association. Yet
they suffered from their own socialization and any serious feminism
would wait for another decade before it would discover its identity in the
character of the R.E.A. The R.E.A. remained captive to the times,
neither giving prophetic guidance, nor any significant "liberal"
alternative.

In professional matters the character of the R.E.A. also remained
flawed. The leadership of the association consisted predominantly of
professors of religious education, all involved in the preparation of
religious educators, known during this period as D.R.E.'s. It is surprising, therefore, how little attention was paid to the developing profession
after students had been trained and placed into church positions.
Granted the literature contained regular articles, editorials and supportive essays regarding the profession of religious education;[97] what was
lacking was any serious attempt on the part of the R.E.A. to organize the
profession into some politically viable professional base. The department of D.R.E.'s remained a stepchild in the R.E.A., never receiving
the full support of the R.E.A. It is ironic to note that the R.E.A. was
primarily concerned with character and social justice issues but left its

own offspring (the embryonic profession) alone without any professional structure for appeal, or substantive programs to build professional security. It is my viewpoint that the character of the association was most flawed in relation to its own family, the children of its creation. The 1930s saw large-scale dismissals of the young religious educational professionals while the parent organization stood by impotent to support the directors of religious education.

It seems to me that there was a second major professional character flaw as well. While the R.E.A. was formed to encourage religious education, during the period of 1923 to 1935 the association lost its moorings and minimized the religious aspect of religious education to the extent that it seriously weakened its ability to cope with the renewed interest in theological matters in the 1930s and 1940s. Two illustrations are in order.

In 1927 Laird T. Hites, editorial secretary of the R.E.A., compiled a "Selected Bibliography in Religious Education." The organization of that bibliography followed this sequence:

1. Body and Mind
2. Religious Education and the Home
3. Learning and Teaching
4. Nature and Principles of Religious Education
5. Organization and Administration of Religious Education
6. Method in Religious Education
7. Curriculum Theory and Construction
8. Testing/Measurements/Surveys
9. Where to Find

One can see how far the R.E.A. had strayed from its earlier character. In this bibliography there was a complete omission of any biblical literature. There was no category of historical criticism. There was no suggestion of religious content that could be construed as being either Protestant, Catholic, or Jewish. The Jewish/Christian theological tradition simply was absent. There was no sign of theological material. Even Hites was aware of these glaring weaknesses. He wrote apologetically about the incompleteness of the selections. But of course the bibliography was published without modification.[98]

It is no small surprise to find that none other than the father of modernism, Shailer Mathews, wrote the following comments just one year later (1928). Mathews was keenly aware of the character flaw. He wrote, "If we are to have leadership in a genuinely religious education, it must be in the field of religion, properly defined, rather than in merely de-theized character study and behavior." Mathews agreed that one could redefine religion to "obviate the necessity of talking about God" but he thought that was only a "triumph of theological amateurs." He suspected that religious education was "in danger of running up a psychological blind alley and calling it a highway to religious truth." Mathews ended his critique with this interesting analogy: "Just as it would be a misfortune if critics and philologians were to be leaders of pastors, so would it be a misfortune if religious education as a movement would be led into the laboratory rather than the church."[99]

But it was even closer to home where the character of the R.E.A. was most questionable. I refer to the financial mismanagement of their basic fiscal responsibility to their own general secretary. For a decade, the R.E.A. continued to operate in debt, ranging from $20,000 to $25,000. By 1935 the organization's indebtedness to Artman exceeded $14,000.[100] The data clearly show that he participated in those decisions and encouraged the association to operate in the red. He had accepted as regular procedure the use of notes of indebtedness in place of salary for several years before 1935. As early as 1928 the association was already $4,000 in debt to the general secretary. By the time he severed employment with the R.E.A. he had mortgaged his home and borrowed money on his insurance.

Finally in 1935 the association faced reality and acknowledged that there was simply no way to continue his service. Ernest Chave reported to the organization: "After a year's struggle, with one creditor suing for payment and more trouble in sight, the executive committee decided to make the creditors an offer of settlement." Chave reported that the agreement reached involved "a forty percent compromise on a basis of ten-year notes without interest. That offer was accepted by all creditors." According to Chave, the executive committee "regretted exceedingly" to have to make this arrangement, and they were especially grieved "to ask our former secretary to make such a sacrifice when he had personally assumed a large note of the association in a previous crisis." Chave went on to point out that Artman was given ownership of *Character* for "an agreed amount to be charged against our indebtedness to him."[101]

The records of the board indicate that Artman settled with a payment of $5000 and legal rights to *Character*.[102] In spite of the regrets that settlement entailed, it cannot be called just. Artman paid a high price for his investment of enthusiasm and his obvious lack of realism. The files contained another document of interest. A special collection raised by the board of the R.E.A. to be given to Artman in November, 1936, amounted to $713.10. According to the letter, Artman was "deeply touched."[103]

My own analysis of that gift is that it represented guilt money to assuage a conscience plagued by a character illness. This marked the second time in the history of the association that the general secretary had to pay a high price for dedication and service. This time there were no testimonials, no journal issue filled with accolades, only a check for $713.10, small payment indeed for a decade of devoted service and small interest on a decade of substantial loans.

There is yet one story to tell related to the essential character flaw of the association. In November, 1932, George Albert Coe raised the issue of indebtedness to Artman. In typical fashion, Coe phrased his comments in behalf of justice for Artman, the R.E.A., and a simple concern for ethical ideals. At that meeting Coe stated: "I understand that our executive committee, instead of paying our general secretary in cash has been paying him in notes on the association." Coe questioned whether that action did "not create an unethical relation between the association and its general secretary." Coe believed that Artman would not take advantage of his financial power over the organization. He saw Artman "as loyal as loyalty itself." But he chided the association for its action. "We should not pretend to be solvent when we are not. We must somehow change this relation to our general secretary and his family."[104]

Nothing however was done to change this indebted relationship. Coe resigned from the board in 1933. His letter of resignation is not in the files, but one can safely assume that this financial issue was related to his departure. Coe was joined in his position by William Clayton Bower who had refused election to the board for this very reason, the lack of fiscal responsibility.[105]

Ernest Chave summarized the issue as follows: "However, after a year's experience, this seemed the only practical way to make any settlement *and to continue the program of the organization*" (emphasis added).[106]

The incident was regrettable and brings to mind the essential thesis of Reinhold Niebuhr's *Moral Man and Immoral Society*. Niebuhr wrote: "Modern religious idealists usually follow in the wake of social scientists in advocating compromise and accommodation as a way to social justice." Niebuhr continued: "What is lacking among all these moralists, whether religious or rational, is an understanding of the brutal character of the behavior of all human collectives and the power of self-interest and collective egoism in all intergroup relations."[107]

So ended the vision of the imperial association. The author of the metaphor, Joseph Artman, suffered more than the association. For the very attempt to create the religious education kingdom had disintegrated under his own best guidance. The character of the association so interested in character was found wanting.

The moral fiber and intellectual integrity failed to bring about just action. The democracy of God had degenerated into discussion method, and the R.E.A.'s commitment to the high ideals of transformation of society by reconstructing values had not proven successful even for the association. Evil in its primal form was yet to be faced. The next decade would assert that essential question more forcefully than even the experience of the Depression. Religion would emerge again, and in the tradition of the prophet, call both the conservative (fundamentalist) and the liberal to a character reexamination both painful and redemptive.

Notes for Chapter III

1. Letter, Joseph Artman to Francis L. Goodrich, July 26, 1929, R.E.A.F.
2. Arthur Cushman McGiffert, "A Teaching Church," *Religious Education* XVI (February, 1921), p. 3.
3. Ibid., p. 7.
4. Ibid., p. 8.
5. Ibid., pp. 7–8.
6. The two documents are "Report of an Investigation of the Religious Education Association" and "Report of an Investigation of the Religious Education Association by the Institute of Social and Religious Research." The first document is not dated. The second is dated February, 1926, R.E.A.F.
7. Ibid., unpublished version, p. A.
8. Ibid., p. 10.
9. Ibid., pp. 21–22.
10. Ibid., selected lists, p. 24.
11. Ibid., p. 46.
12. Ibid., p. 43.
13. Ibid., p. 2.
14. Ibid., p. 4.
15. Ibid., p. 9.
16. Ibid., Part III, pp. 1–22.
17. *The International Journal of Religious Education for Church School Workers* (Chicago: International Council of Religious Education, October, 1924), frontis page.
18. William Clayton Bower and Percy Roy Hayward, *Protestantism Faces Its Educational Task Together* (Appleton, Wisconsin: C. C. Nelson Publishing Co., 1949). The merger joined the International Sunday School Association and the Sunday School Council of Evangelical Denominations into one international association representing approximately 90 percent of American Protestant denominations.
19. Paul H. Vieth, *Objectives in Religious Education* (New York: Harper & Brothers, Publishers, 1930), p. 72.
20. Letter, Shailer Mathews to Mr. Woodward, November 22, 1928, U.C.A.
21. Walter Scott Athearn, *Character Building in a Democracy* (New York: The Macmillan Company, 1925), p. 147.

22. Erwin L. Shaver, "A Survey of Week-Day Religious Education," *Religious Education* XVII (April, 1922), p. 83ff. Note also the June issue of that same volume completely devoted to week-day schools. By the end of the decade, however, it was clear that week-day community schools would not change the essential Protestant educational nonstrategy.

23. See for example Walter Scott Athearn, *The Malden Survey* (New York: George H. Doran Company, 1920). Athearn developed a scorecard evaluation instrument to judge the various church facilities in relation to their usefulness for religious education. The remainder of the book is filled with descriptive pictures, charts, and graphs describing the adequacy or inadequacy of the church education facilities in Malden, Massachusetts, in detail.

24. Walter Scott Athearn, *An Adventure in Religious Education: The Story of a Decade of Experimentation in the Collegiate and Professional Training of Christian Workers* (New York: The Century Company, 1930. The book consists of a careful survey of college and university programs in religious education and a history of the Boston School of Religious Education and Social Service.

25. Joseph Artman commented on this in a brief editorial, "Questions and Answers," *Religious Education* XXVI (October, 1931), p. 597.

26. Athearn, *Character Building in a Democracy,* p. 150.

27. Education department report to President Walter Dill Scott, n.d., Northwestern University Archives. Statistics also contained in *President's Report, 1919–1924, Northwestern University Bulletins,* Archives.

28. David Tracy, *Blessed Rage for Order: The New Pluralism in Theology* (New York: Seabury Press, 1975), pp. 25–26.

29. Sidney E. Mead, *The Lively Experiment: The Shaping of Christianity in America* (New York: Harper & Row, Publishers, 1963), p. 186.

30. Shailer Mathews, *The Faith of Modernism* (New York: The Macmillan Company, 1924), pp. 7–36. All quotations listed in this paragraph are contained in these pages. Other titles by Mathews published during this period include: *The Social Gospel* (1910), *The Individual and the Social Gospel* (1924), *The Atonement and the Social Process* (1930), and *Creative Christianity* (1934).

31. Theodore Gerald Soares, *Religious Education* (Chicago: University of Chicago Press, 1931), pp. 1–17.

32. Robert T. Handy, *A Christian America: Protestant Hopes and Historical Realities* (London: Oxford University Press, 1971), p. 201.

33. Ernest John Chave, *Supervision of Religious Education* (Chicago: University of Chicago Press, 1931), p. 4.

34. Ernest John Chave, *The Junior: Life Situations of Children Nine to Eleven Years of Age* (Chicago: University of Chicago Press, 1925), p. 151.

35. William Clayton Bower, *The Curriculum of Religious Education* (New York: Charles Scribner's Sons, 1928), p. 251.

36. William Clayton Bower, *Character Through Creative Experience* (Chicago: University of Chicago Press, 1930), pp. 240–241.

37. William Clayton Bower, *Religious Education in the Modern Church* (St. Louis: Bethany Press, 1929), p. 204.

38. See reference in Frederick A. Norwood, *Dawn to Midday at Garrett* (Evanston, Illinois: Garrett Evangelical Seminary, 1978), p. 125.

39. Norman E. Richardson, *The Church at Play: A Manual for Directors of Social and Recreational Life* (New York: The Abingdon Press, 1922) and *The Religious Education of Adolescents* (New York: The Abingdon Press, 1913).

40. Norman E. Richardson, *The Christ of the Classroom: How To Teach Evangelical Christianity* (New York: The Macmillan Company, 1931).

41. Ibid., p. 327.

42. Ibid., p. 331.

43. Walter Scott Athearn, *The Minister and the Teacher: An Interpretation of the Current Trends in Christian Education* (New York: The Century Company, 1932). See especially chapters IV and V. These chapters amplify Athearn's early criticism in his letter to the R.E.A. investigation committee. Athearn and Richardson were minority voices in the early criticism of the religious education movement. This was especially significant because they were respected leaders within the movement and the R.E.A.

44. Richardson, *The Christ of the Classroom,* pp. 334–335.

45. Frank M. McKibben, *Christian Education Through the Church* (New York: Abingdon-Cokesbury Press, 1947); *Guiding Workers in Christian Education* (New York: Abingdon-Cokesbury Press, 1955); *Improving Religious Education Through Supervision* (The Leadership Training Publishing Association, 1931); and *Intermediate Method in the Church School* (New York: The Abingdon Press, 1926).

46. For a more complete description of McKibben's work, see Norwood, *From Dawn to Midday at Garrett,* pp. 123, 129, 143, and 169.

47. George Herbert Betts, *How to Teach Religion: Principles and Methods* (New York: The Abingdon Press, 1910); *Social Principles of Education* (New York: Charles Scribner's Sons, 1912); *The New Program of Religious Education* (New York: The Abingdon Press, 1921); *The Curriculum of Religious Education* (New York: The Abingdon Press, 1924); *Teaching Religion Today* (New York: The Abingdon Press, 1934); George Herbert Betts and Marion O. Hawthorne, *Method in Teaching Religion* (New York: The Abingdon Press, 1925); George Herbert Betts, *Foundations of Character and Personality: An Introduction to the Psychology of Social Adjustment,* ed. Raymond A. Kent, published posthumously (Indianapolis: The Bobbs Merrill Company, 1937).

48. George Herbert Betts, *The Beliefs of 700 Ministers and Their Meaning for Religious Education* (New York: The Abingdon Press, 1929).

49. Ibid., p. 43.

50. Ibid., p. 57.

51. Ibid., pp. 72–73.

52. The reference to a "gathering storm" is related to the essential argument of Jeffrey K. Hadden's *The Gathering Storm in the Churches* (Garden City: Doubleday & Company, 1969). Hadden's research portrays the growing distance between lay belief structures and clergy convictions. Betts' study is almost predictive of that development among mainline Protestants.

53. George Herbert Betts, *The Character Outcome of Present-Day Religion; 300 Churchmen Judge the Effect of Current Teaching and Preaching* (New York: The Abingdon Press, 1931), p. 10.

54. George H. Betts, Frederick C. Eiselen, George A. Coe, eds., *Religion and Conduct: The Report of a Conference Held at Northwestern University, November 15–16, 1929* (New York: The Abingdon Press, 1930).

55. Betts, *The Character Outcome of Present-Day Religion,* p. 10.

56. Ibid., p. 12.

57. Ibid., pp. 46–47.

58. Ibid., pp. 101–113.

59. Boardman W. Kathan, "Six Protestant Pioneers," *Religious Education* LXXIII (September–October, 1978), p. 142. Kathan quotes Robert Lynn as referring to the "Yale Studies" as "the most important single set of writings about the history of

American Protestant education. Much of the credit is due to Luther A. Weigle, the architect of the Yale Studies."

60. Luther A. Weigle, *The Pupil and the Teacher* (New York: Hodder and Stoughton, 1911) and *The Training of Children in the Christian Family* (Boston: The Pilgrim Press, 1922). See also Gerald E. Knoff's, *The World Sunday School Movement: The Story of a Broadening Mission* (New York: Seabury Press, 1979), pp. 120–123, for additional comment on Weigle's religious convictions. Knoff's work contains additional data on Weigle's relationship to the world Sunday School Movement (see especially pp. 124, 126, 127, 140, 150, 168–172, and 231–234).

61. Luther Allan Weigle, *The Glory Days: From the Life of Luther Allan Weigle*, compiled by Richard D. Weigle (New York: Friendship Press, 1976), pp. 25, 26. Originally appeared in *Contemporary American Theology*, Vol. II, ed. Vergilius Ferm (1933), pp. 311–339.

62. Vieth, *Objectives in Religious Education*, Appendix 2. This contains a complete bibliography of the major works of the ten authors considered the most significant religious educators of the period (see pp. 295–316).

63. Randolph Crump Miller, remarks made in eulogy for Paul Vieth to the Association of Professors and Researchers of Religious Education, Toronto, November 24, 1979.

64. Paul H. Vieth, *Teaching for Christian Living* (St. Louis: The Bethany Press, 1929) and *How to Teach in the Church School* (Philadelphia: The Westminster Press, 1935). Randolph Crump Miller believes that Vieth's *The Church and Christian Education* (New York: Bethany Press, 1947) was the only "book stating a middle ground between liberalism and neo-orthodoxy" until his own *Clue* in 1950. Letter from R. C. Miller to author, February 14, 1981.

65. I follow the argument of Sara P. Little, "Paul Herman Vieth: Symbol of a Field in Transition," *Religious Education* LIX (May–June, 1964), p. 207. She viewed Vieth as mediator.

66. George Albert Coe, Letters, Yale University Archives. Letters between George Albert Coe and President McGiffert are dated from April 12, 1922 to September 19, 1922.

67. Harrison S. Elliott, *Can Religious Education Be Christian?* (New York: The Macmillan Company, 1940).

68. Philip H. Phenix, interview at Teachers College/Columbia University, New York, August 31, 1977.

69. Harrison Sacket Elliott, "The Significance of Process in the Progress of Christianity," Union Theological Seminary, September 23, 1925, pp. 15–16.

70. Harrison Sacket Elliott, *The Bearing of Psychology Upon Religion* (New York: Association Press, 1927), p. 25.

71. Ibid., p. 77.

72. Harrison Sacket Elliott, *The Process of Group Thinking* (New York: The Association Press, 1928), pp. 1, 18, 21, 186.

73. H. Richard Niebuhr, *The Kingdom of God in America* (New York: Harper & Brothers, 1937), p. 193.

74. "Memorandum to the Committee on Nomination of the General Secretary," January 14, 1925, R.E.A.F.

75. *Religious Education* XX (June, August, 1925), pp. 220, 314.

76. *Religious Education* XXI (June, 1926), pp. 258–260.

77. Theodore Gerald Soares, "History of the Religious Education Association," *Religious Education* XXIII (September, 1928), p. 633.

78. Board of Directors files of the R.E.A., R.E.A.F.

79. Minutes of Religious Education Association Executive Committee, August 10, 1936, R.E.A.F.

80. Minutes of the Board of Directors of R.E.A., October 17, 1930. The minutes indicate that already by that time, Artman had extended personal funds to the organization to the extent of $4,000. This practice continued and ended with the large indebtedness of over $14,000 at the time of his resignation. Undaunted by fiscal restraints, Artman and his staff projected unbelievable expectations. In the board minutes of November 6, 1931, Artman's associate, J. W. F. Davies, projected a necessary budget of $100,000 (p. 2). In November Davies commented on the future growth of the organization: "Mr. Davies then stated his hope for membership of the Association. He was not being optimistic, he said, when he stated that our membership could go to 4,000 in 1933, 6,000 by 1934, 8,000 by 1935, and 10,000 by 1936." The imperial vision was catching! (p. 2, November 25, 1931), R.E.A.F.

81. For a more complete overview of research in religious education during this period, see John H. Peatling, "Research and Religious Education," *Religious Education* LXXIII (September–October, 1978), pp. 101–110.

82. Minutes of the Board of Directors, October 17, 1930, R.E.A.F.

83. *Character and Citizenship: Product of the Community, Creator of the Community*, Vol. 9, No. 1, October 1944, (Chicago, C & C Associates), p. 3.

84. Joseph M. Artman, "Editorial," *Character* Vol. 1 (December–January, 1934–1935), p. 17.

85. See M. L. Fergeson, "Fundamentalism vs. Modernism: The Significance of the Conflict for Religious Education" and George H. Betts, "Give Us the Facts," *Religious Education* XXII (January, 1927), pp. 18–22, 180–182.

86. Harvey C. Lehman and Paul A. Witty, "Church and Sunday School Attendance of Negro Children," *Religious Education* XXII (January, 1927), pp. 53–54.

87. E. Franklin Frazier, "Sex Morality Among Negroes," *Religious Education* XXIII (May, 1928), pp. 447, 450.

88. Minutes of the Executive Committee of the R.E.A., October 30, 1935, R.E.A.F.

89. Confidential minutes of the annual meeting of the R.E.A., April 26–27, 1935, indicate 150 Jewish members and 80 Catholic members. In 1935 there were three Jewish members on the board of directors of 28 members as well as Isaac Landman, vice-president of the R.E.A. One cannot identify a single Catholic on the board during that time. R.E.A.F.

90. Harold D. Lasswell, "The Political Significance of German National Socialism," *Religious Education* XXIX (January, 1934), pp. 20–24.

91. *Religious Education* XXVIII (March–April, 1933), p. 185. The brief, untitled article follows: "Jews and Christians alike have raised their voices in horror, grief and protest over the unbelievably savage persecution of German Jewry. And rightly so! That such persecution is possible in the twentieth century shows what little real advance we have made, in spite of the great civilization which we so pride ourselves on having developed.

"But why this outbreak of primitive savagery? Is the cause back of it all the failure of education in Germany, as in the rest of the world, to develop genuine moral and ethical codes of conduct in the great body of its people? We could be amused, if it were not too serious for amusement, at the inconsistency of the American who displays righteous indignation at the horrors perpetrated in Germany while at the same time himself discriminates against persons of other races and creeds. It is true that we, in America, do not stoop to butchery and bloodshed. We limit our discrimination to exclusion from universities and colleges, hotels, places of amusement, etc., and refusal of employment.

"The problem of preventing the repetition of such an outrage as is now current in Germany is not a problem for Germany alone. All other countries in the world, too, must set their moral houses in order. To the realization of the ideal of a world ethic in which intolerance and bigotry and discrimination can have no place we, as religious educators, must dedicate ourselves.''

92. I have been unable to identify a single article apart from the Lasswell essay which deals with Jewish persecution during this entire period. Yet numerous Jewish authors are regularly represented in every volume in this ten year period.

93. Letter, Hugh Hartshorne to Harrison Elliott, April 6, 1933, R.E.A.F., Board matters, 1933.

94. *Religious Education* XXVI (February, 1931), pp. 97–188.

95. Letter, Adelaide T. Case to Dr. Mann, June 6, 1932, R.E.A.F. Board Minutes, 1932.

96. Kenneth L. Heaton, "Physical and Mental Differences in Relation to Moral and Religious Education," *Religious Education* XXI (June, 1926), p. 285.

97. The regular annual meeting of the Association of Professional Religious Educators in local churches met in conjunction with the annual R.E.A. meeting. But they were always affiliated with, and not the center of, the R.E.A. There was discussion about joining this group with the religious education department of the I.C.R.E. (March 6, 1928 meeting), but the group decided to remain with the R.E.A. Artman raised serious professional questions in the editorial pages of the October, 1931, issue in which he urged that all ministers be trained as education specialists. In the November, 1931, issue, Artman printed two letters from D.R.E.'s which indicated that his editorial of the previous month was interpreted as "abolishing the profession." Both letters pointed to the issue of the lack of status for D.R.E.'s and the apparent need for ordination. They called for R.E.A. support. Artman in turn put the blame on the seminaries and training schools. He, like the R.E.A., side-stepped the issue in real political terms. The D.R.E.'s did not receive sustained support, either from ecclesiastical agencies or from the R.E.A. See *Religious Education* XXVI (November, 1931), pp. 691–692.

98. Laird T. Hites, "A Selected Bibliography in Religious Education," *Religious Education* XXII (December, 1927), pp. 1045–1064.

99. Shailer Mathews in Symposium Issue, "What Is the Task of Leadership in Religious Education," *Religious Education* XXIII (June, 1928), pp. 520–521.

100. Minutes of Board of Directors of R.E.A., April 16, 1936, R.E.A.F.

101. Ernest J. Chave, "Report of the Executive Committee to the Association," *Religious Education* XXXI (April, 1936), p. 144.

102. "Proposal by the Executive of the Board of the Religious Education Association," May 16, 1935, and "Religious Education Association Financial Statements," 1936, Board files, R.E.A.F.

103. Letter titled, "The Artman Fund," November 2, 1936, Board Files, R.E.A.F., 1936.

104. Minutes of the Board of Directors of the R.E.A., November 1, 1932, pp. 7–8, R.E.A.F.

105. Ibid., p. 8.

106. Chave, "Report of the Executive Committee to the Association," p. 144, R.E.A.F.

107. Reinhold Niebuhr, *Moral Man and Immoral Society: A Study in Ethics and Politics* (New York: Charles Scribner's Sons, 1932), pp. xix and xx.

Chapter IV

Aging Liberals:
Old Responses for a New Situation
1935–1952

> It is a lonely and discouraging experience to be a liberal without friends.[1]
>
> Ernest Chave, 1950

> For many, because of certain theological developments in recent years and because of attacks upon religious education, there is a feeling of isolation. For them the association furnishes a rare fellowship.[2]
>
> Harrison Elliott, 1950

The years between 1935 and 1952 probably mark the most difficult period in the history of the R.E.A. The era began in financial desperation. The organization found itself without funds, without a full-time executive secretary, without office personnel, and with a diminished membership (about seven hundred). These internal problems were minor when compared with the surrounding cultural and theological events.

During this period the R.E.A. acknowledged the deaths of Laird Hites, long-time office servant and editor of the journal after Artman's departure, Harrison Elliott, general secretary from 1950–1952 and major figure of R.E.A. leadership during this entire period, and George A. Coe, founder and patron saint of the R.E.A. as well as its honorary president. Others equally important to the movement entered retirement during the late 1940s and early 1950s. The list included long-time R.E.A. leaders, past presidents, and members of the R.E.A. executive committee: Ernest Chave, William Clayton Bower, Hugh Hartshorne, and Luther Weigle. Though a young profession, and a new addition to recognized departments in American seminaries, the major personages of the religious education movement were essentially an amazing group of old, liberal professors.

Leadership in Protestant religious education shifted from the R.E.A. to the I.C.R.E. The unified effort of mainline Protestants shifted to the structure of this well-financed ecumenical agency which remained attuned to the churches and open to the new trends in theological opinion. The R.E.A. became an anachronism amid a growing consensus of American Protestants.[3]

Hard Times:
The Historical Situation

Though the events surrounding the R.E.A. would have been challenging to a generation of young, ambitious professionals, they were overwhelming to the aged leadership of the R.E.A. The aftermath of the Depression continued to shackle the R.E.A. with limited financial options. All organizational, editorial, promotional work, as well as the ongoing clerical chores, had to be done almost entirely with volunteer effort. Many of the R.E.A. central personages were also members of other professional agencies, sometimes serving in leadership positions in both organizations, a kind of "shared directorship."[4] Dual responsibilities taxed the limited energies of aging professionals.

National and international events moved toward World War II. The rise of German national socialism, the advent of Hitler's challenge to Western civilization, and the systematic slaughter of the Jews were actions that did not respond to reason or group discussion methods. The R.E.A. as well as other educational associations stood on the sidelines of human history. Religious education had neither skills nor sufficient moral force to prevent a world-wide holocaust. Old slogans of the "brotherhood of man and the fatherhood of God" appeared as ill-chosen descriptions of inhumane horrors. The entire liberal legacy seemed bankrupt, and there was ample evidence of public confessions by chastened liberals. The *Christian Century*'s series, "How My Mind Has Changed in This Decade" (1939), contained dramatic evidence of humbled liberals either repentant or at least open to modifying their theological-philosophical responses to the new historic circumstances.[5]

None of these confessors, however, were from the executive committee of the R.E.A. There was very little modification of ideas among the R.E.A. leadership. George A. Coe seemed to move even further to the fringe of liberalism throughout this period. His successor at Union Seminary, Harrison Elliott, formed the most cogent defense of the liberal progressive religious education tradition in his major book of the period, *Can Religious Education Be Christian?* Elliott's essay served as the rallying document of the period.[6]

Institutional Ironies

The most encompassing irony of the era seems to have been the inability of the aging liberals to be open to the center of the liberal creed, that is, open to the possibility of change. The R.E.A. leadership seemed incapable of reconsideration of basic theological positions. As youthful seminarians imbibed the "new theologies" of Barth, Bultmann, Brunner, the Niebuhr brothers, and Tillich, the R.E.A. continued to rehearse the ancient creedal statements of the early movement. Even a colleague, respected and admired, was almost ignored as he registered a devastating critique of religious education in his answer to Elliott's question, *Can Religious Education Be Christian?* H. Shelton Smith had raised the Barthian question earlier in the journal, but when his definitive public rebuke of religious education, *Faith and Nurture,* was published one year after Elliott's *Can Religious Education be Christian?* the association and the journal almost ignored the challenge.[7] No transcendent reality could be taken seriously if one continued to operate with an exclusively experiential bias. Claiming to be open and tolerant of truth and varieties of opinions, the R.E.A. denied its own central commitment, that of allowing for another set of predispositions.

When by 1950 the association could employ a general secretary again, they turned to a major, aged mentor of R.E.A. intransigence, Harrison Elliott. They chose R.E.A. orthodoxy over emerging new theologies. They seemed to live in a past period, repeating old slogans, even though the world was struggling with a new metaphor for reality and the presence of the ancient symbol so experientially validated, called sin.

There is yet another historical incongruity about this period. In spite of the inability of the R.E.A. to cope with the new historical and theological circumstances, it did continue to maintain other educational values which seemed initially lost to the new young crisis theologians or the next generation of religious educators. Never viewing education as schooling alone, the R.E.A. continued to challenge the religious educator with a vision of public paideia. In contrast to Protestantism's heresy of individualism, the R.E.A. continued to appeal to a more social under-standing of both sin and salvation.

The strangest irony was surely that, in the presence of cosmic evil and horrendous evidence of human oppression, the R.E.A. aging liberals remained hopeful about the future of democracy and religion, display-ing a more radical form of faith than did the neo-orthodox. Paraphrasing a generally accepted notion of Luther's view of faith, the R.E.A. kept faith, that is, ''hope in spite of all evidence to the contrary.'' The democracy of God was shattered. Voices encircled the R.E.A. with despair and human uncertainty. Huddled together, the remnant warmed their aging souls with party slogans from the past and hopeful optimism (blind faith) for the future. Understanding such party loyalty is surely the only way to interpret this most difficult period in the history of the R.E.A.

Change, the ideal of progressive religious education, would not occur in the R.E.A. circle throughout this period. But strangely, after the war, after the initial victories of the new orthodoxy, there was still a small band of hopefuls loyal to each other and to the vision that the kingdom of God might still become a public reality.

Their students knew better than their mentors the essential faith of the fathers. They would open the association to change and new risks in the next decades for they had been nurtured better than their fathers had hoped for. They believed what their fathers had forgotten, that the most liberal vision was one of change and evolutionary adaptation—not a bad legacy for aged, stubborn, unrepentant loyalists who chose to call them-selves the true believers.

Financial Woes

Financial problems plagued the R.E.A. during this entire period. At the time of the departure of Joseph Artman as general secretary in 1935 the total indebtedness of the association was approximately $24,000. By 1936 the R.E.A. had reached agreement with their creditors and reduced this amount by almost 60 percent to $9,000. The debt was to be paid by budgeting $1000 annually for the next ten years, thus eliminating the debt by 1946.[8] By 1938 the executive committee recognized the impos-sibility of that task. No payments had been made on any of the outstand-ing debt, and money was simply not being generated to eradicate that indebtedness.

The president of the association, Hugh Hartshorne, appointed a com-mittee to resolve the debt responsibility. The committee recommended a plan to raise one-third of the indebtedness over a one-year period and then to request the creditors to accept such payment as full discharge of their debt. The plan was adopted and put into motion. By December, 1938, the committee had raised slightly more than $4000 and all creditors accepted the new settlement, not without some bitterness and considerable personal sacrifice.[9] Ernest Chave wrote to Hartshorne of Artman's reaction as well as his own disenchantment with the plan for debt reduction. "I wonder if the board really visualizes what this means. For instance in the case of Mr. Artman, it says, 'Will you take about $1600 and forget $10,000?' " Chave went on to explain that Artman had been forced to cancel $40,000 worth of insurance. According to Chave, Artman felt he could have continued to direct the R.E.A. with more success than the association was having without his leadership and beyond those practical matters "he (Artman) rankles under the injustice that has been done him."[10]

Nevertheless, by February 5, 1939, the report of the debt committee indicated that all the creditors had accepted the offer and the debt was resolved. The executive committee seemed to justify its decision by its own contributions (in most cases $100 each) and by its commitment to continue to keep the association alive. Having settled the debt, their struggle was by no means ended.

Blanche Carrier, secretary of the executive committee, expressed the sentiment of the R.E.A. board in cryptic language: "Our present income of about $4000 a year permits us to live at a dying rate and no more."[11] The struggle for survival continued. It was compounded by fractured leadership in Chicago, New York, and Pittsburgh. The letters of exchange between the three groups often betrayed misunderstandings and open hostility. The difficulty of decision making was increased because of distance and fragmented responsibility. This condition continued throughout the period even after the election of Harrison Elliott, though Ernest Chave lobbied for a central office throughout these years. Decisions were made by the board in New York, while the executive committee in Chicago managed the office and daily routines of the organization as well as publication of the journal.[12]

The only financial support the association could depend on came from membership fees and subscriptions to the journal. During 1938 the association lost an additional 150 supporting units, 97 members and 53 subscriptions.[13] This loss brought the organization to its lowest membership in the history of the association. Survival was by no means assured even after the debt was erased. The minutes indicate a constant dialogue among the executive committee members during these years over the issue of finances and simple survival. Debates continued over the function and purpose of the organization and its continuance. Yet in the journal the public image was maintained secure and vital.

By the mid-1940s it seemed that the association had turned a corner. Membership reached 1273 inclusive of subscriptions in 1944 and increased by another 200 in 1945. The president, Ernest Chave, was encouraged and finished his term in 1944 feeling that the R.E.A. was "on an upward swing." By 1946, however, F. Ernest Johnson ended his two-year term as president with these cautious words: "As my own term of office ends, I am in a chastened mood. . . . But while we are still solvent, we are hardly more than that."[14]

By 1949 the R.E.A. was again ready to launch out into an expanded program. A mid-century committee was appointed to raise $18,500. The effort was to assure the full appointment of a new general secretary. Optimistic plans were made; publicity was sent to the entire membership. The net results were disappointing. Of the total raised (approximately $11,000), $8,000 represented a Dodge Foundation grant which was negotiated by a relatively unknown young board member, Herman Wornom. Harrison Elliott was elected general secretary and began his work.[15] In Chicago, Ernest Chave wrote discouragingly about the fiscal irresponsibility of the whole endeavor. His words reflect the disillusionment of his own efforts in behalf of the association, his aging realism, and a deep sense of personal discouragement: "You have undoubtedly received the resignation of Weightstill Woods as treasurer. I have talked with him and understand his point of view. He feels that the association is headed for another debt and he refuses to be part of it. I agree with him, but shall not threaten resignation at the moment."[16]

Chave went on to express his ambivalence to the whole project which he thought had not been carefully projected. Elliott had no plan for the future. The board had not set a direction and the entire enterprise seemed to Chave to be ill-conceived and destined to fail. He pleaded for moving all the offices to one location, but that was not to happen until after Elliott's death.

The leadership appeared impotent to solve the long-term fiscal crises of the association. They were not successful in setting a prioritized future agenda for the R.E.A. or its journal. Certainly Chave's concerns for the future and for responsible fiscal planning were on target, particularly in light of past history which he, more than any other member, understood first-hand. His cautions were ignored and Elliott began his tenure as general secretary without financial support from the Chicago group, which for years had been the survival experts in the R.E.A. inner circle. Elliott's premature death after less than a year in office eliminated the potential for another fiscal disaster.

Events Outside the R.E.A.:
The Journal's Response

But the new situation during this period was not filled only with internal distress. More significant, and of greater impact on the future, were the catastrophic events leading to another world conflict. That the R.E.A. was well aware of that possible conflict is clearly indicated by repeated journal articles dealing with the rise of German Nazism. The entire volume of 1937 was largely devoted to that issue.

The R.E.A. journal appealed to reason and in some cases adopted a form of national isolationism in regard to the American entry into the European struggle. James Yard, executive secretary of the midwest branch of the National Conference of Christians and Jews, wrote an article in the journal illustrating such reasoning. The article was titled: "What Happened to Religion and Democracy in a Totalitarian State?" He outlined the results of totalitarianism upon German religious life. He pointed to the courageous stands of Barth and Niemoller in their defense of classical Christianity, in defiance of Hitler and Nazism. Yet, when he raised the question of America's role in the struggle against totalitarianism, he became a strict isolationist. He appealed for an open struggle against bigotry and minority repression in the United States. He advocated the pluralism of a multi-ethnic America. He supported the preservation of a free press and wrote in strong defense of full employment. To preserve all these important values, he finally argued that at all costs "we must make sure that the United States keeps out of the next European war."[17]

In that same issue, Blanche Carrier and Amy Clowes, both religious educators at Northwestern University, made similar appeals in behalf of prevention of an "Authoritarian State." Their argument was representative of the blandest kind of liberal progressive rhetoric. In an effort to increase Christian tolerance, they argued that German nationalism and the advent of Nazism was a reasonable response to the unfair armistice agreement of World War I. Attempting to understand international developments in terms of an individual model of psychological development, they excused German nationalism as the natural order of psychological development. "She [Germany] develops a martyr complex; she feels righteously justified in building up every reserve against her enemies."[18] Then in an incredible appeal, implying that world events could be solved by Christian goodwill and democratic group process, the authors wrote: "It is the essence of Christianity that with an understanding eye and heart the Christian can cut straight through the circle and transform the antisocial elements by a positive goodwill that heals the confusion at its source."[19]

Such rhetoric deserved Reinhold Niebuhr's assessment of liberalism as "a kind of blindness." Carrier and Clowes were aptly described by Niebuhr's criticism. He believed liberals were blinded by allegiance to these six convictions:

1. Injustice is caused by ignorance.
2. Civilization is becoming more moral.
3. Individual character is the guarantee of justice.
4. Appeals to love, justice, goodwill, and brotherhood will bring reform.
5. Goodness which brings happiness will overcome selfishness and greed.
6. War is stupid, therefore enlightened persons will not wage war.[20]

Carrier and Clowes surely fit Niebuhr's analysis; they recommended their view to the "family of nations" and the authors really seemed to believe that this procedure would solve world crises. The article ended with an appeal for intelligent action, a release of inhibition by free discussion, a development of tolerance by democratic processes, and finally a reduction of tension by cooperation and goodwill.

The article was a splendid exhibition of liberalism betrayed by its ethical mischief. There was neither the courage or conviction of prophetic idealism, nor was there the authority of an absolute ethical value apart from the romantic ideal of talking together in group process. Finally all ethical solutions seemed to consist of group process and psychological adjustment. The article, while certainly not representative of the best of Protestantism mainline liberal response, is a fair illustration of liberal religious education progressivism at its most popular level. The authors seemed to imply that the solution for preventing authoritarianism in national politics was really as simple as using "psychological principles of emotional and intellectual guidance."

Such articles were public appeals for deserved conservative criticism. The Evanston religious educators seemed to invite the kind of criticism that was sure to come. Educationally, they had opted for a simplistic group process methodology. Philosophically, they had espoused a viewpoint about human nature that contradicted much historical evidence in addition to ample psychological evidence of the period itself. Theologically, they projected a piety that Christian goodwill was sufficient armor to face the real world of intolerance, bigotry, inhumane values, and cosmic evil. They seemed romantically unaware of the swirling events that would soon make their vision understandably ridiculed. There were, however, other voices from Chicago, from Evanston, which countered their romantic vision and presented a more realistic liberal approach.

Three such articles were contained in the same volume. Each revealed a more realistic liberalism, already chastened by the events of history, but still devoted to the ideals of human potential and critical rationality. Victor Yarros' "Religion and the Totalitarian State" used the most popular cliches of religious education rhetoric to critique the romantic oversimplification of liberal piety. He called for a prophetic posture between the religious community and that of the state. "Religion divorced from life; religion afraid to face and criticize governments and outworn institutions plainly inimical to the essence of religion; religion satisfied with Sunday sermons, rhetoric, and a little charity; religion which prates of the Brotherhood of Men as the corollary and deduction from the Fatherhood of God and does nothing for the ideal of brotherhood. . . . This sort of religion is worse than no religion at all."[21]

Yarros advocated a "Christ against culture" view of the relationship between the church and society. He argued for the disestablishment of religion in public life, certainly a critical liberal position in light of Protestant domination in the development of American religion and culture. Though still optimistic that the German nation would not allow for the long-term continuation of Nazism, Yarros almost revealed a conservative theological bias; he appealed to the divinity of Jesus and the biblical roots of Christianity in biblical Judaism. The entire article was supportive of a revitalized religion, related to life and history and capable of standing over against culture in protest and criticism. There was no retreat from the liberal vision of a better world. There was a change in the perception of how that world might come about. He called for liberal action in politics and life, rather than the divorce of religious theory from life issues. Any attempt by religious forces to return to theological quietism was, according to Yarros, self-defeating. Religion would be judged by its empirical relevance.[22]

George Albert Coe's articles throughout this period (1930s) continued to represent the most cogent liberal religious education party line. His brand of liberal progressivism always remained radical and usually "against the grain." In a brief half-page comment, "Let the Convention Wrestle with Political Totalitarianism" (1937), Coe was able to cut through volumes of words and target the essence of his liberal religious position over against the potential emergence of totalitarianism.

He suggested that the proposed convention should examine the drift toward Fascism in the United States by a critical review of judicial decisions, laws, administration acts, state initiated propaganda, and illegal violence. He warned against the idealization of the state. He urged that the R.E.A. might even move toward "actual resistance," and finally cautioned against "public school education for citizenship" with a clear inference that such teaching deserved careful review in light of the potential for national indoctrination.[23]

Finally there was in that same issue a balanced viewpoint expressed by Laird T. Hites, the faithful R.E.A. office manager. In an analysis entitled "On the Psychology of War," Hites argued for the following four basic premises:

1. War results from psychological drives that are basic to human nature. Therefore war is inevitable.
2. Those same drives that provoke war are fundamental to all other forms of civilized achievement: security, fear, protection, survival.
3. Pacifism cannot prevent war if only successful in the United States, indeed such a position would in all likelihood promote war.
4. The dialectic between the militarists and the pacifists in the public debate throughout the United States is desirable, for it serves to check the excesses of the other.[24]

Hites' article drew on the findings of depth psychology and though there is no historical verifiable relationship between his conclusions and the early work of Reinhold Niebuhr, his argument for the continued dialectic of militarism and pacifism seemed identical to Niebuhr's prescription for justice in *Moral Man and Immoral Society*.

One detects subtle shifts among the R.E.A. leaders reflecting the conscious or unconscious impact of the social situation upon the reasoning and traditional positions. Nowhere is that evidence more apparent than in the area of theological development where the challenge to liberal religious education was so serious. The more threatened, the more defensive the posture of the religious educator seemed to become.

New Theologies and Old Liberal Absolutes

Between the years 1935–1953 (the 1935 meeting lacked a quorum of members but was recorded as a "convention"; it was in fact a very small meeting), the R.E.A. never managed to host a major successful national convention. Several were planned, some didn't materialize, and those that did were poorly attended. What appear in the journal to be major affairs were in fact small meetings. (Such a meeting as the 1948 Pittsburgh conference had "about one hundred and fifty" members.)

Apart from Laird Hites, part-time editor, business manager, office clerk, and loyal advocate, the R.E.A. lived during this period on a subsistence budget rarely larger than $4,000 during any annual period. The conventions, field visits of the general secretary, and promotional materials had to be abandoned. Ernest Chave and Harrison Elliott managed brief leaves from their respective academic institutions to visit old R.E.A. loyalists and lobby for the development of local chapters as a substitute for a national annual fellowship. Historical identity was not maintained by public events. Rather, behind the scenes countless meetings were held in New York, Chicago, and Pittsburgh to promote leadership and historical continuity. All were attended voluntarily without reimbursement by the R.E.A. All were acts of personal devotion by the faithful.

In those sessions, often tense and conflicting, the inner circle of R.E.A. patriarchs brooded over the developing circumstances encircling their once secure liberal enclave. There was a life-death dialogue throughout this period, revolving round the essential questions of the R.E.A.'s reason for being. The key participants were Elliott, Hartshorne, Chave, Bower, Coe (usually by mail), and Israel Chipkin.[25]

As early as 1937 William Clayton Bower (revealing his own personal loyalties) suggested that the R.E.A. had lost its distinctive character and ought to merge with the International Council, thus eliminating any continued dialogue with either Jews or Catholics.[26]

In 1938 President Hartshorne wrote to Chave addressing Chave's position that the R.E.A. needed to be more concerned with its philosophy. He admitted that the association was indeed "weak on the philosophical end" but argued that the most important value of the R.E.A. was its primary concern for educational method rather than theory or theology.[27] And in the meeting of the executive committee, held January 21, 1938, Mrs. Henry Nelson Wieman proposed that the R.E.A. become the "religious section of the Progressive Education Association or the National Education Association." She received some support from McKibben of Northwestern. In that same meeting, suggestions were made that the R.E.A. incorporate its journal with the advisory section of the I.C.R.E. Neither suggestion was adopted.[28]

In 1939 Herbert L. Seamans, college secretary of the National Conference of Christians and Jews, wrote to Ernest Chave and raised the recurrent question of the R.E.A.'s relationship to Catholics. He was correct in his observation that the only effective work in the R.E.A. had been between Jews and Protestants, rather than among Catholics.[29]

In February of that same year Bower finally uttered what must have been implicit in the minds of some R.E.A. members for a long time. Bower is recorded having said: "Religious educators need a theology, and we have not yet had it. Most of our group is working along, uncritically accepting some vaguely defined form of liberal theology." Bower continued: "We have not yet worked out a satisfactory theology on which we can base our educational method. The time has come when, without theologizing our movement—which would be a tragedy—we must seek an intellectual and theological basis for it."[30]

In another undated document (probably 1940), Bower outlined his theological viewpoints. He criticized the "neo-supernaturalists" as potentially destructive to the cause of religious education. Their theology could only lead to irrational chaos and the advent of a new form of indoctrination, coercion, and propaganda. He proceeded to raise a significant number of questions regarding the challenge for religious education. He suggested that the liberals needed to make more of the "beyondness of experience." He acknowledged that if sin were an inappropriate theological term, perhaps there was some need to acknowledge the "deep pathos of life." Had liberals been too intellectual over the emotional side of human experience? Had religious education become superficial in its denial of any serious reconsideration of the tradition? Much of Bower's position was seconded by Walter M. Horton (R.E.A. board member), who extended Bower's questions in a mini-defense of the emerging neo-orthodoxy.[31]

In a March, 1940, meeting of the New York branch of the R.E.A., a discussion centered on the adequacy of the major religious education metaphor for democratic interaction, the "democracy of God." In some interesting Jewish-Christian exchanges, the group began to renegotiate the old R.E.A. synthesis. Consider this exchange.

A Mr. Owen suggested that democracy rested not in theology but in "faith in man." Alexander Dushkin, founder of the College of Jewish Studies, Chicago, modified that sentiment indicating that in rabbinic thought the emphasis was upon a "partnership of man with God." Cole countered Dushkin's emphasis and noted that the Jewish motif of a suffering God provides a new way to look at democratic religion. And Rabbi Israel Chipkin, director of the American Association for Jewish Education, went so far as to "emphasize the value of old terms." Throughout that entire report there is indication that the Jewish view seemed to negotiate between the religious position of God's transcendence and the other liberal Protestant ideal of God's immanence, but in such a way as not to threaten the traditional religious education alliance between Reform Jews and mainline liberal Protestant educators.[32]

In that same year, the board of directors considered strategy matters based upon a four-page syllabus, probably prepared by Elliott. That document labeled the R.E.A. as liberal and then revealed the obvious but seldom public confession that the "Catholics do not participate because of these very assumptions of the association."[33]

Earlier that same year in another April meeting, Herbert Seamans again raised the Catholic issue with a small group meeting at Union Seminary in New York. His question was straightforward. "How can you possibly reconcile the difference to bring about real cooperation when Catholic education inevitably results in attitudes of intolerance?" Again a Jewish member, Israel Chipkin, served as the key negotiator of the group and outlined an agenda for dialogue with varieties of religious progressives. Chipkin noted that if one built conversation and cooperation around certain issues one could continue the interfaith movement. Those areas of consensus would be: "God, Brotherhood of Man, Dignity of the Individual, Democracy, Peace, (and) Social Justice."[34]

The Catholic theological position emerged more vividly in the notes on a conference on religion and higher education, prepared by Ross Snyder. A person identified simply as "McQuade," when asked the Catholic viewpoint, responded: "The Catholic feels that we must move away from a relativistic liberalism. The relativist will always refuse to commit himself and move through the conformative mind to reality. This is not merely our opinion about the thing. Tolerance to the Catholic is 'forebearance in charity of those who are wrong.'" No response by the group was indicated.[35]

The Catholic metaphysical bias again troubled the association in 1944. In a letter from F. E. Johnson, president of the R.E.A., to Harrison Elliott, Hugh Hartshorne, and Paul Limbert, all members of the R.E.A. board, Johnson did some obvious "behind the scenes" Protestant lobbying. A certain Mr. Desvernine had been accepted as a new member to represent the Catholic tradition. Johnson's estimate of Desvernine was a little less than evangelical. "He seems to be full as a tick of Aristotle, and he assured me that if anyone rejected the supernatural nature of man there was no basis for discussion." Johnson's reason for writing his colleague was equally candid. "Now I am putting this before you, not because I think any blow-up is inevitable, but in order that we may be prepared." Of course what was being threatened was the philosophical, unwritten credo of the R.E.A. And between Johnson, Hartshorne, and Elliott there was no misunderstanding as to what that position entailed.[36]

By 1946 William Clayton Bower was willing to go so far as to abandon the interfaith ideal of the association if such interaction threatened the creedal agenda of the R.E.A. Bower wrote to President Johnson as follows: "I would favor the R.E.A. going forward on a frankly liberal basis irrespective of the formal interfaith tradition of the association." Bower was advocating a fellowship open to persons "of all faiths who are in sympathy with its (R.E.A.) ideals, but abandoning the ideal that its constituent elements as a base line are Catholics, Protestants, and Jews."[37]

Bower's candor was refreshing. He seemed to acknowledge that the R.E.A. did have a specific liberal agenda. Indeed, though the R.E.A. consistently and publicly denied any formal creedal position and insisted on the open exchange of ideas, the truth was revealed in the behind the scenes exchanges just reviewed.

Its faith, in brief, rested in the conviction that the only pursuit of truth which was acceptable was that of scientific experimentation. The only reality of religious conviction was that of experimental humanism. If God were a consideration, God was only to be met in the interaction of other human beings. Any metaphysical posture that would not conform to this empirical position was not acceptable. The notion of transcendence or revelation was an unacceptable category because of the epistemological bias of scientism. The clearest indication of this antimetaphysical bias was seen in the association's failure to involve Catholic Christians and its open anti-Catholic nonpublic prejudices.

Neo-orthodoxy:
Of Liberal Parentage

The advent of neo-orthodoxy, while important and significant, was for a time at least one step removed from R.E.A.'s institutional doorstep. The Catholic presence, once sought after, continued to incite the discomfort that would grow into serious proportions when confronted with the onslaught of the neo-orthodox challenge throughout the forties and fifties.

Neo-orthodoxy had its historical roots in the liberal rather than the orthodox tradition. Wilhelm Pauck once noted that "orthodox theologies give rise to more orthodoxies; liberal theologies give rise to neo-orthodoxies."[38] If I understand that sentiment correctly, Pauck was indicating that the thrust for change and reconsideration is birthed in liberalism rather than orthodox epistemologies. Liberals are open to new evidence; they are concerned about the word of God in the cultural experience, while conservative orthodoxy is interested in the preservation of a tradition, devoted to an epistemology of repetition and rehearsal of the exactness of the tradition.

That certainly was true of the advent of European neo-orthodoxy. The liberal tradition began the theological task by examining the cultural context of God's activity. The neo-orthodox critique of modernism and positivistic evolutionary optimism grew out of a realistic reexamination of the European cultural situation. Liberalism might explain the peaks of human development, and it might explain the dark side of contemporary life. Neo-orthodoxy could claim the liberal tradition for an exacting, searching critique of the social conditions of life. That evaluation pointed to a dialectical conclusion. The human condition was no longer perceived as optimistically as the liberal had once pictured it. The evolutionary tide did not inevitably lead toward a more humane world. Indeed, the experience of western Europe revealed the opposite direction. World War I had ravished Europe, and the early symptom of the rise of Nazism in Germany pointed to a bleak future. The single most evident characteristic of the human condition seemed to point toward a reality that the orthodox tradition had called sin.

The neo-orthodox theologian operated with liberal assumptions in another significant way, equally critical of liberalism, but using the same epistemological method. The neo-orthodox biblical exegesis methodology was precisely that of the liberal colleagues. In fact, both Barth and Bultmann were essentially biblical theologians, exegetes, and their early work had to do with exegesis rather than with the systematic reinterpretation of the theological tradition. Their training was in the most liberal tradition of German biblical scholarship.

If there was a shift in their view of Scripture, it was in regard to the hermeneutical question rather than the exegetical. Surely the neo-orthodox accent of the precondition of faith to interpret the biblical tradition was closer to orthodoxy than to the liberal's intention of objectivity. Yet the hermeneutical difference grew out of the exegetical understanding. The Bible seemed to the neo-orthodox to insist on the qualitative difference between the divine and the human, and the only bridge to cross that intellectual/spiritual chasm was the analogy of faith.

Faith was understood in biblical terms as an essential gift of grace, a reliance on the indwelling of the spirit. Faith did not hunt or pursue God by scientific analysis of human life; rather faith received the self-disclosure of God in the mystery of responding to the word-event of Jesus. Faith was not progressive attainment; faith was receiving the presence of the living word, Jesus, by the gift of the spirit, the spirit of Christ.[39]

There was an existential cast to the self-understanding of the neo-orthodox theologian. This is particularly true in the work of Rudolph Bultmann. The human condition provided the material for the self-understanding of evil and inauthentic existence. The word of God, the

Gospel, provided the possibility of faith. To trust that revelation and act upon it in freedom and dependent security was the act of faith. The task of demythologizing the word of God was in behalf of the Gospel, so that in hearing the "good news" without the offense of premodern, prescientific biblical categories, one might live in authentic faith. The exegetical task served the preaching task so that faith might be formed in response to hearing the word of God.[40]

The liberal ultimately built a sophisticated natural theological system of thought from humankind to God. The religious education enterprise during the first two or three decades of the twentieth century in the American experience was a splendid example of that kind of theological system. One would come to know God, or the kingdom of God or the democracy of God, through the natural process of social interaction and the experience of love. God's immanence was celebrated with a tendency to ignore the ambiguity of human experience, overlooking the presence of evil, denying the existence of original sin, turning away from the sight of contradictory evidence.

Such a posture was more difficult after World War I and impossible after the Holocaust and World War II. But the corollary must also be noted, that the basic insights of the neo-orthodox position were culturally conditioned. It is no historical secret that the genesis of neo-orthodoxy grew out of the dramatic failure of the human enterprise in western Europe. The quest for the divine, however, led—for the neo-orthodox—to a new understanding of the demonic and a new sense of the "otherness" of the divine, the absence of God in the human marketplace. It should not be surprising then to find the germinal neo-orthodox word to grow out of European soil. The bombshell that shattered the liberal theological world was Karl Barth's commentary on the Epistle to the Romans, published in 1918. One can find the basic outline for the next two decades of theological debate in that work. Barth's *Romans* was published in English in 1933 in its sixth revision.

While not written as a critique of liberalism, consider the following exegetical results aside of the contemporary liberal theological majority opinion in the 1920s. Barth argued as follows. The Gospel, the message of God's love in Jesus, is of God, not humans. The Gospel is not a "religious message to inform mankind of their divinity." God is "utterly distinct from men."[41] The Gospel requires faith to be any real Gospel. "It can therefore be neither directly communicated nor directly apprehended." Barth appealed to the Reformation understanding as he pointed to the paradox of faith in the life of the Christian. "When God makes alive, he kills; when he justifies he imposes guilt; when he leads us to heaven he thrusts us down into hell."[42] Barth understood the paradoxical center of faith; to experience the grace of God, one must experience the tragedy of Good Friday.

As to the human condition, Barth was equally pessimistic. "Sin is that by which man, as we know him, is defined, for we know nothing of sinless men. Sin is power, by it men are controlled."[43] Barth points to the negative, to the impossibility of the human condition for good or for the divine or for any communication with the divine from human's side. Naturally there was no way out, only certain death and the accusing word of God's wrath.

The resurrection of Jesus was not to be understood as a historical fact to either assert or deny. Neither made much difference. Rather, in faith the resurrection was understood as God's meaning for life. Barth's dialectical style is illustrated: "Sin is the final meaning and life of this life. But then Christ died. God is the final meaning and death of death. God who stands beyond the death of this life." Being one in Christ's death and resurrection frees one from the death of this life to live the "risen life." "The power of the resurrection is the key, the opening door, the step over the threshold."[44]

Barth's radical epistemology turned the tables on scientific liberalism. Instead of searching for God, God searches for us. "Let us set aside our investigation of God. He searcheth us. Our mind is never right."[45] One can imagine the difficulty of the liberal to assimilate such a radical denial of the entire scientific enterprise. But Barth was not interested in that enterprise. He was interested in asserting the biblical view that God was in control of the divine human encounter. "Measured by the standard of God the dignitaries of men forfeit their excellence and their serious importance—they become relative; and even the noblest of human, moral, and spiritual attainments are seen to be what they really are—natural, of this world, profane, and materialistic."[46]

Barth, writing in *Christian Century* two decades later, noted his changed political standing. He acknowledged his radical politization in light of the event of Hitler. While he seemed to admit that dimension of change, he did not feel he had changed substantially, only in terms of those who interpreted and reviewed his books. Barth wrote, "But I should like to be allowed to say that anyone who really knew me before should not now be so much astonished."[47] That sentence seems on target in light of the testimony of these words from the 1918 *Romans* commentary. "This is uprightness before God, and it contradicts all our petty, sophistical questionings concerning why God is God. The man who fears lest the divine sovereignty may remove human responsibility or desires that it should do so must be reminded quite plainly that he stands before the judgment of God as a sinner."[48]

By the end of the 1940s Barth's theology found its way into mainstream American Protestant church curriculum. The most significant influence upon mainline Protestant religious education was probably the development of the Presbyterian *Christian Faith and Life Curriculum* (1942–1947). Under the careful theological guidance of James Smart, that curriculum successfully introduced the basic neo-Reformation concerns into the mainstream of Protestant religious education materials.[49]

Can Religious Education Be Christian?

Neo-orthodoxy's influence was pervasive, as illustrated by the impact upon almost all of the authors polled by *Christian Century* in the series "How My Mind Has Changed." Though assuredly most of the writers rejected or modified their total agreement, the majority did acknowledge the influence of the new dialectical theory upon their own positions. It was no accident that Barth was asked to end the series, for he had been most influential in initiating a reconsideration of basic liberal theological traditions.[50]

On the American side of the Atlantic, neo-orthodoxy (or neo-Reformation theology) was most notably represented at Union Seminary in New York by both Reinhold Niebuhr and Paul Tillich. Long a dominant liberal Protestant institution, Union now became the center of some of the most creative theological discussions in American Protestantism. That conflict and ferment must of course have been felt by the major religious educator of the period, Harrison Elliott, successor to Coe's position in religious education at Union Seminary. So it was both natural and understandable that Elliott would accept the challenge and publish the most responsible and eloquent defense of liberal religious education against the significant threat of neo-orthodoxy.

Elliott's book, *Can Religious Education Be Christian?* was by far his most careful work. In both style and content it was superior to any of his other published writings. For the most part it was a serious attempt to do justice to the challenge of neo-orthodoxy and to offer a careful positive defense of the liberal religious education tradition. The book grew out of Elliott's Ph.D. dissertation, written at Yale under the direction of Hartshorne and Weigle, which probably explains the historical thoroughness and accurately balanced description of positions. The liberal religious education movement could not have asked for a more capable defense. Responses indicated joyful relief. Ernest Chave applauded: "Elliott proves that religious education can be Christian."[51] The journal, *Religious Education,* asked Coe, patriarch of Protestant religious education, to write the review, and Coe did so with relish. He praised the book and celebrated its publication, indicating his approval.

"On the negative side" Coe thought Elliott had proven that neo-orthodoxy misused the Bible, ignored church history, perverted psychological knowledge with "guesses and hunches," and finally "ascribed divine authority" to what really was "opinion of the neo-orthodox writers themselves." "On the positive side" Coe thought that Elliott's brand of progressive religious education despite misunderstandings "springs factually considered from assured knowledge, not from guesses nor from any new-fangled dogmatism."[52]

Coe was still praising the book a year after the review, and he wrote Elliott expressing his conviction that Elliott's book had targeted the issues. "That your book hits the bull's-eye becomes more and more evident," Coe wrote as he extended his criticism of F. E. Johnson's *Social Gospel Re-examined*. Coe rejected Johnson's attempt to mediate between the neo-orthodox and the religious education tradition.[53] Certainly Harrison Elliott had not done so; this is the critical value of the book. Elliott met neo-orthodoxy with the social tradition of religious education, and finally the book must be read as that kind of challenge. The book was a fascinating description of two schools of thought regarding the nature of Christian truthing.

The first eight chapters of Elliott's book were historical sketches of the development of religious education within the Protestant liberal tradition. Woven throughout that history was descriptive evidence of the neo-orthodox position, particularly as expressed by the work of Brunner, Niebuhr, Barth, and Tillich. The latter seven chapters were descriptions of the current liberal religious education theory, relying on the major voices of the movement: Coe, Hartshorne, Bower, Chave, and others. The backdrop of the entire book was the shadow of neo-orthodoxy and its rejection of liberal Protestant natural theology. The plot of Elliott's story was admittedly a defense of progressive religious education and its component social method of nurture.

Elliott's description of neo-orthodoxy was balanced and fair for the most part. He acknowledged the difference between neo-orthodoxy and American fundamentalism.[54] He accepted Niebuhr's view of social egoism and noted the parallel position of Coe and Niebuhr on the issue of the human predicament.[55] (I have noted in earlier chapters that Coe had reserved a category for sin, especially in his *Social Theory of Religious Education*.) Elliott found interesting similarity between Coe's view of God's immanence and Tillich's approach to the "ground of being."[56]

His criticism of neo-orthodoxy, however, was not so gentle. According to Elliott, neo-orthodoxy was a form of Protestant neo-scholasticism, an appeal to some kind of ultimate scriptural authority. He rejected neo-orthodoxy as another form of indoctrination with potential to set religious education back into a new form of Herbartianism.[57] Any attempt to appeal to revelation or transcendent authority was rejected. He was critical of Barth's and Brunner's insistence that only the "believer can truly interpret the Scripture." "In other words, they insist that the only study of Scripture which can be authoritative is that which accepts their particular approach." To his credit he does acknowledge the fact that "liberals and religious educators have also been guilty of attempting to fit the Scripture to their particular patterns."[58]

The argument against neo-orthodoxy was best summarized as a defense of the liberal religious education system of natural theology. Elliott claimed that God was to be met in human experience. He disavowed the possibility of revelation or any transcendent or supernatural experience; God was to be known through the "experience and the reverent search of men."[59] He advocated the use of the Bible without any preconceived opinions. He still believed that the kingdom of God could happen. He acknowledged the potential for human reconstruction. He opted for love and goodwill. "Therefore the goal is truly social, for it is that approximation which is possible to human beings in their social arrangements of the Kingdom of God in which love is manifested in all social relationships." He continued, "Confidence in the success of these human endeavors is based upon the Christian belief in the limitless resources of God which are available to individuals and groups who meet the conditions for their release."[60]

Elliott ultimately answered his question, *Can Religious Education Be Christian?* with a resounding yes! He rehearsed all the old beliefs in the kindgom of God, the brotherhood of man, the magic of love, and the natural relationship of persons to the divine. In short, Elliott never seemed able to confront the radical nature of a Christian understanding of sin. In his rejection of any formal principle of authority in Christian judgment, he seems to have abandoned any chance for serious social criticism or any authentic prophetic posture for the Christian message.

The weakest segments of the book deal with educational method and realistic outcomes. Here he parrots his mentor, reviving the rhetoric of the past rather than dealing with the charges of large-scale failure by the liberal religious education establishment. For the four decades of religious education had not brought the kingdom into being, not within the church and certainly not in American society. Somehow, blind to the failures of liberal religious education, he appeared unable to confront the dark side of human life and the fallibility of the best of human intention. In light of the next half-decade to come, he would be faced with the embarrassing truth of the failure of liberal Protestantism to provide a viable basis for social salvation.

Can Christian Education Be Religious?

H. Shelton Smith was for a brief period of time a colleague of Elliott's at Teachers College, right across the street from Union Seminary (1928–29). He was part of the inner circle of the R.E.A., a member of the board of directors and a regular contributor to the journal, writing both articles and book reviews. From the early 1930s he represented the loyal minority within the R.E.A. His interest was more theological than educational.

Smith's major religious education work, *Faith and Nurture,* was published in 1941, just one year after Elliott's *Can Religious Education Be Christian?* The book was a frontal attack on the religious education tradition, particularly the work of Coe and Elliott. The references to both authors were numerous and usually critical.[61] Chosen to be a selection of the Religious Book Club, the book received public attention from the religious education community as well as from the general reading public. Perhaps the most muted response to Smith's book came from the R.E.A. itself. The book was reviewed in *Religious Education* (unfairly, I believe) by Edward Ames. The review did not describe the book, but linked Smith with the other orthodox critics of religious education. What could have evolved as a constructive dialogue between Smith and Elliott did not occur, at least not in the pages of *Religious Education.*[62]

Smith was unrelenting in his criticism of religious education, and although the book was by no means a capitulation to dialectical theology, its most barbed criticisms often sound very much like the larger neo-orthodox critique of liberal theology. Smith noted his indebtedness to Reinhold Niebuhr, and as one reads the book it is not difficult to note the similarity of the argument.[63]

Smith set the stage for his critique of religious education by stating clearly what he believed was the crisis for the religious educator at this time in history. While American theology was in the process of internal reconstruction due to the challenges of neo-orthodoxy and the larger cultural criticism of liberalism in general, religious education "simply reiterates the characteristic tenets of liberal education." Smith believed this defensive attitude could only serve to disallow any modification or change among religious educators to meet the new theological and cultural realities.

He then proceeded to sketch the history of liberal Protestantism in the American context, linking the religious education theological attitude to that of the nineteenth-century religious liberalism with little modification. The key focus of early liberalism—divine immanance, growth, goodness of man, and the nonhistorical Jesus ("in other words, the real Jesus is a twentieth-century modernist"[64])—continued to be the faith of modern religious education. Smith went about attacking each of those theological presuppositions.

He believed that the liberal religious educator had turned the kingdom of God into an anthropocentric kingdom. Smith named the enemies: Coe, Elliott, Dewey, Bower, Soares. Coe's "democracy of God" and Elliott's "growing process" are, from Smith's view, antithetical to Christian faith. They involve "a denial of God as transcendent from human creatures."[65] The sovereignty of God is reduced to democratic human agreement. In so doing, Smith argued, the religious educator had equated the kingdom of God to a particular social order, American democracy. Such a view was, according to Smith, sheer romanticism.[66]

Smith believed that humans were creatures of God made in the image of God. While rejecting the naturalism of John Dewey, Henry Nelson Wieman, and William Clayton Bower, Smith did not repudiate the value of the natural sciences. He did, however, reject the limited perspective. "Naturalistic liberalism has failed to see man in the full dimension of his existence."[67] Smith pointed out the absence of sin as a category of theological understanding for liberal religious educators and argued that the biblical image of humankind was one of humans in rebellion, not only against one's neighbor, but against God. He was careful to note that Coe did allow for sin, but in the development of his thought that notion receives little attention.

Smith accused the religious education movement of losing its evangelical focus; "it is without an adequate evangel." He believed that the Christian revelation of God in Jesus Christ was the "ultimate meaning and destiny of human existence."[68] Rejecting the relativism of experimentalism, he criticized Sophia Fahs and Blanche Carrier and their methodology of inductive questioning as a "form of vacillation, cowardice, or superficiality."[69] Smith believed that the biblical witness called for a Gospel of repentance and deliverance from God's side rather than from human's. Rejecting the notion that humankind could build the kingdom or that social reconstruction could change human nature, Smith called for a religious education content true to the biblical view of deliverance and grace. Abandoning American Protestantism's "moral-

istic and self-help Gospel,'' he advocated a return to Pauline understandings of faith and grace. Moving close to a classical Lutheran
paradoxical understanding of grace, Smith wrote: ''A god whose
'wrath' against human sinfulness is sharper than a two-edged sword is
yet a God who does not reckon the repentant believer's trespasses
against him. This paradoxical truth eludes every canon of human reason, yet it is the wisdom of the Gospel.''[70]

Smith's last chapter was a detailed rejection of progressive experimentalism as a method for religious education. Basing his critique on a
biblical understanding of a theocentric world view, a fallen creation, an
imperfect human nature, and a divine revelation of deliverance in Jesus
Christ, Smith concluded that progressive religious education experimentalism was in fundamental conflict with the Hebrew-Christian faith.

> For Christian faith, as already indicated, envisages human society within a
> framework that is theocentric. It sees man from a perspective that includes
> the empirical natural order, but also transcends it. It expressly denies that
> human values can be adequately understood as to their origin, worth, or
> destiny within the frame of a purely empirical democracy. With equal con-
> viction it rejects the idea that the source of deliverance from sin, mean-
> inglessness, and frustration had its center in humanity.[71]

Smith's exacting criticism was balanced, cautious, and for the most
part accurate. However, his references to ''classical Christianity'' seem
undefined and vague. His method of referring to Bible texts for support
of his position was probably not adequate to persuade any of his liberal
opponents to modify their positions. Ames' review in *Religious Education* correctly noted that weakness in Smith's book, and surely for those
who were looking for defense, the best defense was to illustrate Smith's
apparent appeal to authority by biblical reference.[72]

The essay, moreover, was not an attempt to reconstruct religious
education method, except by implication. (One could only conclude that
religious education should be more biblical and evangelical.) So while
an important statement of the weakness of progressive religious education and a passionate appeal to Christian biblical traditions, Smith's
seminal work remained only a theological critique of the general religious education nonsystematized creedal position and not an agenda
for a new program of Christian education.

Others would have to assume the task of building a new strategy for
religious education. Unfortunately for religious education, Smith's future interests turned away from religious education to history rather than
to the difficult task of building a religious education theory congruent
with his biblical neo-orthodox viewpoint.[73]

The Mature Liberal:
Bower's Middle Way

What Smith had managed to do was drive a significant theological wedge between the experimentalistic humanism of John Dewey and the progressives and the more theological understanding of Christian experience. In rejecting Dewey's method as inadequate for Christian education, Smith had forced the religious educators to reconsider their methodological tasks. That such a reconsideration happened is indicated by a marvelous exchange between Smith and Bower only a year after the publication of *Faith and Nurture*. The essays are contained in the journal, *Religion and Life*, and seem a natural extension of Smith's argument. (*Religious Education* ignored the conflict between Smith and Elliott, a telling rebuke to Smith's effort.)

Smith's title, "The Supremacy of Christ in Christian Nurture," hints at his basic argument. Religious education must become more Christian, less liberal, and certainly less progressive. Smith focused on the creedal foundation of progressive pedagogy which he attributed to the work of John Dewey. Smith summarized seven key ideas of Dewey. Education according to Dewey was a social process through which the community shares its values with the growing child. The aim of school was growth, or "continuous reconstruction of experience." Education was about present living problems, not "preparation for future living." The process and goal of education are the same, growth. The "child's own social activities" are those that unify the curriculum. Learning "is free active self-expression on the part of the child," and the basic method of social progress is what Dewey called "democratic education."[74]

Smith rejected this progressive methodology as both rationalistic and moralistic. Against such a salvation he posited a high Christology, a theology of the cross. Smith understood the cost of redemption. The injunction to use one's intelligence and practice love only "add frustration and confusion to our already distraught existence," he wrote.

Bower's essay "Christian Education After Nineteen Centuries" contained no reference to progressive methods, no appeal to psychology or educational theory, no scientific data to support experientialism, and no mention of John Dewey. Instead, Bower began his essay with a discussion of Jesus' ministry, pointing out the immediacy of Jesus' life and how he viewed his relationship to God and persons of supreme importance in the present moment. Bower argued that Jesus rejected the tradition and authority of the past and filled the present experience with new values.

He proceeded then to sketch, historically, the development of New Testament theology and the nature of church creedal development through the intervening centuries. He argued that the church had replaced experience with tradition and in so doing had lost the creative impact of the religion of Jesus. "Thus the church in its traditional educational programs has come dangerously near to substituting literature for life, tradition for a present and living experience of God, and indoctrination for a creative facing of the issues of present living in terms of growing and dynamic spiritual values."[75]

Bower reiterated the objectives of religious education as accepted by the International Council which stressed the development of a Christlike personality, a reconstruction of society to approximate the kingdom of God on earth, and the use of tradition for understanding the present and building a fellowship within the church for renewal and support. He concluded his essay with a type of humility seldom practiced by his religious education colleagues. "This, whatever its defects in theory and practice, (is what) modern Christian education is seeking to accomplish." Bower noted that Christian education had been "distorted and dominated by tradition and authority" for nineteen centuries, but that "modern Christian education is seeking to approximate Christ's way of education by coming to grips with the experience of growing persons where they are confronted by reality." That place was the setting where "God is creatively at work" in history, "where tradition is undergoing reconstruction in the light of emergent insights and of growing values."[76]

Henry Van Dusen, professor of systematic theology at Union Seminary, wrote a brief analysis of the two essays. He caught the curious fact that both authors were appealing to a Christological base. Van Dusen introduced his essay with the insightful observation that religious education was the youngest of all the seminary disciplines. In comparing the religious education movement to the period of adolescence, he noted that youth are usually the most inclined to the newest novelty and most radical in their sense of loyalties, yet least able to let go after the passing of the fad. He pointed out that religious education had given full allegiance to modernity and conformed to the tides of early twentieth-century liberalism. He understood the fact that in all likelihood religious education would be the last branch of religious disciplines to "admit disillusionment with the axioms of the age." He suggested that Smith's work in general was a moderate voice from within the religious education movement calling for maturity of change.[77]

Then he proceeded to target the interesting irony of the two essays. Smith charged religious education with misplaced loyalties, abandoning the Christian tradition and the particular revelation of Jesus Christ for a modern, humanistic experientialism, a baptized version of John Dewey's progressive theory. Bower, on the other hand, did not refer to Dewey or progressive method. Instead he had argued for historical continuity to the living Jesus and his method and understanding of religious values and faith. Though Bower's understanding of Jesus and Scripture may have been incorrect or biased, both authors, without reviewing the other's article before publication, appealed to an understanding of the Christ event or to a specific mode of Christology. According to Van Dusen, Bower's view assuredly reflected nineteenth-century liberalism, and Smith's was surely influenced by neo-orthodoxy.

Van Dusen expressed surprise at the viewpoints of both authors, particularly those of Bower. If Bower's view represented the essential thinking of the movement, then Van Dusen seemed to lend support to that view. For Van Dusen reminded his readers: "Before deciding against their immediate liberal heritage, Christians do well to remind themselves that the century which was largely under the spell of this view of Christ and his kingdom was, in Professor Latourette's phrase, "the great century—incomparably the century of greatest advance in every aspect of the Christian movement's influence upon mankind."[78]

Understandably then, Smith's theological attack was threatening: "Modern religious education feels that it is fighting for its very existence."[79] The problem with Bower's essay was that he had ignored the essential difficulty of religious education's methodology; that is, the capitulation to a secular methodology. Whatever his motive, Bower had recast the movement in theological language and avoided much of the criticism which he must have known would have come his way after reading Smith's *Faith and Nurture*. Bower's theological description was credible. It was not, however, truly representative of the majority of religious education theorists of the period, certainly not of Elliott, Coe, Fahs, Betts, or Chave—some of the dominant voices in the R.E.A.

Smith's book did not affect the central leadership of the R.E.A. The old faithful remained for the most part unrepentant liberals. Even as late as 1960 Bower affirmed his continuing liberal bias. In responding to Kendig Cully's assessment of the new theological climate of the 1960s, Bower replied, "By no means have all in Israel 'bowed the knee to Baal.' "[80]

The Romantic Liberal Response

Two illustrations will suffice to show how romantic the liberal progressive bias remained throughout the period among some of the R.E.A.

principals. The first was the publication of Chave's *A Functional Approach to Religious Education* (1947), which Chave chose to label "my Gospel."[81] A review of Chave's gospel shows clearly how entrenched the commitment to liberalism remained even after World War II.

Chave rejected any form of transcendent salvation. "The functional approach emphasizes the responsibility of man for a large share in his own salvation."[82] Chave offered a "naturalistic and functional" approach to religious education. What Chave meant by naturalism was clearly a humanistic form of natural theology. He called for religious education that emphasized the creative experience and identified God as "the name for the most important phase of one's cosmic environment on which person-social life is dependent." Chave concluded: "God is not denied, and the naturalist is neither agnostic nor atheistical but functional, adjusting himself to the creative orderly processes of life which he experiences in daily living."[83]

Chave defined the content of the divine as "the essential nature of the growth process evident in the spiritual realization of latent human possibilities."[84] The outcome of functional religion was listed accordingly:

1. Sense of worth;
2. Social sensitivity;
3. Appreciation of the universe;
4. Discrimination in values;
5. Responsibility and accountability;
6. Cooperative fellowship;
7. Quest for truth and realization of values;
8. Integration of experience into a working philosophy of life;
9. Appreciation of historical continuity; and
10. Participation in group celebrations.[85]

One might note the absence of any theological content or traditional categories of religious language. Yet Chave would argue that he had "not done away with anything that was real or vital in the familiar theological concepts of God, sin, salvation, Jesus, will of God, spirit of Christ, eternal life, prayer, forgiveness, sacrifice, Bible as word of God, revelation, inspiration, sanctification, heaven, hell, supernatural, sacred or holy."[86]

In spite of his denials, Chave had really abandoned the historical religious tradition of Christianity or Judaism. His closing paragraph illustrates how far his progressive liberalism had led him. Chave talked about the real world, a dynamic world in which atomic forces ban all securities, a world of masses of increasing expectations. "We live in a world not of one book, but of many significant books, not of one religious culture, but of plural concepts and practices." There is not "one God but many gods . . . the hope of the future is in a spiritual unity directed to specific tasks of gigantic size."[87]

I find Chave's humanistic religion vague, sentimental, and almost irrational. What Chave had effectively done was reduce religion to the routines of human existence, turned God into a symbol of growth potential, and turned religious education into an incomprehensible experience in spiritual uncertainty.

Sophia Fahs serves as the second illustration of one bearing the signs of aging romantic liberal progressivism. Her many books for children as well as her volumes in religious education are for the most part classic liberal progressive statements completely unaffected by the theological movements of neo-orthodoxy during the period of the 1940s and 1950s.[88]

A confirmed naturalist, she viewed the religious education process as one of natural discovery in contradiction to any form of authority or indoctrination. For Fahs "vital religion lives in the totality of experiences."[89] Rejecting revelation or any transcendent possibility of otherness, Fahs remained loyal to the humanist value of creative experience and the related concept of the immanence of God. She never lost her optimism or hopefulness. Consider these sentiments: "A cosmic God— if there be one—must be closer than hands and feet. Nearer than a mother to her unborn child. Our relationships are boundless. They are cosmic like those of God himself. We too are invisible, intangible, and beyond understanding." Then in a more universal mood she continued: "Our new hopes of a world brotherhood—when once they take deep root and spread in our common social consciousness—will give us new songs to sing, new experiences to celebrate, new depths of feeling to explore, and new devotions to fire our zeal."[90]

Sophia Fahs remained a Unitarian liberal progressive throughout her career. Both Fahs and Chave maintained their social convictions throughout their careers. In this partnership they passed on the R.E.A. heritage which always promoted some form of public piety concerned with the whole rather than the individual, always stressing the corporate rather than the single solitary soul.[91]

In spite of these criticisms there was a noble quality about the liberal progressive educator in the struggle of the 1940s. Although I am generally negative in regard to their theological perspectives, so unchangeable and dogmatic, I do admire their devotion to the public task of religious education. Their vision of a democratic religion sustained the primal R.E.A. dream when others abandoned the social task and accented the more narrow perspective of personal salvation and private sins. One can readily criticize the theological sterility of the aging liberals, but one must admire their social consciousness.

The Future Belongs to the Young

Leadership for the 1950s would not be forthcoming from the re-petitious liberal rhetoric of the R.E.A. voices of the 1940s. Nor would it emerge from the strident voices of neo-orthodoxy. The conflict between the two positions seemed to generate more heat than light. Stewart G. Cole, in reviewing Chave's *A Functional Approach to Religious Education* for the journal *Religious Education,* caught that dilemma in these words: "It is somewhat unsure of its grounds for introducing many of the concepts that are central in historic Christianity. How can the functional approach and the metaphysical viewpoint be accommodated?"[92]

Old liberals shunned such accommodation. Young neo-orthodox religious educators were equally uninterested in compromise. Why should they be when victory seemed so complete? Some central mediating position between the two extremes was necessary if any new creative religious education movement was to emerge. That task was accepted by another generation of religious educators, new to the religious education establishment, but due to become heirs to that tradition.

Three such persons emerged during this period as potential leaders. All of them were members of the R.E.A. One was later to assume the Horace Bushnell Chair of Christian Nurture at Yale University and serve for many years as editor of *Religious Education.* Another (by far the oldest of the three) was to become a successor to Harrison Elliott at Union Seminary. The third was to become general secretary of the R.E.A. All relatively unknown during the early 1940s, each emerged into significant leadership positions during the 1950s and 1960s. What each had in common was a moderate theological perspective and boundless energy, both necessary for the future of any developing movement.

Randolph Crump Miller began his religious education career as instructor in the areas of philosophy of religion and Christian ethics at the Church Divinity School of the Pacific in 1936. He ended it forty-five years later as Horace Bushnell Professor of Religious Education at Yale University. His early theological outlook was sketched in *What We Can Believe* (1941). As co-editor of *Christianity and the Contemporary Scene* in 1943, he began to sketch out a new position in religious education. Miller wrote two of the essays in that book, one dealing with theology and the other with education. Those two concerns dominated his entire professional career and influenced the development of the entire American Protestant religious education movement.

Miller called for a "central trend" which would incorporate the values of neo-orthodoxy and maintain the virtues of the liberal tradition. Believing that such a balanced view would recognize the tragedy of the human condition without denying the hope for renewal inherent in the event of Jesus Christ, he called for a synthesis of science and Christianity, a reworking of liberal Christology and a new vitalized biblical theology.

In his chapter on Christian education, Miller attempted the same mediating position. He took issue with H. Shelton Smith's position that the movement's key enemy was John Dewey. "By this I mean we must show how the fundamental insights of progressive education can be made consistent with the Christian way of life and belief."[93] Miller did not accomplish such a synthesis in that brief article or in later volumes. He did manage to plead for more theology, for more biblical concern, and went so far as to advocate a return to indoctrination. "In the last analysis, there must be a greater amount of theological indoctrination, but it must be good theology."[94] Miller seemed, in retrospect, to have sketched his life's work. He advocated a new "understanding of the organized relationship between content and method, involving theology, evangelism, and action."[95] While the essay did not come close to solving those challenges, it did set forth a prospectus for the future.

Miller continued to stress his central theological position as editor of a small volume, *The Church and Organized Movements* (1946), and in a second book, *Religion Makes Sense* (1950), he chose the same middle position appealing to both faith and reason, to the fruits of the neo-orthodox critique, and to the heritage of the best of liberalism. Miller again posed the same educational question: How can method be related to content? The major interest of those books was theology rather than religious education.[96]

Miller was at this point in his career very much a person of his time. Influenced by current attitudes, he still shared some latent anti-Catholic sentiment born of earlier Protestant prejudice. In caustic language, Miller asked: "If Mary had been so perfect as modern Roman Catholics now believe, we might expect Jesus to have taught the Motherhood of God, but there is no reference to such teaching."[97] He wrote disparagingly about Catholic centralized power and saw such development as a threat to "the historic alliance of Christianity and democracy."[98] And while Miller extolled the virtues of Catholic universalism, he had harsh words for American Catholicism: "This view of the Church is a big one, and it is the liberal's belief that 'the Church has never been

Catholic enough,' for almost all who use the name 'Catholic' are among the most sectarian and divisive in Christendom.''[99]

Miller reflected the liberalism of his mentors, generally open-minded until threatened by some form of authoritarianism or doctrinal allegiance significantly different from their own, be that fundamentalism, neo-orthodoxy, or Catholic confessionalism. But he was young, and there were years of ecumenical growth ahead. He seemed to mature to those challenges as his influence widened and deepened.

Miller's first significant religious education publication, *The Clue to Christian Education* (1950), really began his long career toward the development of a theological method consistent with the best of the ''central tradition.'' He acknowledged his indebtedness to H. Shelton Smith's *Faith and Nurture*. Committed to Smith's challenge to develop a theology of religious education and a methodology that would be congruent with such a theology, Miller tried to avoid the old pitfalls of indoctrination or naturalism. He articulated his central position as follows:

> But if neither content nor indoctrination provides the clue, how can theology be at the center of the curriculum? The answer is that theology is not at the center. The center of the curriculum is a twofold relationship between God and the learner. The curriculum is both God-centered and experience-centered. Theology must be prior to the curriculum. Theology is the ''truth about God-in-relation-to-man.''[100]

The remainder of the book outlined that viewpoint. Miller sought to bring theology and progressive method together. In his phrase defining theology as ''the truth about God-in-relation-to-man,'' Miller had tried to forge the beginnings of a theory that would bring concern for both the intellectual task of theology and the social task of Christian experience.

That phrase also pointed to the key dialectic of Miller's entire theoretical viewpoint. While earlier liberals had focused primarily on the nature of social relationships in the task of Christian nurture, Miller pleaded for a theological basis for educational methodology. Continuity with the past liberal tradition was preserved. Miller would not abandon the key insights of the religious education movement. But he would extend those social concerns to enrich and empower the experiential basis with an evangelical theology. At the beginning of his career, he tried to walk between both camps, religious education and neo-orthodox theology, particularly defined by the Niebuhr brothers, and specifically as related to the doctrine of man. As his career unfolded one noticed his theological modification and the enrichment of his experiential concerns.

The second and oldest of the sons of the aging fathers was Lewis Joseph Sherrill, who began his career in religious education at Louisville Presbyterian Theological Seminary and ended his work as professor of religious education at Union Seminary, New York. His appointment was almost symbolic of the future trend in religious education, initiating a shift from social theory to psychological insights as the basis for educational practice. Sherrill's work was rooted in a conservative, evangelical tradition and over time moved from educational and theological concerns to a serious consideration of the insights of depth psychology for the task of religious education. Uninterested in developmental behaviorism and experimental psychology, he turned his interests to the insights of Jung, Freud, Adler, and other psychoanalysts.

Adult Education in the Church (1939)[101] was a practical manual about the task of adult education in the life of the Protestant parish. There are no references to the progressive giants of the R.E.A. movement. Rather, the book represented a practical, straightforward, common sense approach to adult education, built on the basic conviction that the task of the church was teaching the truths of Scriptures.

Understanding Children (1939) was more heavily psychologically oriented. Sherrill drew from Betts, Piaget, Jung, Gesell, Hall, Jersild, and Chave to describe the developing nature of the children. Sherrill, however, saw no inherent conflict between psychological theory and the basic tenets of the Christian tradition. The book ended with a chapter on Christian fellowship, where Sherrill argued the case for Christian community. Psychological health became the way to Christian maturity; Christian relationships became the avenue to psychological health.

Sherrill believed that ''when a child trusts an adult and lets himself go in affectionate response (this act) is remarkably like a thing that was constantly happening when Jesus was among men.'' A child, Sherrill argued, ''needs this very same faith in our Lord, this confidence and trust which persons felt in the days of his flesh.'' Sherrill believed that a child's faith in some adult ''is a gateway into the greater redeeming faith in God.'' The opposite of that reality would be equally true, that a ''child's lack of faith in his adults is one of the surest ways to mar or break his personality and character.''[102]

Opening Doors of Childhood (1945) continued along the same ideological lines, using the best in current child development theory in partnership with a traditional Christian theological basis. Relationship with God grew out of a psychological analogy. Children needed a sense of security and companionship, Sherrill maintained. But these psychological components were not antithetical to Christian fellowship. They were supported by the Christian experience of forgiveness.

Sherrill advocated the use of the Bible with children, but with adult discretion. He advocated careful selection of stories to correspond to the developmental level of the child. He placed much of the responsibility for religious education on parents, and the book was filled with stories and anecdotes from parish life. The style was folksy, often practical, with direct suggestions. Written in lay language, the effort was a successful attempt to help parents and teachers act out their faith convictions with a deeper awareness of the psychological impact of their relationships upon children. Sin was an accepted reality in Sherrill's view, as was forgiveness. Balancing theology with psychoanalytic theory, always in complementary fashion, he used psychoanalytic theory in behalf of his theology.[103]

The last of Sherrill's books in this period was *The Struggle of the Soul* (1951). His effort projected the life development of the Christian from early childhood through all the stages of life until death. Again, Sherrill's work was that of synthesis. He cast the task of maturity into the image of pilgrimage. Pilgrimage was a way to affirm both the transcendent and the human aspect of growth into maturity.[104]

His work was much more individualistic than that of Elliott, Coe, Chave, and others. Yet throughout his work he stressed the nature of the Christian community as the place of faith formation.[105] Certainly we have a new direction in his work from the social theory of earlier religious education theorists. Because of his psychoanalytic orientation, the accent was on the individual rather than the community or the larger cultural context. That influence we shall note continued into the 1950s and marked a new direction in religious education theory at odds with the more social theory of the majority of R.E.A.'s early leadership. Turning away from a cultural basis to a more theological basis and a more individualistic psychological orientation, Sherrill's early work is illustrative of much of what was to come in future decades; depth psychology replaced social theory as the paradigmatic location for future strategies of religious education.

Herman Wornom, the third of our third-generation liberal heirs, was least known and least influential during this period before he became general secretary of the R.E.A. He had served as director of religious education in a number of parishes between 1925 and 1937. From 1942–1946 he served as a professor of religious education and director of field work at the Pacific School of Religion in Berkeley. In 1946 he was appointed executive secretary of the Department of Christian Education of the Protestant Council of the city of New York. Soon afterward his name began to appear on lists of R.E.A. meetings in the New York area and in meetings of the executive committee of the association.

A document dated January 15, 1951, indicates that he was instrumental in drawing up a grant proposal for $8,000 for the R.E.A. mid-century campaign. That grant gave the R.E.A. a new lease on life, opening the door for the possibility of a full-time general secretary and making possible a larger program.[106]

After Elliott's death the association turned to Wornom for leadership. The announcement of his appointment was listed in the May–June 1952 issue of *Religious Education*.[107] That issue followed the memorial issue devoted to George Albert Coe who died November 9, 1951.

It seemed a fitting irony that Wornom began his career in such close proximity to the death of two of the most loyal progressive religious education liberals, Elliott and Coe. It was surely the end of an era. Wornom's leadership would chart new directions and bring new energy into the troubled association. The neo-humanists were fading from the scene, and a new period of change for the R.E.A. was about to commence.

Later in his life, Wornom assessed this period as that time in the history of the association where the humanists "had almost killed the association."[108] He viewed his own leadership as a more moderately centered position, comfortable with a renewed interest in theology and a growing concern for the institutional church as well as the broader community, but loyal to the continuity of the social values of the R.E.A.

There are few records which indicate the selection process which resulted in Wornom's position as general secretary. He himself had noted that Chave and others disapproved of his appointment.[109] In all likelihood that is true. He surely would have been at odds with the humanism of Chave at this point in his career. Wornom brought youthful energy, excellent administrative skills, and boundless optimism to his new job. These virtues were desperately needed by the aging leadership of the R.E.A. A period had ended, and a new time was only beginning. In 1952 there were few data on which to base hope. The future was blurred, the new leader unknown, the financial health of the organization shaky, the leadership aging, and the times disjointed from the old rhetoric of liberal optimism.

*   *   *   *   *   *

Throughout this period, circumstances seemed to limit the effectiveness of the R.E.A. Finances limited the outreach of the organization. Volunteers edited the journal, called the meetings, visited the loyalists in the field, promoted the organization, lobbied for new members, and attended the annual, discouraging meeting. Conventions were abandoned. Yearly gatherings were poorly attended, although there were moments of "rare fellowship." The times were hard.

Optimism faltered as the United States entered another world conflict where evil prevailed and the horror of inhumanity to humanity filled the newsreels of local movie houses. Prophetic voices spoke against the evil with new conviction. They hearkened to a word of God and were not afraid of principalities and powers. Their kind grew throughout the forties and shattered the liberalism of American Protestantism with a new awareness of the dark side of human life. They confronted the "Christ of culture" theorists with a new challenge. They taught that the situation was worse than one imagined and the good news was better than a simple matter of reconstructed human values. They held "Christ against culture" so that it might be transformed, not by human enterprise, but by the divine intervention of the God of justice and mercy.[110]

The R.E.A. remained for the most part captive to its liberal, progressive history. The leaders repeated the truths of the movement. They appealed to democracy, brotherhood, and love, and continued to look for the presence of God in the sciences and in the human situation. They were passed by, ridiculed, and taunted. They repeated time-worn phrases, but out of context. They turned at the end of the period to their aged leader and most articulate advocate, Harrison Elliott, for salvation and renewal, for leadership and guidance into a new day.[111] A year later he died, and his death was followed only months later by the death of Coe, the patriarch of the R.E.A. family.

Funerals are times for remembering. And young R.E.A. leaders would remember the stories and the achievements of their fathers. Their convictions would not be forgotten. They would be changed. Their creeds would not be rewritten; they would be edited. Their language would be modified but not abandoned. And the democracy of God would remain an image to achieve in a new way and in a new place through a new language of relationships, in the community of the church. The dreams would be transformed, but not forgotten.

Notes for Chapter IV

1. Ernest J. Chave, "What Does R.E.A. Mean?" unpublished essay, R.E.A.F., October 23, 1950. The essay was later published in *Religious Education* with this sentence deleted. See letter from S. P. Franklin to Harrison Elliott, November 22, 1950, R.E.A.F.

2. Harrison Elliott, "A Report from the General Secretary," *Religious Education* XLVI (January/February, 1951), p. 4. Elliott wrote these sentences as indication of the

first need for continuation of the R.E.A. Other expressions followed, all of which summarized his reflections on his visits to the "field" in the fall of 1950.

3. For a comparison of the I.C.R.E. during this period see William Clayton Bower's and Percy Roy Hayward's *Protestantism Faces Its Educational Task Together* (Appleton, Wisconsin: C. C. Nelson Publishing Co., 1949) and *The Study of Christian Education* prepared by the Committee on the Study of Christian Education, (Chicago I.C.R.E. Office, 1946–1947).

4. The concept of "shared directorship" was suggested to me by Charles Kniker, Professor of Education, Iowa State University, Ames, Iowa. As we shall note later in the chapter, a number of key R.E.A. figures held major positions in other related agencies; thus their influence was both enlarged and occasionally over-extended. The idea of shared directorship is best illustrated by joint leadership in the R.E.A. and the I.C.R.E. The 1936 *Annual Yearbook* of the I.C.R.E. lists all these R.E.A. members as I.C.R.E. associates: Ernest Chave, Hugh Hartshorne, F. Ernest Johnson, Otto Meyer, Frank McKibben, H. Shelton Smith, Luther Weigle, Paul Veith, William Clayton Bower, Blanche Carrier, Harry C. Munro.

5. See *Christian Century*. The articles ran in weekly issues from January 18, 1939, to September 20, 1939. The last two segments were written by the father of neo-orthodoxy, Karl Barth.

6. Harrison S. Elliott, *Can Religious Education Be Christian?* (New York: The Macmillan Company, 1940).

7. H. Shelton Smith, *Faith and Nurture* (New York: Charles Scribner's Sons, 1941).

8. Ernest J. Chave, "Report of the Executive Committee to the Association," *Religious Education* XXXI (April, 1936), p. 144.

9. Report of the Debt Raising Campaign Committee to the Board of Directors, February 5, 1939, R.E.A.F. Published in *Religious Education* XXXIV (April–June, 1939), pp. 115–116.

10. Letter from Ernest Chave to Hugh Hartshorne, January 25, 1938, R.E.A.F.

11. Minutes of Executive Committee, December 14, 1939, Blanche Carrier, Secretary, R.E.A.F.

12. See exchanges between Chave and Hartshorne, January 1, 1939, and January 3, 1939; between Chave and Franklin, October 11, 1950, and March 13, 1950; Laird Hites to Ernest Chave, April 27, 1948; and Leonard Stidley to Franklin, November 20, 1950, R.E.A.F.

13. "Financial Movement," January, 1939, R.E.A.F.

14. Report of the President, Biennium, 1944–1946, R.E.A.F.

15. Letter from Harrison Elliott to Chave, April 13, 1951. Even Elliott was skeptical of success. He wrote: "It is as yet by no means certain that we can make good on an expanded program of the R.E.A. with a General Secretary. We have a respite of probably a year because of the Foundation gift of $8,000," R.E.A.F.

16. Letter from Chave to Franklin, October 11, 1950, R.E.A.F.

17. James M. Yard, "What Happens to Religion and Democracy in a Totalitarian State," *Religious Education* XXXII (January, 1937), pp. 13–16.

18. Blanche Carrier and Amy Clowes, "Education Approaches to the Prevention of an Authoritarian State," *Religious Education* XXXII (January, 1937), p. 22.

19. Ibid., p. 23.

20. See Niebuhr's "Editorial," "The Blindness of Liberalism" in *Radical Religion*, Vol. 1, #4 (Autumn, 1936), Editor Reinhold Niebuhr, p. 4. Published by the Fellowship of Socialist Christians, New York. Niebuhr edited the journal (renamed *Christianity and Society*) until its final publication Summer, 1956, Vol. 21, #3.

21. Victor S. Yarros, "Religion and the Totalitarian State," *Religious Education* XXXII (April, 1937), p. 98.

22. Ibid., p. 97.

23. George A. Coe, "Let the Convention Wrestle with Political Totalitarianism," *Religious Education* XXXII (April, 1937), p. 85.

24. Laird T. Hites, "On the Psychology of War," *Religious Education* XXXII (April, 1937), p. 107.

25. The R.E.A. files throughout this period probably were the personal papers of Harrison Elliott. Most of the letters and minutes are part of his personal collection of correspondence. I have not been able to locate any personal Elliott papers apart from the R.E.A. files.

26. "Minutes of the Meeting of the Religious Education Association" held at the Madison Avenue Presbyterian Church House, Friday, December 17, 1937, R.E.A.F., p. 6.

27. Letter from Hugh Hartshorne to E. J. Chave, November 29, 1938, R.E.A.F.

28. "Minutes of the Meeting of the Executive Committee (and some board members and guests)," June 21, 1938 in the R.E.A. office, p. 1, R.E.A.F.

29. Letter from Herbert L. Seamans to Ernest J. Chave, April 10, 1939, R.E.A.F.

30. "Meeting of the Board of Directors of the R.E.A.," February 5, 1939, p. 4, R.E.A.F.

31. R.E.A.F., no title, no date, in 1940 file folder, pp. 6–8, R.E.A.F.

32. "The Religious Education Association, New York, Metropolitan Area, Summary of Discussion," March 4, 1940, pp. 1–3, R.E.A.F.

33. "Suggestions on Policy and Strategy," discussed by the Board of Directors of the R.E.A., Buffalo, New York, May 5, 1940, p. 3, R.E.A.F.

34. Conferences on Strategy, Union Seminary, April 17, 1940, pp. 1–4, R.E.A.F.

35. Notes on Conference on Religion and Higher Education, Morning Session, n.d., prepared by Ross Snyder, pp. 1–2, R.E.A.F.

36. Letter from F. Ernest Johnson to Harrison Elliott, Hugh Hartshorne and Paul M. Limbert, October 19, 1944, p. 2, R.E.A.F.

37. Excerpt from a letter written by William Bower to the president of the association, attached to a letter to the membership of the R.E.A. from Johnson, April 20, 1946, R.E.A.F.

38. Wilhelm Pauck is quoted in David Tracy, *Blessed Rage for Order: The New Pluralism in Theology* (New York: Seabury Press, 1975), p. 27.

39. Ibid., pp. 27–31.

40. James D. Smart, *The Divided Mind of Modern Theology: Karl Barth and Rudolf Bultmann,* (Philadelphia: Westminster Press, 1967). This is a careful discussion of the development of Barth's and Bultmann's thought from early agreement to divergence and conflict.

41. Karl Barth, *The Epistle to the Romans,* translated from the sixth edition by Edwin C. Hoskyns (London: Oxford Press, 1933), p. 28.

42. Ibid., pp. 38–39.

43. Ibid., p. 167.

44. Ibid., p. 207.

45. Ibid., p. 317.

46. Ibid., p. 77.

47. Karl Barth, "How My Mind Has Changed," Part II, *Christian Century* LVI (September 20, 1939), p. 83.

48. Barth, *Romans,* p. 83.

49. William B. Kennedy, "Neo-Orthodoxy Goes to Sunday School," *Journal of Presbyterian History* Vol. 58, #4, (Winter, 1980), pp. 326–370.

50. For example, see Albert C. Dieffenbach, "No Need for Panic," *Christian Century* LVI (August 23, 1939), pp. 1019–1022; Halford E. Luccock, "With No Apologies to Barth," LVI (August 9, 1939), pp. 971–974; Georgia Harkness, "A Spiritual Pilgrimage," LVI (March 15, 1939), pp. 348–351.

51. Chave is quoted in Kendig Brubaker Cully, *The Search for a Christian Education Since 1940* (Philadelphia: Westminster Press, 1965), p. 19. Cully chooses to start his story with a review of Elliott's *Can Religious Education Be Christian?* In a sense Elliott's book and the rejoinder by H. Shelton Smith, *Faith and Nurture,* were watershed events that marked the beginning of a new decade of religious education theory, even though largely detained among R.E.A. members until after Elliott's death in 1951.

52. George A. Coe, "Book Review of Harrison Elliott's *Can Religious Education Be Christian?*" *Religious Education* XXXV (October–November, 1940), p. 239.

53. Letter from George A. Coe to Harrison Elliott, January 12, 1941, R.E.A.F.

54. Harrison S. Elliott, *Can Religious Education be Christian?* (New York: Macmillan Company, 1940), p. 10.

55. Ibid., p. 182.

56. Ibid., p. 275.

57. Ibid., p. 13.

58. Ibid., p. 113.

59. Ibid., p. 115. Elliott believed that there was a progressive revelation, though always tied to "natural religion." Robert Lynn typified Elliott's approach as a "unitarianism of the Holy Spirit," that is a developmental approach to God through centuries of religious history (experience), though not limited to Christian religious experience. Interview with Robert Lynn, February 18, 1981, Lilly Endowment, Indianapolis, Indiana.

60. Ibid., p. 321.

61. Cully, *The Search for a Christian Education Since 1940,* p. 24.

62. Edward S. Ames, "Book Review of H. Shelton Smith's *Faith and Nurture,*" *Religious Education* XXXVII (January–February, 1942), pp. 60–61.

63. H. Shelton Smith, *Faith and Nurture* (New York: Charles Scribner's Sons, 1941), p. ix.

64. Ibid., p. 19.

65. Ibid., p. 47.

66. Ibid., p. 59.

67. Ibid., p. 76.

68. Ibid., p. 105.

69. Ibid., p. 113.

70. Ibid., p. 169.

71. Ibid., p. 201.

72. Ames, "Book Review," p. 61.

73. See Albert C. Outler's essay, "H. Shelton Smith: An Appreciative Memoir," in *A Miscellany of American Christianity: Essays in Honor of H. Shelton Smith,* ed. Stuart C. Henry (Durham, North Carolina: Duke University Press, 1963), pp. 1–23. Outler notes that Smith never produced his "sequel" his own "alternative constructive theory of Christian nurture," and Outler is also correct in his criticism that no one else (outside the progressives) had done so.

74. H. Shelton Smith, "The Supremacy of Christ in Christian Nurture," *Religion in Life* XII (Winter, 1942–1943), pp. 32ff.

75. William Clayton Bower, "Christian Education After Nineteen Centuries," *Religion In Life* XII (Winter, 1942–1943), p. 44.

76. Ibid., p. 47.

77. Henry P. Van Dusen, "Religious Education in Crisis," *Religion In Life* XII (Winter, 1942–1943), p. 48.

78. Ibid., p. 52.

79. Ibid.

80. Cully, *The Search for a Christian Education Since 1940*, p. 16.

81. Letter from Ernest Chave to the members of the Board of Directors and Standing Committees of the R.E.A., January 2, 1947, R.E.A.F.

82. Ernest J. Chave, *A Functional Approach to Religious Education* (Chicago: University of Chicago Press, 1947), p. v.

83. Ibid., p. 120.

84. Ibid., p. viii.

85. Ibid., p. 22.

86. Ibid., p. 57.

87. Ibid., p. 145.

88. Sophia L. Fahs and Mildred T. Tenny, *Beginnings of Earth and Sky* (Boston: Beacon Press, 1938); Sophia L. Fahs, *From Long Ago and Many Lands* (Boston: Beacon Press, 1948); Sophia L. Fahs, *Leading Children In Worship* (Boston: Beacon Press, 1947); Sophia L. Fahs and Dorothy T. Spoerl, *Beginnings of Life and Death* (Boston: Beacon Press, 1938); Sophia L. Fahs, *Today's Children and Yesterday's Heritage* (Boston: The Beacon Press, 1952); Sophia Fahs and Helen Sweet, *Exploring Religion With Eight Year Olds* (New York: Harper & Brothers, 1930); and Elizabeth M. Manvell and Sophia Fahs, *Consider the Children How They Grow* (Boston: Beacon Press, 1940).

89. Fahs, *Today's Children and Yesterday's Heritage*, p. 29.

90. Ibid., p. 217.

91. See Edith F. Hunter's *Sophia Lyon Fahs, A Biography* (Boston: Beacon Press, 1966), for a respectful positive interpretation of Fahs' life and work.

92. Stewart G. Cole, "Book Review of Ernest Chave's A Functional Approach To Religious Education," *Religious Education* XLII (July–August, 1947), p. 252.

93. Randolph Crump Miller and Henry H. Shires, eds., *Christianity and the Contemporary Scene* (New York: Morehouse-Gorham Co., 1943), p. 197.

94. Ibid., p. 149.

95. Ibid., p. 201.

96. Randolph Crump Miller, ed., *The Church and Organized Movements* (New York: Harper & Brothers Publishers, 1946) and *Religion Makes Sense* (New York: Wilcox and Follett, 1950).

97. Miller, *Religion Makes Sense*, p. 98.

98. Ibid., p. 130.

99. Ibid., p. 296.

100. Randolph Crump Miller, *The Clue to Christian Education* (New York: Charles Scribner's Sons, 1950), p. 5.

101. Lewis Joseph Sherrill and John Edwin Purcell, *Adult Education In the Church* (Richmond, Virginia: John Knox Press, 1939).

102. Lewis Joseph Sherrill, *Understanding Children* (New York: The Abingdon Press, 1939), p. 205.

103. Lewis Joseph Sherrill, *The Opening Doors of Childhood* (New York: Macmillan Company, 1945).

104. Lewis Joseph Sherrill, *The Struggle of the Soul* (New York: Macmillan Company, 1951), pp. 6ff.

105. Ibid., pp. 148–149.

106. Memorandum from H. E. Wornom to a foundation in New York City showing the validity and timeliness of a specific plan of the Religious Education Association and so justifying the appeal of the R.E.A. for a grant of $8,000 to implement the plan, January 15, 1951, R.E.A.F.

107. *Religious Education* XLVII (May–June, 1952), p. 178.

108. Interview with Herman Wornom, August 30, 1977.

109. Interview, August 30, 1977.

110. The references are to the book by H. Richard Niebuhr, *Christ and Culture* (New York: Harper & Row, 1951), where Niebuhr outlines five types of relationships practiced between Christianity and culture. The R.E.A. movement was clearly reflective of the "Christ of culture" type (see pp. 83–108).

111. Letter from Lawrence C. Little to a member of the R.E.A., September 28, 1950, in behalf of the Mid-Century Expansion Fund Committee. Little's phrase is in capital letters: "A NEW DAY HAS DAWNED FOR R.E.A." (R.E.A.F.).

Chapter V

The Domestication of an Ideal
1952–1970

> Perhaps the time has come for religious educators to recognize the interrelationship of doctrinal problems and moral issues, of personal morality and social morality. The R.E.A. and its journal has dealt very little over the past ten years with the educational approach to the great social issues of our time. Perhaps the time has come for our journal to give major attention, via symposia, to problems of race, the morality of nuclear warfare, the social causes of juvenile delinquency, etc.[1]
>
> Herman Wornom, 1963

> For the earth always carries its end within it . . . . But may we rather see, through the crumbling of a world, the rock of eternity and the salvation which has no end.[2]
>
> Paul Tillich,
> *The Shaking of the Foundations,* 1948

The 1950s marked the painful involvement of the American experiment in South Asia. The Korean war began and ended in national dismay. Few really believed that war, any war, was any longer the last or the most justified of wars. Nothing was certain, no one was to be trusted, everything needed surveillance. Treaties were to be protected, alliances guarded, and solemn agreements held in constant vigilance.

The Vietnam war followed and extended the terrifying truth. The United States was not the ''democracy of God'' nor for that matter ''God's best footstool'' to use a phrase of earlier times by President Eisenhower. Few dared claim a kind of historical purity anymore, once the heritage of a young democratic experiment.

Race riots sparked the volatile kindling of broken promises, and

147

students disrupted academic functions throughout all of society. Columbia University witnessed the student takeover of the most powerful symbol of power at an academic institution, the president's office. Union Seminary, across the street, handled the rebellious student matter more reasonably. They caucused in Church-like fashion and turned a major share of traditional responsibility and power associated with administration or faculty into the hands of the students.

West of New York, Chicago police beat down the young and sometimes innocent outside the amphitheater, while inside the Democratic party chose Humphrey and Muskie over the flower children's candidate, Senator George McGovern. He had promised to lead this youth counterculture to some mythical, unattainable Camelot of the earlier Kennedy dreams. But Parousia was not to happen in these times; rather Watergate, and Kent State, and Richard Nixon, and assassinations: Martin Luther King and John and Robert Kennedy. These were surely times to shake foundations.

In this same period the R.E.A. grew to its largest number in the history of the association. At the end of the period Herman Wornom would end his career as leader of the R.E.A. with the most appropriate public success, the largest convention in the recent history of the R.E.A., attended by more than 1500 members.

What is less visible but equally true was another reality, that somewhere during these successful years the association strayed from its larger ideal—that of public pedagogy and a significant commitment to the solutions of social ills. The public democratic ideal of the founders became a strategy for internal affairs, a way to organize conventions and workshops, a way to pursue ecumenical goals and not alienate anyone in the process.

The Administration of Herman Wornom

Though there is an abundance of data of primary records kept carefully by Herman Wornom during this period, there is hardly any evidence regarding the selection of the new general secretary after the death of Harrison Elliott. One small set of minutes labeled "confidential" included the names of several men who might be considered for the vacancy, but among the thirteen names suggested there is no mention of Herman Wornom. The only other item which reflects some of the thinking of some members of the executive committee is a brief suggestion by Rabbi Levinson that the committee might think about the possibility of selecting a layperson. A small group was selected to serve as a screening and selection committee. No other records indicate the remainder of the process, how or why Wornom came to be selected.[3]

The announcement of Wornom's election appeared in the May–June, 1952 issue of *Religious Education*. The brief biographical sketch of the new general secretary indicated that Wornom was not a layman but a clergyman, forty-nine years old, with more than twelve years of experience as a local director of religious education.[4]

In that same issue the newly elected general secretary addressed his first formal words to the association. In that letter he added significant data which seem important in understanding his selection and the future direction of his efforts in the Religious Education Association. He identified himself solidly with the association, indicating that he had held membership for twenty-eight years before becoming secretary. Setting forth his four major aims—strengthening the local chapters, increasing membership, planning the 50th anniversary convention in 1953, and increasing the financial support of the organization—Wornom seemed to have already established his goals (after only 28 days in office).

The new general secretary ended his letter by claiming solid continuity with the R.E.A. historical tradition. He told the membership that Harrison Elliott was his personal friend, his major mentor at Union Seminary, chairman of the executive committee of the Department of Religious Education of the Protestant Council of New York, (supervisor of Wornom's position with the council) and his most intimate advisor "until the week of his death." "Because of what I owe to Harrison S. Elliott, I am especially happy that I am privileged to help carry on some of the association's projects which his sudden death left unfinished."[5]

Wornom developed many of the same personal qualities of his mentor, Harrison Elliott. His endless correspondence betrays a personal thoroughness rare in even intimate private communication. This quality of administrative thoroughness is most notable in Wornom's care of budgetary detail. Every inquiry, every bill, every expense was scrutinized before payment. Fiscal responsibility was the hallmark of his term as director. At no time during those eighteen years did the association overextend its resources (a common malady of earlier administrations).[6]

In the general area of decision making, the new general secretary most clearly evidenced the training of his mentor, especially in the skilled use of group processes to arrive at democratic decisions. Convention committees would number in the thirties and forties, and the evidence from those minutes indicates that Herman Wornom really believed in consensus theory and in the group's responsibility for the actions of those decisions. One sees the same democratic process unfolding in the early preliminary research efforts of the "round tables" where Wornom gathered folks together to talk and listen. He assumed something in that very process was worth doing. Here surely was a late liberal vision at work around the conference table.[7] The great social questions might remain unsolved, but the educational academic debates were a more manageable arena for the practice of public pedagogy.

Wornom was committed to the scientific ideals of his intellectual mentors as well. The evidence of that commitment will become clearer as later in this chapter we review his dramatic successful efforts to stimulate new research in religious education. Perhaps Wornom's chief success was in just this arena, yet his allegiance to the sciences was certainly more circumspect and tempered than that of his earlier predecessors. He saw the sciences in service of religious education, not as primary in setting theory or goals.

Herman Wornom did not write a great deal in his career as the general secretary—no books and only a few articles. But his prose was unmistakably clear when he did choose to write. In regard to science and religious education, he concluded: "A scientific approach to certain problems of religious education was established as a primary policy of the R.E.A. in 1903. This emphasis has developed over the years. At mid-century R.E.A. recognizes that science cannot provide the goals of religious education but that it can be highly useful in determining the means and method."[8]

His was a reasoned, cautious viewpoint, willing to acknowledge the benefits of the empirical effort, while yet maintaining the priority of philosophy and theology for setting goals of religious education. There was a certain mid-path balance about Wornom's position. This was true of all aspects of his administration, but certainly evidenced in his evaluation of the scientific in pursuit of religious education principles and directions.[9]

He was able to draw upon all the diverse resources of the membership and he constantly expanded those resources. In his extensive travels on behalf of regional chapters, national conventions, or research-related matters, his itinerary always was filled with new contacts. He was an ambassador of democratic goodwill. In one such visit to Cambridge in 1962, Wornom would manage in a two-day period to have meetings with Wesner Fallaw, Paul Tillich, David McClellan, Gordon Allport, Timothy Leary, Alan Watts, Donald Shriver, Robert White, Rose Eileen, Dana Farnsworth, Harvard Crimson offices, Erik Erikson, as well as a dozen others.[10]

He filled his trips with interesting persons and seemed to relish being in the presence of the most important persons in religion and education.

Perhaps Wornom's extensive flirtation with higher education and its chief leaders was somehow compensatory for his own incompleted doctoral degree work. Wornom recalled that on at least one occasion a Teachers College professor derided him because of the lack of academic credentials.[11] Even so, he always seemed at ease with academics, ecclesiastical judicatories, public education officials, and all the rest of the R.E.A. constituency. He embodied the old R.E.A. notion of "causing things to be done." His life and administration was more like that of a catalyst than of a primary element.

Wornom's relationship to the common layperson and the anonymous director of religious education was not nurtured with equal enthusiasm. While he courted the academic intellectuals and gained support from some ecclesiastical elites, his relationship to laypersons seemed suspiciously manipulative. Lay committees were organized in major cities primarily to raise funds for the association. The rhetoric of the early Religious Education Association for a working partnership between lay and professionals had largely disappeared and the association developed under Wornom's leadership into a single-minded professional organization with little attention or regard for the lay teacher or interested lay advocate so important in the early years of the R.E.A.'s constituency.[12]

In an interesting exchange of letters between a layperson, James Gallagher of the La Farge Institute, Brother Gregory Nugent, president of Manhattan College in New York, and Herman Wornom, the issue becomes quite clear. Gallagher had attended one of the lay group meetings chaired by Nugent to recruit a new lay contributing membership. After the meeting he wrote to Brother Nugent who had assisted Wornom in making the R.E.A. presentation at the meeting. He saw the obvious image of the association as one that appeals to the professional educator. He then raised the question of the R.E.A.'s intention regarding lay members. Did they want lay members simply as a way to balance the budget, or was the R.E.A. really interested in recruitment of laypersons as full participants in the association? If so, he argued, then the R.E.A. would have to arrange programs specifically designed for lay members in far greater proportion than in the past. He spoke of the intimidation of the lay person in the presence of the professional religious educator, and indicated that full participation would demand sharing as "first-class" members, not just as paying participants. Since Gallagher said he spoke for a number of men present at the meeting, the letter seemed important and demanded a response.[13]

In a discreet four-page reply, Herman Wornom made a detailed defense of the R.E.A.'s genuine interest in full lay participation. He reviewed some key conventions where lay issues were discussed. He described three significant lay members on the board of directors (surely the exception, not the rule in the otherwise clerically dominated organization). His argument was probably not all that convincing to Gallagher since he ended the letter with a summary explanation of the financial appeal for lay support. Lay members were indeed welcome to attend meetings, but they were most welcome to contribute fifty to a hundred dollars as contributing members.[14]

While Wornom's letter made a fair case for lay interest on the part of the association, the lay membership card was clearly geared to interest contributing members for the sole purpose of financial support. Laypersons were asked to join and contribute as "lay friends" in significantly larger amounts than the professionals.[15] The separation of lay members into a new category of "contributing" narrowed the earlier vision of the association.

Another characteristic of Wornom's administration was the lack of support or encouragement for the average religious educator in the parish. Wornom's own efforts were, as we shall see, devoted largely to research pursuits and higher education interests. And though he himself had spent long years as a religious educator and more than a dozen of those as unordained, there is little evidence that he was a strong advocate of the practitioner of religious education. One makes this judgment by negative or silent data. Wornom simply did not publish any essays or editorials which could serve as advocate of the developing professional. Wornom knew as well the jealousy of denominational judicatories. He was not about fighting losing battles.[16]

Wornom fell prey to the elitism of the leadership of the association, almost entirely consisting of professionals who concentrated their attention on those who taught the front-line religious educators, the seminary and college professors. The association showed little interest in the parish religious educator throughout this period and neither in convention nor journal does one find any continuous support for the profession created by the first generation of Religious Education Association leaders. This is all the more surprising in light of the fact that Wornom was really the first practicing religious educator to assume office as general secretary. The parish professionals would have to turn elsewhere (usually denominational affiliations) for a support base for their practical vocational concerns. The R.E.A. would not nurture its own, at least not in terms of traditional professional characteristics: status, training, salaries, appeals structure, unionization, or ecclesiastical lobby. The union card in the new profession that counted remained the credential of ordained clergy, and Wornom's decision regarding his own status seemed to reflect that reality. He too became ordained, to "prevent any road blocks" to his professional future.

Wornom was a master of compromise and pragmatic about his task to build the R.E.A. His ecumenical success is vivid testimony to that ability. Throughout his career he aimed for compromise, always maintaining the nonactivist structure of the R.E.A., always insisting on its character as an association only interested in religious education, its single mission. Yet as the sixties unfolded, he too was caught up in the larger issues of the time. A poignant exchange of letters between Wornom and Wesner Fallaw in 1965 highlights his personal estrangement from the United States' involvement in Vietnam and his frustration at any effective recourse of action as a professional or as a citizen.[17]

By 1970, very near the end of his tenure as general secretary, Wornom made a serious decision to enter the anti-war lobby. For the first time in recent history of the association, the general secretary took a public political stand, in this instance on behalf of ending the war in Vietnam. His action marked a radical break with the actions of past general secretaries. Never before had the general secretary taken such a public stand on such a controversial issue. Wornom's action was more reminiscent of George Albert Coe's consistent political interest and social concern.

On May 11, 1970, Wornom sent out a public letter addressed to the president, chairman of the board, and chairman of the executive committee of the R.E.A. advocating support for the Church-Cooper and McGovern-Hatfield amendments, which bills limited funds for further hostilities in Vietnam and Cambodia. He informed his immediate superiors that the letter would be circulated to other R.E.A. leaders across the country.

Always cautious, Wornom hedged his action with this qualifier: "In sharing the above information with you and others, I do not express any official policy of R.E.A. I do, though, as general secretary feel a responsibility to share with you information which has come to me which might be useful in ending the war. As a result of telephone calls to a small sample of our members, I have found that they all want the information and suggestions I have made above."[18]

But the apology was hardly either necessary or adequate. His passion against the war and his encouragement for political lobby action was of course closer to the R.E.A.'s early ideology than the safer operating style of the association in the thirties and forties, always to remain outside the real arena of political conflict. On the issue of the war, Wornom took a stand, a courageous posture quite unlike any other action of his long eighteen-year secretariat.

That the action was new and untraditional is attested to by the presence of letters of protest to his circulated letter. Two such letters (still in the R.E.A. files) indicate the volatility of Wornom's action. A Dominican Sister wrote: "As a member of the R.E.A., I deeply resent your letter of May 11 re(garding) proposed legislation to withhold funds for military operations in southeast Asia." She continued, "I believe in supporting the lawfully elected President of the United States; further, I resent and deplore the fact that you would use the R.E.A. membership list to propagandize your point of view."[19] And a Southern Baptist wrote: "The interesting thing about all of this to me is how the academic community falls in line for the very thing the Communist movement has openly admitted to be their strategy." The writer suggested this alternative: "It appears to me that the religious educators of America could make a far better contribution by setting an example to discourage window breaking, fires, and other means of destruction and try to bring some degree of unity."[20]

The files also contain supportive letters from George McGovern, Alan Cranston, and a cross-section of R.E.A. members. The Jewish Students for Peace wrote: "We share your sense of urgency in developing widespread support for the Hatfield-McGovern amendment."[21] The Rev. James J. Doyle, C.S.C., wrote: "I want to congratulate you for taking the initiative in sending information of the Washington efforts to end the war in Vietnam/Cambodia. This is the kind of service which I feel the R.E.A. can well expand."[22]

Herman Wornom's last significant action as general secretary might well have been his most characteristic. Here was a man who tried to achieve consensus and effect change by the long process of nurture, research, and institutional change. But when finally up against an intolerable situation, his liberal instincts prevailed, and he acted alone, courageously, at a time in his career when he could have easily left office without conflict or rancor. Wornom's last political act (actually very circumspect) could certainly point the way for the future. The R.E.A. might yet become a significant lobby agency in the politics of the public, certainly a vision shared by George Albert Coe and William Rainey Harper in their own day and in their own way. On the other hand, one might argue that Wornom had little to lose, since he was so close to retirement. In balance, Wornom's action, basic to the core of his person and convictions, was in fact all the more noteworthy in light of his age and general disposition to avoid conflict and enhance unity.

Religion and Higher Education

From the time of its origin the R.E.A. always had a professional section on higher education open to those members whose vocations found them in a university or college setting. The original genius of the organization certainly grew out of the consensus of such scholars. Herman Wornom knew that history and built upon it early in his tenure as general secretary. In a meeting of the Committee on Religion in Higher Education of the R.E.A. held April 22, 1954, Wornom outlined that past history and urged the need for continued emphasis of religion in higher education. He understood the growing interest in the subject of higher education, and he saw that discussion as a new opportunity for revitalizing the R.E.A.

Though the R.E.A. was limited in budget and staff, Wornom suggested that the association could serve as a leaven to stimulate the needed dialogue between religion and higher education. Decrying the "secularizing of American culture" and the "deterioration of literature in American life" he saw publications, pocket books, radio, television, art, drama, and music all together as participants in the decadent process of cultural vulgarization. And with a biased salvo at the sciences, he added, "God is no longer our sovereign. The social process and statistical averages have become our gods."[23]

Wornom linked the problem of culture with the plight of the university, and it is clear that he felt the university was the precise place where solutions to those problems ought to be found. His sentiments, though not crafted in impressive prose, echoed those of Harper in his appeal that the university serve the culture as prophet and messiah, somehow acting as the social conscience and arbiter of social ills.

Wornom knew that the problem of culture and religion was much larger than higher education, but he argued, "Yet leaders of higher education concerned with religious values might well take the lead in analyzing our predicament." Higher education should, according to Wornom, explore the problems "especially church-related and independent higher education." Wornom believed that the task of higher education was to "bring the insights of religion to bear on solving the crisis."[24]

The meeting at which Wornom spoke those words resolved to plan a series of regional seminars ("round tables") to explore the topic of religion, culture, and higher education. The detailed planning was left up to the general secretary and a small committee. By 1963 Wornom was able to report to the association that five such "round tables" had been held in major U.S. cities and that he had represented the R.E.A. at more than twenty related workshops at university campuses throughout the United States.[25]

The first such seminar met in New York at Columbia University on November 26–27, 1954. The agenda was loosely structured. Conversation revolved around three issues: the question of Judeo-Christian values in contemporary American culture, the role of higher education in fostering those values, and what changes in higher education would seem useful to strengthen those basic Judeo-Christian commitments.

The membership of that conference consisted of more than forty professors and leaders in American higher education, representing various disciplines in the university: natural sciences, social sciences, history, literature, philosophy, religion, medical science, law, education, journalism, engineering, business administration, and theology. Wornom had gathered an illustrious group of scholars with no other agenda except to talk together about their concerns over the issue of the relationship of the religious tradition to the nature of higher education. Abraham Heschel joined Wilhelm Pauck, Philip Phenix, Harry Jones, George Shuster, Gertrude Driscoll, and others in what must have been most interesting conversation.[26]

Much debate revolved around the role of science and religion, but there was little consensus. There was great diversity over what the basic Judeo-Christian values were, or if they were yet descernible in this culture. Several suggestions were made regarding the universities' role in support of those values, but there is no evidence that any consensus or agreement was reached, at least not at this meeting. Liberal arts and humanities were cited as potential areas for enrichment and as natural allies to the religious concerns of the theologian and the religious educator.[27]

In the summary of a second round table held in Chicago several months after the New York meeting, the same issues remained unresolved. What are the essential Judeo-Christian values? How does one gain consensus at a time of pluralistic diversity? How or what makes a university really a universe of discourse? How do the values of free inquiry and indoctrination or authority of religious convictions reside on the same campus or in the same faculty? What sort of moral power, if any, does the university maintain?[28]

It is difficult to assess the historical success or failure of those five round table efforts. One side effect, though not planned, was realized. Walter H. Clark, the chairperson of the committee, wrote to Herman Wornom late in 1954 and indicated that there were some real residual values: "We have given a practical demonstration of the genius of the R.E.A. by creating an atmosphere in which members of differing faiths can discuss problems of great import and mutual concern. I feel that there is no doubt but that the seminar has increased our stature in the minds of many well-placed persons."[29]

Wornom's own stature was certainly enhanced by the seminars as well. After the early sessions, he was called to lecture widely on the subject of the seminars, "Religion and the University and College Campus." His general speech (in different editions) was a summary of the viewpoints of the R.E.A. conferences. The difficulty of that reportive effort was significant, as there were more than three hundred fifty participants at those round tables. Wornom's conclusions were conventional generalizations, hardly new to the practitioners of higher education:

1. Departments of religion and faculties must be strengthened.
2. Cross departmental concerns between religion and the several disciplines need to be enhanced.
3. Professional education and religion need to explore new relationships.
4. Religious training ought to be provided for those in secular faculties.
5. The university needs to provide an open climate for rehabilitation of the Judeo-Christian heritage in the minds of faculty and students.[30]

Wornom's interest in higher education did not diminish as the years went on. By 1958 he had visited more than twenty institutions specifically to determine the relationship of religion to the general curriculum of the institution. In close cooperation with Henry E. Allen of the University of Minnesota, Wornom drew up a major research proposal to study the place of religion in the curriculum of the state institutions. The proposal called for a full-time director for one full calendar year and a suggested budget of more than $110,000. Unfortunately the proposal never materialized, but Wornom's interest did not wane.[31]

Researching Religious Education

Research became the theme of Wornom's next ten years. John Peatling, in reviewing that research history, is absolutely correct in according Herman Wornom the compliment of "vision and friendship" for the serious religious education researcher.[32] It was also in this arena that Wornom was most successful financially. The story that unfolds is singularly significant for so small an association. Wornom's mark falls on all of the proposals, all of the efforts, all the details, and all of the successes. Though never the researcher nor the technician, he always remained the manager behind the scenes, making possible for others what would not have been possible without the support of the R.E.A. He again embodied the old vision that the R.E.A. "caused things to happen."

From 1959 onward Wornom was able to build a most creative partnership with the Lilly Endowment, stimulating useful research in religious education with grants that ultimately totaled more than $200,000. These funds allowed the association to set up a five-point program to stimulate research in religious education and character development, long an interest of the association since the early Hartshorne-May studies of the 1930s.

Under the general secretary's leadership and the ongoing supervision of the research committee of the R.E.A., five steps of research were begun and persistently completed. Stage one involved a simple research survey of all major research in religious education recently completed. That study completed in cooperation with the Character Research Project of Union College was reported in the May–June, 1959 issue of the journal. More than three hundred fifty research projects were briefly reviewed. The service provided the researcher quick access to all the major research in religious education and character development.[33]

The second task was somewhat more formidable and in typical Wornom fashion involved a democratic survey of leaders of religious education throughout North America. The participants were asked one question: "To state and describe problems the solution of which you believe to be critical for the progress of religion and character education."[34] More than one hundred fifty responses were received.

As I reviewed those diverse suggestions I was struck with these observations. I expected and found many proposals on teaching method and learning theory. I expected to see the influence of neo-orthodoxy in the research proposals which dealt with the nature of humankind or the religious curriculum. Those influences were present. There was a large group of research suggested relating to the family, marriage, and sex, all of which one could indeed anticipate. No surprises!

It seems curious, however, that under the suggestions for research related to the "Training of Religious Educator Professionals and Volunteers" not a single piece of research was offered to determine any normative quality about such training. There was no recommendation related to the professional competence and training of clergy. It is strange that research so critically important to the future of the religious education profession was not explored. There were no questions about the key professional areas of status, identity, stability, competence, and financial security, all ongoing struggles of the professional religious educator.[35]

The other interesting aspect of the report was titled "The Relation of Religion and Culture; The Problems of a Religious Culture vs. a Secular

Culture.'' One can clearly see the discontinuity between such a perspective and that of the founders of the R.E.A. By 1960 it was apparent that (at least in this sample) religious education tended to view the secular world as enemy opposed to the values of religion. Neo-orthodoxy had surely left its mark. What is also clear, but perhaps not as apparent, was the subtle implication of such a viewpoint. If one operates from a ''religion vs. culture'' premise, one surely will be involved with institutional church priorities rather than public strategies for cultural formation. There was a kind of religious provincialism about the suggestions; many relate to institutional structures, to questions of preservation of styles of religious education, to concerns for the church or synagogue, rather than any vision of a religious America. Visions of a public paideia were domesticated into styles of church renewal.

It is instructive to note how the loss of that vision turned the profession inward to self-preserving activities and rituals. It was probably easier to study character development, teaching methods, or learning theory than to raise the more difficult questions of transformation of a culture. The research suggestions are indicative of a great divorce between the religious educator of the fifties and those of the first generation of the association's founders. One can only wonder if the problem of pluralism had really diminished any communal effort to recoup the grand ideals of the older vision. Researchers, at least, were not interested in that sort of question.

The third step of the process to stimulate research was completed during the summer of 1959. Nine social scientists working three weekends during that summer reviewed all the research proposals from a social science viewpoint. Their task was to convert all those proposals into workable hypotheses for the social science researcher. Their objective was to edit and combine proposals into some meaningful pattern which would become stimulus for the profession. Those members represented the top R.E.A. social science researchers of the period including: O. Hobart Mowrer, Ernest Ligon, Dorothy Lee, Walter Clark, Robert Havighurst, Joseph Fichter, and others. Herman Wornom joined the group as administrator, his typical role throughout all these proceedings.

The researchers refined the suggestions, added a number of their own and published a report on their work in a monograph entitled ''Highlights of Recommendations for Research,'' edited by Herman Wornom.[36] The report was published in *Religious Education* and more than ten thousand copies were distributed beyond the journal subscription. Its import was certainly to open the arena of religious education and character development to a larger scientific world.

Wornom's popular ''Highlights'' was even more successful financially. As he reported to the association, "When the Lilly Endowment received the 'Highlights' report in October, it immediately sent R.E.A. a check for $56,000 to carry forward the fourth stage of its program to stimulate research."[37]

A seminar to assist potential researchers in their designs and project developments known as the Cornell workshops was held during the summer of 1961 on the campus of Cornell University. Potential participants came from all the several denominations represented in American religion. More than one hundred fifty persons applied, of which approximately fifty were chosen for attendance. Those select persons along with a dozen social science researchers spent twelve full days in August working on their individual research proposals. Approximately 70 percent of the workshop time was devoted to personal study of small group interaction to aid the researcher in his/her design. The key papers presented to the participants were published in a *Religious Education Supplement*.[38] The entire collection of research proposals was printed in a book, *Research Plans*, edited by the workshop director, Stuart W. Cook, and published by the R.E.A.[39]

After the Cornell conference there were more suggestions than there was money available for future plans to stimulate research. The last day of the workshop was spent in gathering such proposals and the more than eighty participants were not shy about their expectations. Research conferences and workshops were suggested, continued publication of current research in religious education was encouraged. Several opinions were voiced regarding recruiting and training of future researchers. Speculation suggested that the R.E.A. would need between fifty and one hundred thousand dollars annually to support such ambitions. There was additional encouragement that the R.E.A. enlarge its staff to include a full-time research director.[40]

Herman Wornom was elated, for most of these goals paralleled the early comprehensive plan of the R.E.A. adopted several years before. The fifth step called for "setting up a continued full-time, multifaith organization to foster research in religion and character education by existing ecclesiastical bodies and academic institutions."[41] The R.E.A. had not clarified details as to the nature of such an organization or its structure, support system, authority, etc. There was little certainty about how this development would materialize. The R.E.A. had limited resources, a committee and a persistent, stubborn general secretary. Those assets hardly seemed adequate to launch a full-time research agency.

The R.E.A. research committee met early in the fall of 1961 and authorized a strategy committee to look at all those future plans and plot strategy for fulfilling step five. As one reviews those minutes it becomes clear that the two central protagonists at that meeting were Robert Havighurst of the University of Chicago and Herman Wornom, the general secretary. Wornom stuck tenaciously to his agenda to gain full approval of the recommendations of the Cornell meetings. Havighurst at one point in the meeting called Wornom a ''masochist'' and suggested that the general secretary was ''torturing himself with his stick-to-it-ness.'' Wornom defended his style and kept the meeting's single-minded direction to resolve the future R.E.A. research task.[42]

Late in the meeting Havighurst made a long speech in behalf of his viewpoint before he had to leave the meeting to return to Chicago. He encouraged the committee to establish a department of research but only with a part-time person. He warned that the essential placement of such a department was a university setting, not a professional organization. He urged R.E.A. to hire a part-time person who would be able to maintain relationships with a university as well as serve the R.E.A. He cautioned, ''I feel that there is some possibility and even danger of bureaucratizing the R.E.A. business a bit . . . . Keep the association as an instigator and catalyst, but don't try to build up an organization.''[43]

Wornom obviously disagreed and doggedly pursued his own agenda. The conclusion of the debate was strictly in keeping with Wornom's viewpoint. The R.E.A. would apply to Lilly and attempt to fund a three-year appointment of a part-time (two-thirds) director. Negotiations with Lilly began, and by 1964 Wornom had managed enough financial support to launch the last of his research goals. A department of research was initiated under the supervision of a part-time director. The prospectus for the research department was extensive. The department would supervise an annual supplement to *Religious Education,* would stimulate writing and critique of research, would develop a handbook on research methods, and would conduct conferences and workshops. The director, in addition, would serve as a kind of R.E.A. research advocate to disseminate research information and interest. He would encourage (Wornom's major concern) dialogue between social scientists, theologians, and religious educators. A final function and probably the most important was the administration of the ''Lilly Research Training Fellowship Program for Empirical Research.'' The research director would administer the selection and distribution of those grants and monitor the ongoing research of those Lilly fellows.[44]

The R.E.A. advertised for the position of director of research in the fall of 1964. The specifications involved a two-thirds time position for three years with a starting salary of $7200. The person chosen should be in his thirties, competent in research, a churchman able to work with all denominations and types of persons. His work was fourfold—to work with denominations, seminaries, and graduate schools to encourage research in religious education, to work directly with persons to stimulate research, to administer the R.E.A. research training fellowships, and to attempt to develop another research planning workshop similar to the one held at Cornell in 1961. The funding of the position was totally supported by a grant from the Lilly foundation.[45]

A careful selection process ensued and the appointment was finally given to Merton Strommen who began his work with the R.E.A. November 1, 1964. His position was half-time, the remainder of his time being devoted to the organization he had founded, "Lutheran Youth Research." The announcement of Strommen's appointment outlined his duties. He was to serve as catalyst, not researcher. His major task was to administer the Lilly postdoctoral fellowships.[46]

Strommen seemed the ideal choice for the position; indeed, his three-year tenure with the R.E.A. was most productive. He brought to the task widely acclaimed skills as evidenced by his recently published *Profiles of Church Youth*. Strommen seemed to embody all the qualities the R.E.A. needed. He could raise money, he could write proposals, he knew research, he knew the church, he was an excellent administrator, and he was interested.

The selection was excellent. Over the next three years he administered the unique Lilly fellowship program for postdoctoral empirical research. Those fellowships went to numerous religious educators whose work and professional reinvestments in the discipline have been more than modestly significant. Persons like Milo Brekke, Paul Maves, Ray Fairchild, and D. Campbell Wyckoff were but a few of the recipients.

By 1966 Strommen had written and submitted a $100,000 grant proposal to the compliant Lilly Endowment for the study of national youth values, an ecumenical extension of his work on *Profiles of Church Youth*. The proposal was declined because of the similarity of the project to the work of the Character Research Proposal, already funded by Lilly.[47] Funds were simply no longer unlimited. The R.E.A. tried several other foundations, all without success. Strommen's work was not to extend beyond his three-year appointment.

The major publication project begun by Strommen while with the R.E.A. was completed even after he had left office in 1967. What Strommen managed to do over those years was collect, organize, and edit a massive volume: *Research on Religious Developments: A Comprehensive Handbook*. The book itself was published by the R.E.A. in 1971 and remains a tribute to the careful work of Strommen and the impact of the R.E.A. research support system. Representing all segments of American religious life, the book encompassed a vast, diverse map of research interests and attainments. The book became the most comprehensive compilation of research findings in religious development to date.[48]

That publication, painfully nurtured into print late in Wornom's administration, was a culminating victory for more than a decade of efforts. Strommen had been the editor of the volume and had done most of the critical work on the volume, but it was Herman Wornom who managed the publication printing maze as the project seemed to falter late in its development.[49]

The research program had more than succeeded. There were interesting side effects as well. Early in the fall of 1961, Walter Houston Clark, the chairman of the committee, raised this question: ''How to raise the prestige of the discipline? I think this latter problem is a very critical one. As long as religious educators are second-class citizens you will be swimming against the stream. The discipline itself must have prestige. You need vigorous and independent minds.''[50]

Wornom's research stimulation was helpful in solving that problem. Crucial to any discipline is the need for a solid foundation of key ideas and core data upon which to build the paradigms for truthing. Religious education for the most part lacked that base in the early fifties. By 1970, under the R.E.A. stimulus, Strommen's work had gone a long way to enrich the profession and add prestige and credibility to the discipline of religious education. Research and researchers became the basis once again, as in the early days of the organization, to renew the profession with academic respectability and professional competence. Herman Wornom could lay claim to a large part of that emphasis and success.

Ecumenical Efforts:
On Dealing with Catholics and Cardinals

Herman Wornom's dogged efforts in the area of research were equaled by his successful ecumenical efforts, particularly noteworthy before Vatican II (1963) when ecumenicity became an institutional agenda for Catholics as well as liberal Protestants. The letters between the general secretary and the Catholic archdiocesan leadership of Chicago serve as a model of Wornom's efforts throughout the country.

In 1952, when Herman Wornom took leadership of the R.E.A., no one could really claim that the association was truly ecumenical or multifaith. The great majority of the members and officers were liberal

Protestants, certainly not even representative of the mainline conservative Christian bodies. (Note the total absence of fundamentalist and conservative Evangelical groups.) Until 1952 there was but one article which appeared in the entire history of the journal written by any member of the Lutheran Church Missouri Synod, a synod noted not only for orthodox faith, but also for the largest Protestant school system in the United States.[51]

Nondogmatic Jews and antidoctrine Protestants formed a developing partnership throughout the history of the R.E.A. The same dialogical ease never emerged with Catholics prior to the secretariat of Herman Wornom. In fact, as late as July 7, 1954, there were only three official Catholic members among the one hundred R.E.A. members from the entire metropolitan city of Chicago, which contained one of the major concentrations of Catholics in the entire country.[52] Yet by 1966 Wornom was able to report that the convention which had just met in Chicago registered more than 1200 full-time participants of which 75 percent were Catholic, 20 percent were Protestant, and 4 percent were Jewish. By then Wornom would chide his Protestant sisters and brothers in forthright language: "This eagerness of Catholics and lesser concern of Protestants and Jews for ecumenicity clearly marks out a task for the future for the Religious Education Association and for Protestant denominations; namely to get Protestant religious educators more involved in ecumenical affairs." Wornom continued: "First of all, they need to understand the significance of the ecumenical movement, not just for ecclesiastical structures but for the dynamism of religious thought and action in our time."[53]

In fact, the Catholic attendance was so high at that Chicago convention that the Catholic president of Newton College of the Sacred Heart wrote Wornom with these words of concern: "I hope that Catholics will not take over the organization, and if it becomes necessary to establish a quota for the next meeting, please let me in."[54]

By 1967 more than one-third of the national membership consisted of Catholics.[55] An examination of Wornom's dealings with the Chicago hierarchy is instructive to understanding that unusual success in the recruitment of Catholics, particularly in light of other Protestant failures in dealing with Catholics in ecumenical efforts.

One gains an early impression of Wornom's style and straightforward approach in a letter dated June 29, 1954, from the office of the Church Federation of Greater Chicago. The Rev. Hughbert Landram wrote to congratulate Wornom on his visit with Cardinal Stritch and added, "I haven't even seen him in all these years, let alone having an audience." He caught Wornom's caution as well. Yes, he would "take the whole matter in stride as you suggest."[56]

On July 7, 1954, Wornom wrote to the Cardinal explaining the R.E.A.'s approach to religion, a question that the Cardinal wanted to explore. Wornom made clear that the R.E.A. espoused no theological perspective, was open to various theological nuances, but was committed to a theistic viewpoint.

He took pains to reject the naturalism associated with the organization during the thirties and forties, a perspective he correctly identified as related to the University of Chicago R.E.A. leadership. No, the R.E.A. was not interested in converting Catholics to becoming Protestants. Yes, the R.E.A. believed in God and was not part of the dreaded "modernism" which so threatened believing Catholics. He asked for the Cardinal's blessing and support in gaining Catholic membership for the newly organized Chicago chapter.[57]

The day after he posted that letter, Wornom read the *New York Times* and clipped an ominous article entitled "Stritch Cautions of Unity Session." The news report indicated that Cardinal Stritch had forbidden Catholic clergy and laity from participation in the World Council of Churches meeting in Evanston, Illinois. Stritch's objection to attendance revolved around the issue of any acknowledgement by Catholics that they were also "searching for the truth of Christ." He rejected such a position and insisted that the full truth of Christ was revealed in the Roman church. "It (this unity) is found in the Roman Catholic Church and in her alone. She and she alone is the true Church of Jesus Christ."[58]

Wornom hastily addressed another letter to Cardinal Stritch after reading the morning *Times*. He referred to the article, even included a copy for the Cardinal and proceeded to delineate the character of membership in the R.E.A. He noted that the R.E.A. was not an ecclesiastical organization. Membership was among individuals, not representatives of any church ecclesiastical authority. Church unity was not an R.E.A. problem. Within the R.E.A. one did not seek agreement of doctrine or dogma. Wornom even went so far as to claim, "So far as the R.E.A. is concerned there would be no quarrel with the statement which the *New York Times* quoted from you this morning."[59] Many R.E.A. leaders would probably not have agreed with Wornom's assessment and would have taken exception to the Cardinal's pronouncement. R.E.A.'s conventional consensus held the key notion that no position was the absolute truth, but all parties were open to honest exchange of ideas and positions with a view toward compromise and consensus. Nevertheless, Wornom was wooing a Cardinal and his efforts were successful. The membership need never know the extent of the concession.

By August 27 Wornom had received what he needed to recruit Catholics in Chicago. An official letter from Cardinal Stritch not only indicated that the Cardinal had no objection to the R.E.A.'s inviting key

Catholics into membership, but included the marvelous statement, "You are perfectly free to invite the Catholics you mentioned or any others to take part in your chapter."[60] Wornom now had official authority to solicit Chicago Catholics for R.E.A. membership.

One must also note that the R.E.A.'s open interfaith character was indeed most palatable for such a compromise and in that sense the association had a certain genius that other ecumenical agencies did not. R.E.A. was not about church unity or ecclesiastical debate. It was rather in the best sense a free forum for ideas of all persuasions. Wornom had accented that genius and won. Wornom met again with Cardinal Stritch in March of 1957. His purpose was clearly successful, he needed and received the Cardinal's goodwill regarding the proposed convention in the fall of 1957. By then the program planning committee and other major decisions involved many Chicago Catholics. Wornom wanted the Cardinal to know those developments and he wanted his support. He even requested some official word of encouragement in the *The New World*, the diocesan paper.[61]

Shortly after Albert Meyer's (successor to Cardinal Stritch) appointment as archbishop of Chicago in 1958, Wornom began a series of letters to the newly appointed Chicago leader. He reviewed his cordial relationship with Cardinal Stritch and asked for the same support from Cardinal Meyer. He indicated that he had information that there was some objection to Catholic membership in the Chicago R.E.A. chapter and wanted to negotiate some resolution if indeed there was some serious problem. He argued from precedent, using past correspondence to document his viewpoint. On October 24, 1960, Cardinal Meyer wrote to Wornom and accepted the position that had ensued under Cardinal Stritch. Nothing had changed. The R.E.A. had full permission to pursue membership with Chicago Catholics.[62]

Wornom's relationship with the Chicago hierarchy held fast through the Meyer years and continued with the advent of Cardinal Cody. He met Cardinal Cody at a brief luncheon in February of 1966 and proceeded to initiate a long series of letters and excellent working relationships. Wornom was able to solicit Cardinal Cody's presence to serve as speaker at a special gathering of prominent Chicago laypersons, all in behalf of the R.E.A.

Wornom's success in Chicago was duplicated in other settings throughout the Catholic Church. His mission was of course made easier after Vatican II, but his contacts and support of the early ecumenical efforts were all groundwork for stimulating the later deluge of Catholics that happily joined the R.E.A. They came interested in open ecumenical dialogue and sometimes met with lukewarm Protestant and Jewish responses. Wornom was ahead of his time and set a solid foundation for continued ecumenical work within the R.E.A. built on mutual respect and professional care about relationships and institutional structural nuances.

"A Language of Relationships": Religious Education 1952–1970

The R.E.A.'s journal *Religious Education* was edited by two persons during the Wornom administration. Leonard Stidley became editor in 1947 and remained so until his death in 1958. It is difficult to assess his impact on the journal because his personal articles and editorials were insignificant in comparison to his management and editing skills. Stidley, like Wornom, never wrote any books, published few articles, reviewed few books for the journal, and edited the R.E.A. journal during the long period of transition from the lowest ebb of R.E.A.'s life to the vibrant years of the mid-fifties. He charted the journal from the period of waning liberalism into the period of new theological interest and neo-orthodox convictions.

His gifts to the journal were hard work, careful editing, and creatively assembled symposia of significant interaction and interest. In fact, the typical Protestant-Catholic-Jewish symposia idea became during his ten-year editorship the mark of the journal. Yet it might have been the only way to move gently toward a truly ecumenical dialogue. Most often the symposia were simply position papers rather than any serious interaction of ideas (e.g., "Group Education," July–August, 1953, or "Case Studies in Religious Education," March–April, 1956). One wishes that the structure of the symposium might have been more dialogical.

Stidley was often able to gather interesting contributors of his period, but the potential interaction (ecumenical dialogue) rarely happened. One such example, the symposium on "Philosophy of Education and Religious Values," November–December, 1953, had articles by Reinhold Niebuhr, Will Herberg, Leo Ward, Harry Broudy, Robert Ulrich, Ernest Chave, Donald Butler, Loise Antz, Randolph C. Miller, and Elmer George Homrighausen, all religious personalities with distinctive and unique positions. But none of those viewpoints were seriously debated in the symposium.

Niebuhr called for a radical revision of public education, a creative shared-time concept where the three major religious traditions would form a totally new partnership with public education. Ward argued for a universal "religious literacy," a kind of unbiased religion in general style of public religious education. Ernest Chave inveighed against neo-orthodoxy and wrote in behalf of his own "functional approach" to religion. He advocated public debate and for opportunity to confront critical theological and pedagogical differences in open conflict. He challenged the R.E.A. to become such a fellowship, yet participated in a symposium which by design did not allow for that exchange.

Randolph C. Miller opted for a theological approach to religious education and set about in his typical manner to attempt to use the best insights of the new theology without losing the social and democratic aims of the former liberalism. He called for the primacy of theological concerns and secondary emphasis upon methods. He argued that methods flow from theology rather than the reverse position that methods dictate theological interest.

E. G. Homrighausen, neo-orthodox religious education professor of Princeton, followed with an essay which argued that theological matters were surely primary but needed to be in tension with a concern for the whole Christian community. "Christianity is a culture consisting of song and symbol and biography and literature and color and many other things." At the same time, advocating a social perspective on the place of the environment, he never explored the difficult culture question nor attempted any strategy for such a public solution. The pedagogy of the public was finally a closed community for him, a kind of "Christ against culture" position where the Christian ideal was formed in a small reality, the church.[63]

And so what could have been a most creative dialogue of opinion and purpose was really a series of unchallenged opinions that were never joined in debate or solution. For the most part that style of symposium filled almost every issue throughout Stidley's editorship. The journal was indeed a deposit of ecumenical ideas and diverse values. It was not, however, a forum for free exchange and interaction of ideas except when one or another author would insist on making it such. Those instances were the delightful exception and must be judged as self-motivated rather than as the result of editorial policy.

One such exchange illustrates what could have been under a different kind of editorial policy. The symposium took place during a period of an acting editor. In the November–December, 1959, issue, Kendig Brubaker Cully, in his usual candid manner, carefully outlined the changes in theological disposition among religious educators during the previous two decades. He noted the shifts in emphasis to theological concerns and the positive influence of various styles of neo-orthodox theologies. He called this a reconstruction process, a gathering together the best insights of the new biblical theology and the critical transcendent character of the neo-orthodox position. He noted the general abandonment of the earlier liberalism and the widespread new efforts toward some moderate consensus around a biblically based neo-orthodox continuum.[64]

Six months later in the July–August, 1960, issue an aged William Clayton Bower took sharp issue with Cully's article. Although agreeing with Cully about the new theological trend in religious education, Bower noted that liberalism was by no means dead. Bower pursued the liberal pre-neo-orthodox R.E.A. position so long a hallmark of the journal. He advocated the old standard argument for a religious education based in experience, one which took current history seriously and one that was grounded in the communal experience of society. He called for a religious education that was based on primary experience, rather than religion based upon the "end products of past Christian experience." He urged the use of theology and tradition but in the way of Coe and Elliott, as an experiential task always tied to current experience. He disallowed the transcendent-immanent dialectic and called for a position that acknowledged that there was really only one God-reality and that was found in the present history of firsthand human experience. God was to be met in the living present, or God was not to be met at all.[65]

The article was a powerful argument for the renewal of old R.E.A. values. It challenged Cully's theological view, expanded upon it, clarified the question and made a strong case for a more socially oriented education. Bower had not lost his capacity for clarity. His point was pressed logically; he was not opposed to the new theological interests (he had much earlier called attention to the need for theology). He rather pressed the question of theological usage and practice. His theological method always grew out of experience and back into the tradition, rather than the neo-orthodox notion that God's intervention in biblical history was the starting place for theological discourse. Unfortunately those sharp exchanges of ideas did not often happen during the editorship of Stidley. It would remain the task of his successor to modify the symposium structure to allow and encourage debate and exchange of ideas.

Randolph Crump Miller assumed official editorial duties in the fall of 1958 and continued in that capacity until 1978. If Herman Wornom dominated the R.E.A. behind the scenes as promoter, manager and missionary of moderation, then it is equally true that Randolph Miller's values became the R.E.A.'s editorial grid through which the public, professional image of the journal was maintained. For countless members who never made a convention, never participated in one of the major committees, for that large majority, the R.E.A. was the journal, and the journal was an extension of the editor. For better or worse during the next twenty years of editorship Miller molded the printed image of the association by his decisions, selection of articles, writers, and reviewers.

Miller confided to me that though he always worked with an editorial committee of some sort and remained in close contact with the general secretary the major decisions about choice of author or article were always primarily his.[66] He chose to publish those articles that he felt important at that time in the history of religious education. Granted, there were vague editorial policies, but when all was said and done the decision that mattered was what Miller decided. And as far as I can determine from the minutes of the various editorial committees, his decisions were rarely questioned and never challenged. His personal choices, decisions, and biases fill those twenty years of *Religious Education*. It is to those very themes that we now turn.

The basic difference between Miller's editorial qualifications and those of his predecessors was the fact that Miller was primarily an author. Over the years, Miller has written more than eighteen books as well as a large number of professional articles. In one way the journal became for Randolph Crump Miller a kind of extended forum, a place to test ideas and check responses. His personal contributions to the journal throughout the years of his editorship were numerous and set the tone for the journal's emphasis.

Kendig Cully was right when (in 1959) he singled out Randolph Crump Miller as the most important person in reviving theological interest in the field of religious education since H. Shelton Smith's *Faith and Nurture* of the early forties.[67] Miller's *Clue to Christian Education* was an announcement of a future theological program. Throughout Miller's two decades of editorship, theological themes dominated his work and influenced the journal. Upon Miller's retirement as editor of the journal in 1978, James Michael Lee, a contemporary religious education theorist, was asked to comment on Miller's contributions. He paid tribute to Miller's contribution as primarily bringing theology back into the concern of religious educators. That assessment was indeed most accurate.[68]

Miller's analysis of religious education was that it lacked a serious theological basis. Five years before he became editor of the journal, he set forth his view of this problem. Religious education was a theological discipline, and if it were to gain importance in the seminary and the church, it must again first give allegiance to the theological task. The article was an open defense of the new neo-orthodoxy. Miller made short shrift of the Dewey disciples of a generation of religious educators (the historic mentors of the R.E.A.). He claimed their problem was a lack of theology. Because of a loss of theological grounding, religious educators were misled by Dewey's "instrumentalism." In perhaps one of the most succinct statements of religious education theory ever written, Miller describes the task for religious education: "Its problem is to describe adequately the existential situation, the religious predicament, to which the Christian Gospel has the answer. Its task is to make a theology which describes this relationship relevant to the learner of whatever age, and thus to bring the learner into a right relationship with God within the dynamic fellowship of the redemptive community."[69]

Miller's success as an author grew throughout his career as editor of the journal. Unquestionably, by the mid-seventies Miller had gained the reputation of the modern father of Protestant religious education, and he had as well a sizeable Catholic following. He had become the "dean of Protestant religious education," a title which acknowledges something of his influence and his acceptance within the field.

Randolph Crump Miller is one of those happy souls, those "once born" Jamesian Christians who seemed to be alive providentially for their time. His interest, training, and convictions matched the times. Theological concern was revived with the advent of the new orthodoxy. New biblical studies and new theologies swept the American seminaries throughout the fifties and sixties. Miller was a person who fit his period. He was able to articulate the concerns of those around him, and because he was singularly clear in his prose and unpretentious in his style his arguments and assessments became the rallying point for Protestant American religious education.

There were a host of other related figures who more or less agreed with Miller's viewpoint. Miller's theological clue for Christian education was shared by a goodly group of other theorists. Lewis J. Sherrill's contributions certainly were early companions to Miller's moderate neo-orthodoxy. But there were others as well; Reuel Howe, Ellis Nelson, James Smart, D. Campbell Wyckoff, and Iris and Kendig Cully are but a few of those who seemed to be writing in much the same vein.

Miller's theology was for the most part always moderate. In this enterprise he seemed a natural partner with the general secretary, Herman Wornom. Miller's theology was personal, relational, and institutional. Being a Christian happened in a Christian environment. Method and theology were not antithetical. Theology and praxis belonged together, doctrine and living were two sides of a unified process.

Miller's theology was never essentially prophetic or militant or even counter-cultural. Thus the themes of difficult social issues never dominated his books or his articles. Rather, Miller's concerns were primarily (certainly until his most recent period of "process" theological concerns) the nature of the Christian experience with God in Christ as lived out in the setting of tbe church. One might criticize Miller for not taking as seriously as he might have the first task of his definition referred to earlier. Sometimes it seems Miller did not describe adequately the existential situation, but rather dismissed its seriousness and difficulty. Controversy rarely surfaced in Miller's generally cheerful world view.

Miller's theology represented a domestication of the great liberal themes of his religious education forefathers and mothers. While Coe and Harper and other first-generation religious educators would hope to change a society and a nation with a vision of God's democracy, Miller would opt for a much more reasonable and pragmatic goal, that of concentration on the Christian community called the church. Miller adapted to cultural pluralism.

The social aspects of Ernest Chave and William Clayton Bower's work were not lost on Miller. They were incorporated in a new, more realistic dimension. He could not take on the whole culture, but he could be concerned about the institutional church. Surely Miller affirmed the transcendent; yet as his theology moved consistently to that of process thought he continued to note the importance of the radical dimension of the immanence of God in empirical relationships. The relationships which were redemptive were those of believers, those within the church.

The abrasive language of Coe's social reform or cultural parousia changed in Miller's thought to a domestic language of relationships. He had not rejected the importance of the social in religious education, he had relocated it. The nudge for faith was the dogmatic tradition, the Gospel. And the process of faith happens in the context of the home and the church, the place where persons live out their faithful relationships.[70]

Miller held a melioristic ideal that the world could indeed change. In *Christian Nurture and the Church* (1961) Miller argued that the task of Christian nurture was to take the pupil "from the world to the church and send the Christian back to the world." In the community of the Holy Spirit the learner is nurtured into mature Christian responsibility. Then s/he is sent back to the world to change society according to Christian values. Miller's series of sermons *A Symphony of the Christian Year* (1954) contains several essays which give explicit advice for Christians in dealing with injustice in society. Within the Christian community, Christians are equipped for responsible citizenship in the real world.[71]

Miller's characteristic stance was moderate. Conditioned by modern empirical method, influenced by neo-orthodoxy, modified by developmental process thought, and genetically nurtured by the loving, personal experience of his own formative years, Randolph Crump Miller wanted to keep the best of several traditions. He began his religious education mission as a messenger of transition. He criticized his spiritual fathers, but never left them. And in his most recent stage, scientific empirical process thought, he has gone full circle to affirm the important dynamic of the immanence of God in all human experience. Miller's own personal ecclesiastical commitment and his strong biblical interest continued to force him to a balanced, middle-road position. He was the apostle of resolution, attempting and usually succeeding in bringing positions and persons together into an agreeable relationship.

As one surveys the themes of the journal by decades, some interesting trends are apparent which I believe simply underline the themes of Miller's interests and how those interests were reflected in the composite of the journal *Religious Education*. The numbers of articles dealing with theology rose noticeably during the fifties and sixties. One can note the gentle domestication of social concerns. In the decade of the sixties, ten articles dealt with personal morality, twelve articles with sexuality, forty-two with ecumenical concerns, and two with the question of nuclear war.[72]

The journal seemed somehow disconnected from the larger social problems (Wornom's observation). During the critical fifties when blacks were making national strides in politics, in the courts and in education, there were but two articles on the race question. In the decade of the sixties there were forty-two articles that dealt with the question of race, a large percentage of those in one single issue, a symposium on race published in 1964 (twenty-eight articles).[73]

The journal took few stands on any of the significant social issues throughout the fifties and the sixties. One might interpret that position as consistent with the history of the association. R.E.A. was not an organization with an active political or public ideological position. Hence there could be no open editorial or position on any of the critical social or theological issues of the times.

But the question is not resolved so easily. The noncontroversial position of the journal was the hidden agenda of the editor and the association. By selection or rejection of an article, a social-political decision was made. It is my personal conviction that the journal under Miller's editorship tended toward quietism, and dealt with safe questions and issues that were unrelated to the difficult social problems of public pedagogy. Wornom's criticism of the early sixties did not change the content or context of the journal. The important issues of the times were not engaged: the role of women, the horrors of the Holocaust, the question of the justice of war, the serious questions of nuclear destruction, or the draft. These social (educational?) issues did not dominate the journal's interest; rather, education issues, questions of learning, development, theological matters, and endless Protestant-Catholic-Jewish perspectives on higher education, teaching methods, and church strategies, and so forth, occupied the major portion of the journal. (In fairness to Miller, one must note that these issues do indeed surface frequently in the seventies, but that period is beyond the considerations of this study.)

But even those noncontroversial themes always avoided the real ecclesiastical world of denominational interests or divine claims for authority or absolute truth. Somehow none of the serious Protestant-Catholic-Jewish issues were ever really debated: not the question of papal infallability, nor the question of the messiahship of Jesus, nor the question of the Americanization of Protestantism. None of these issues ever surfaced, at least not in conflict and open dialogue.

It seems the essential failure of the R.E.A., historically and in the journal, had remained. Because there was no solid ideological base except the illusive notion of free exchange of ideas, there never developed a significant platform for social reform or social correction. Without a mature philosophical grounding the association floundered, drifting from conventional wisdom to the most recent educational fad. The R.E.A. became captive to its own institutional success, it worked for and through power structures that it really never challenged or criticized. The prophetic ideals of Harper and Coe became domesticated, adaptation became a way of institutional life.

The language of relationships was useful for organizing church groups, for conducting conventions, and for running ecclesiastical organizations. Relationships were important for church strategies and religious education methodologies. But the relationship language of Miller or the relationship practice of the R.E.A. never related to the social setting of a great deal of public education.

In summary, Randolph Crump Miller's ideal R.E.A. member was loving, biblically informed, prayerful, careful about relationships both with God and with neighbor. They were persons involved with church work, for that was the arena of redemption and of God's meeting. The pages of *Religious Education* were ultimately pages and articles of optimism, above the clamor of the social chaos that shook this republic during the decades of the fifties and sixties.

R.E.A. members were good persons—happy, reborn Christians clinging to the providential care of God, assured that at least among the covenanted in the chosen flock there was peace and tranquility. Though all hell might break loose outside those walls, within the chosen chambers one could conduct research, run seminars, debate public school religious education strategies, and hold endless symposia distanced from the anguished outside. Yet even in that R.E.A. comfortable world, the best of all worlds, even there the foundations would finally shake and the end of the Wornom years would find the association challenged by the real world.

The trouble would not generate from the journal, not from the R.E.A. councils of the elites, the committee on higher education, on research, or the executive board. Rather, the challenge would come from the members, the common nameless members who gathered occasionally in convention to listen and learn from the experts and be enthused and stimulated and sent home filled with new vigor and hope. It was ultimately a convention that shook R.E.A.'s staid foundations. Here the full R.E.A. congregation would meet, and issues untouched by the journal would surface and challenge the association to renew its historic mandate, the development of a public paideia.

The Gatherings of the Faithful

From 1935–1953 the R.E.A. really had no full-fledged major national convention. There was a usual annual or semi-annual meeting, a gathering of the inner-circle faithful to determine that they would keep going without a general secretary, with limited budget, and with unpaid contributions of officers and journal editor. When Herman Wornom was chosen general secretary after the unexpected death of Harrison Elliott, one of his first major tasks was to bring the association back together in a golden fiftieth anniversary convention (1953). The convention would serve as some kind of symbol to link the association to the glories of the past and to project the R.E.A. into the future, one filled with new promise and renewed excitement.

This convention was Wornom's first challenge and one that would mean much for his future success and leadership of the R.E.A. In typical Wornom fashion, he set about with meticulous democratic plans; decisions were always group decisions. A convention committee was formed in New York, closer to Wornom and distanced from Pittsburgh, the city of the convention and the center of the R.E.A. executive board during that period, as well as home of the R.E.A. president. Wornom's close friend, F. Ernest Johnson of Teachers College, became chairperson of the convention committee. The committee consisted of twenty-two notable members such as Israel Chipkin, editor of *Jewish Education;* Hugh Hartshorne, Yale Divinity School; Paul Maves, Drew Theological Seminary; Lewis J. Sherrill, Union Seminary; George B. Ford, pastor of Corpus Christi Church, New York; and a host of others. The committee included Catholics, Greek Orthodox, Jewish, and Protestant members. Most were university persons or ecclesiastical bureaucrats; only one member was a common practicing director of religious education.[74]

Wornom not only organized the convention in cooperation with those twenty-two members, but extended the convention committee by adding and soliciting names of corresponding members from all parts of the United States and Canada, so that the convention "may reflect the thought of our membership across the nation." These persons would review convention plans, comment on them and return their criticism to the committee. They would also be asked to promote convention attendance and help secure new members for the association.[75]

Wornom collected sponsors for the convention, an impressive list of more than fifty university and college presidents who promised to be in attendance or send a message to the proceedings. The list included the presidents of Ohio State, Carleton College, Notre Dame, Howard University, Princeton Seminary, Southern Baptist Theological Seminary, University of Missouri, Northwestern University, Tuskegee Institute, St. Louis University, Union Seminary, Teachers College, Columbia University, Jewish Theological Seminary, Yale University, and the dean of Harvard Divinity School.[76]

Wornom submitted a budget of $16,000 for the convention and field organization which was to follow up after the convention to recruit new members. (That additional support system never materialized.) The actual expense of the convention itself was budgeted at approximately $7000.[77] That was surely a somewhat more realistic figure than original plans for the convention which called for a budget of $32,000. Wornom's realism and fiscal conservatism seemed already evident, and such realism surely was welcome in an organization historically overextended by its ambitions.[78]

Wornom was able to finance that 1953 convention through the fees of registrants, the support of sponsors, and the contributions of several foundation grants. In his appeal to foundations, Wornom used the rich history of the association; he highlighted the support of nationally recognized university presidents. He underlined the ecumenical aspects of the convention. He had received Bishop Dearden's (Pittsburgh) support which he used to negotiate funds for the anniversary celebration. The appeals were successful and several modest grants eliminated any R.E.A. loss on the convention.[79]

The convention theme "The Place and Adequacy of Religious Education in our Times" was aptly chosen as a way to keep faith with the past and announce publicly that the R.E.A. would be about future criticism and support of religion in education and the practice of the best education in the arena of religion. The speakers of the convention included Henry Van Dusen of Union Seminary; Paul Reinert, president of St. Louis University; Isaac Berkson, Harry Broudy, Will Herberg, Donald Butler, and a host of others. Key sessions were held around the themes of "Crisis of Religion in Education," "Religion and Philosophies of Education," "Strategies for Making Adequate Provision of Religious Education for All Our Young," "How to Improve the Status and Provision of Religious Education." Seminars were held on philosophy, on agencies of the religious education, on the question of religion in public schools, on the parochial school (no representative from the Lutheran or Evangelical traditions were on the program), church and synagogue, and other agencies. There were twelve seminars, the last of which was on the place of theology in religious education, chaired by Randolph Crump Miller with resource persons such as Elmer Homrighausen, Alexander Schmemann, and Mary Janet Miller.[80]

The four issues of the journal preceding the convention ran articles related to the theme of the convention. After the convention, Wornom editorialized about the success of the meeting. More than four hundred persons registered, and more than five hundred attended evening sessions. Reports from members and nonmembers were all laudatory. The board was ecstatic and complimented Wornom on his excellent administration in carrying out all the details of the successful convention.[81]

The March–April issue of *Religious Education* carried the speeches of the convention and all the seminar reports. Hugh Hartshorne, past president of the association, cautioned the R.E.A. against becoming an "institution with a program." He encouraged the free exchange of ideas, even though he acknowledged the fact that the profession lacked a strong philosophical and research base.[82] Hartshorne wanted an open forum, but held no brief for a research-oriented institution. In fact, Hartshorne had spoken against a research committee in the board of directors meeting held at the convention.[83]

Perhaps the most dramatic proposal to be uttered at the convention came from Eugene Carson Blake in his address on public education. He must have alienated several of the publics present. He spoke clearly against parochial schools. He called for a reintroduction of religion into the core curriculum of the public school. His language was surprisingly blunt and candid: "I believe all religious persons, forces, and institutions should press for the reintroduction into the heart of the curriculum and life of our public schools belief in God as Creator, Ruler, Judge and Father." Blake qualified, "This is not a proposal for the sectarian teaching of religion. It can be based on a common area of agreement. It can be based on the Old Testament."[84] Blake had managed to put a little stress on ecumenicity; he had, as one reporter put it, given "the fraternal bonds their sharpest tug" of the convention.[85]

Wornom's summary of the convention was more than self-congratulatory. He used the convention and its proposals to sketch out his future agenda for the association. If one reads carefully his essay "A Program for Exploration and Discovery," printed in the postconvention issue of *Religious Education,* one will find there Wornom's early priorities: his intention to stimulate local chapters; second, the embryonic idea for the round tables, and even hints about a massive program in stimulating research. Little did anyone know at that point that this new general secretary had really outlined his administration's agenda for the next two decades.[86]

There was one other noteworthy presentation which seemed cautionary and even prophetic for the association's future. The closing essay by Mildred McAfee Horton addressed the convention on the topic of "Many Means to the Highest Value." In a kind of neo-evangelical appeal she noted that all the objective teaching about religion was not really at the heart of religious education's problem. To teach religion one had to help people know religion as experience and conviction, not as object or content. She called for a rebirth of faith among religious educators and implied strongly that the essential problem of religious education was a matter of a loss of faith of the practitioners.[87]

Her essay was reviewed in *Christian Century* which raised the same issue of faith in compelling words about her speech. The reviewer was obviously moved by the experience. "Mrs. Horton brought the needed evangelical reminder that none ought to be at this effort if it is for him just a means to accomplish even such lofty ends as the salvation and redemption of Western culture . . . . Rather because of faith or, in the words of Theodore A. Gill, 'because an eternally necessary relation is compellingly perceived.' "[88]

Horton was addressing the central problem of the R.E.A. All success, all research, all technologies were futile if in fact there were few believing professionals. No wonder her words fell so strikingly upon her hearers. She reminded the professional that it is not professionalism that really nurtures if there is no charisma, no gift, no faith. Her words were eloquent and they were needed.

There were four other conventions held during the administration of Herman Wornom. Each drew more participants than the one before. Each grew in ecumenical character. Catholics, once a minority in R.E.A. membership, became a large majority in R.E.A. convention attendance. Catholic and Jewish participants were well represented; for the first time in the history of the association they were a part of the planning and the program. Now one could call the R.E.A. an interfaith association with integrity.

The themes for the conventions were stimulating and reflected the issues of the times. In 1957 the convention considered "Images of Man in Current Culture"; in 1962, "Contemporary American Morality and Religion and Character Education"; in 1966, "Ecumenical Revolution and Religious Education"; and in 1969, "Our Divided Society, A Challenge to Religious Education." The 1969 convention came toward the end of the Vietnam war, after the assassinations of Robert Kennedy and Martin Luther King, after the Chicago Democratic convention, amid the black revolution and at the beginning of strident voices being heard throughout the land from the Third World. Even the R.E.A. would have to listen; the tremors were close to home. All of these meetings were great successes. Each convention met in Chicago, the historical birthplace of the association. There were some regular high-level participants. Each gathering saw and heard from some eminent American Jewish leadership. The speakers usually included Abraham Heschel, Marc Tannenbaum, and Eugene Borowitz. Catholic regulars included Ann Ida Gannon, B.V.M., Gerard Sloyan, and Philip Scharper; and the Protestants gathered the faithful "Randy" Miller, Martin Marty, D. Campbell Wyckoff, Ellis Nelson, and many others.

There were other regular features. Under Wornom's leadership the conventions became showplaces of democratic processes. There were always the major presentations, as well as numerous seminars. Here common persons could talk and be heard and respond. The summaries of those sessions filled the pages of the postconvention journal, and they also found their way back to the executive board. There is good reason to believe that Wornom took those minutes seriously as evidenced by his reaction to the 1953 convention. The responses became his agenda for the next decade.

Other strategies became common practice during the Wornom years. Preconvention issues of *Religious Education* were always filled with articles relating to the convention topic. Regular promotional announcements occurred before the convention, and after the meeting all the major essays and papers were published in the journal. The dominant membership of the convention program committee was always the same: truly ecumenical, largely male, almost entirely academic or high-level ecclesiastical types. The Wornom conventions were carefully planned and meticulously orchestrated.

In all of the eighteen years of Wornom correspondence, minutes, and countless boxes of files, I have noticed only one serious conflict between Herman Wornom and his colleagues in the R.E.A. And that issue involved the careful planning of the 1969 convention. The conflict reveals the minute care for detail that Wornom brought to his convention tasks. Whatever he planned was done with exacting accuracy. The incident also reveals the social tremors that seemed closer to the sheltered walls of the R.E.A.

Originally Wornom had proposed the theme for the convention be titled "Religious Education—A Unifying Force in a Divided Society." That theme was accepted by the executive committee as early as October 11, 1968. On April 2, the committee changed the word "Unifying" to "Creative" at the strong urging of David Hunter, president of the R.E.A. There was little discussion and the issue seemed trivial, except to Herman Worman.[89]

At first Wornom accepted the change, but two days after the meeting, April 4, he addressed a letter to each of the members of the executive committee. He explained in detail the reason he now felt the earlier wording was superior. He argued that the convention should serve a unifying purpose. He also felt "unifying" was the antithetical word to divided and therefore a superior word choice simply on the matter of clarity of idea.

Then in a moving paragraph, Herman Wornom revealed the real agenda of his complaint. Wornom wrote: "A major part of my ministry in R.E.A. has been devoted to playing a unifying role between diverse groups. In working for the convention for next November (my last) I would like more fully than ever to be engaged in exploring the unifying potential of religious education." Wornom personalized his argument, "During the traumatic experience of last spring, when Dr. Martin Luther King and Robert Kennedy were assassinated and when Morningside Heights, where I live, was in continual turmoil with student protest and police action and brutalities, I almost decided that I would not have the strength and will to undertake another convention." But Wornom wanted one last chance to make a difference. "However, when the executive committee agreed on October 11, 1968, that the convention theme should be on religious education as a unifying factor in a divided society, that presented a strong challenge and I felt that I could give myself wholeheartedly to planning and administering a convention on that theme."[90] He requested the board's permission to be the final authority of choice of exact title for the convention. He wanted the word "creative" changed back to the original unifying word. In a memorandum dated April 10, 1969, Wornom noted that six of the seven members responding gave him full responsibility for the final wording of the convention theme.[91]

The seventh member, R.E.A. President David Hunter, responded on the ninth of April. In a strongly worded letter, Hunter took Wornom to task. He would not agree with Wornom's request for this final responsibility. He wanted a special meeting of the executive board. He wrote: "The executive committee voted and the vote ought not to be rescinded except by the executive committee in meeting."[92]

Wornom replied the same day. He rejected the idea of a special meeting. His challenge to his board chairperson was emotional and loaded. He threatened resignation: "I am saying to you that if this trust is not given, I am ending my 17 years of service with the R.E.A. this spring."[93]

Whatever Wornom's personal motives for his behavior, his written record stands. He was dismayed by the events that seemed to shatter his world and he wanted this convention, like others, indeed like the major Wornom moderate agenda, to unify this broken, shaking society. What he could not have known in those spring days was that the fall convention of the R.E.A. would not accomplish even his fondest wish. Rather it would shake the very foundations of the association that he sought so valiantly to protect and nurture. This last Wornom gathering would bring all the stress he felt on Morningside Heights into the convention halls of Chicago and challenge the R.E.A. as never before in all its history. Strange irony that what set out to be a unifying experience became a shattering experience, and precisely because of some of the best planning of his entire career.

Shaking Foundations:
The 1969 Convention

As usual, Wornom worked with a large convention committee of thirty-three persons (two women), chaired by Philip Scharper.[94] Major addresses were given by Alvin Pitcher, Jesse Jackson, Alan Geyer, Oswald Bronson, and Whitney Young. But perhaps more importantly the convention was one of "loud minorities."[95] Young people were vocal. Women were assertive. Seminars bristled with tension and conflict and the resolutions were presented to the entire convention for debate and decision. The R.E.A. was to be challenged from the "field" by the average day-to-day member of the association.

The convention dealt with controversial issues: blacks, minorities, white racism, generation gaps, American world power, and Vietnam. The seminars raised questions about racism, sexism, drug-related issues, American military power, the draft, and related strategies that educators might use in an effort to turn the direction, to unify society and heal the wounds of fracturedness.

The words that sounded from the convention were angry words; they were words of prophecy, of indignation, of no-holds-barred criticism of the church and of the R.E.A. itself. The collage of words was surely as mixed as the participants but the central theme was alarmingly clear. Something had to be done. Business was not as usual; finally the quakes had caught up with the R.E.A. itself.

Alvin Pitcher called for "compensatory opportunity" which he candidly accepted as discrimination in reverse. "It's un-American and it's probably unconstitutional." He advocated black power and black business. He called for a new liberalism, one that came with compensatory opportunity, black power, and black separation.[96] He did what he intended to do, he shook some "white folks'" foundations.

Jesse Jackson followed his mentor and spoke of "Christianity, the Church, and Racism." The screws tightened as the words cut closer to the audience, those pious religious persons gathered to listen, finally to listen! Jackson wasted no time in getting to the point. "There is a great gap between Christ and Christians. The American church by and large has failed our God, at least the God of the Scriptures."[97]

He was not nice about his language. The ring of his prose was more than shocking in the midst of the congregation of the R.E.A. "You have been Americans, yes; you've had a commitment to the flag, yes, but not to the Cross. . . . Witch doctor, that's what Nixon is, nothing but a witch doctor. . . . Man is not justified by getting crucified, and I'm not justified by living to be old, and no one is safe save those the Lord allows to come into his Kingdom through grace which is basically a bunch of shit." Jackson's prose was that of the black movement and he used it well. His imagery and metaphor must have shattered even the most professionalized among his educated congregation. He ended his address with typical Jacksonian rhetoric.

"In the midst of it all, my confidence that some people call arrogance is my trust and absolute belief in God. Even if he does not deliver us tonight he's able." Jackson continued, "The wheel in the middle of the wheel is ever so clear to me. Our little wheel with our connected bones from our body spins toward justice, however slowly. There's a great Babylonian wheel outside of us moving toward injustice." Jackson's rhetoric went beyond symbolic reason. "And then there's the Third World wheel moving toward justice. And there's a fourth wheel whom we've never seen face to face. Those hanging down are God's legs, and he's overlooking us all, willing to throw his loving arms of protection around us if we would but serve him.'' Jackson called for a ''moral mandate'' to resist evil. He urged a united oppressed people who would organize powerfully enough ''to have the Christian young men of the nation to resist war and the ministers to declare it over. Then the presidents would have no choice but to study war no more.''[98]

Whitney Young, director of the National Urban League, flew to Chicago to deliver his word. He came closely guarded with continued police protection.[99] His word urged the convention to action. Though not as strident as Jackson, Young was equally challenging. He urged the R.E.A. to root out racism in its own profession. He advocated political education and laid part of the responsibility for a lack of it at the feet of the R.E.A. He urged R.E.A. members to learn from the black educational experience, for there one would see ''a knowledge of the survival capacity of the scars of people who have lived for centuries with injustice. Their skills and discoveries might inject new blood that could stop the increased tide of racism.'' He challenged the R.E.A. to change history, urban and social.[100]

And the convention heard from young people, striking out in anger and rage. They wanted to be heard, and they wanted someone to listen. Their solutions were unclear, and they were not sophisticated about the issues or the solutions. But they were direct and simple about the moral question and the moral imperative. They were against war and for peace, they were against racism and for justice. They were activists and they wanted a piece of the action. Their voices were heard as well as those of adults in the many resolutions which grew out of the convention seminars. Those resolutions were the voice of the association, finally made public in an open way in calls for radical changes within the profession of religious education and in the organization of the R.E.A.

Their words were gathered and compiled after the convention was over by the general secretary. They fill seven pages of single-spaced prose. Some of the key recommendations which emerged were the following:

R.E.A. was urged to strive for a wider participation with blacks and minorities, to establish a task force to review history texts in an effort to correct misimpression of white racism.

R.E.A. was urged to take a position on the legality of consenting homosexual practices.

R.E.A. was urged to publish more material about drug abuse and drug usage.

R.E.A. was urged to lobby for an end to the war in Vietnam by direct political activity. (Fourteen recommendations dealt with the question of America's military power and the Third World.)

R.E.A. was urged to recruit young persons and allow them significant roles in the association.

R.E.A. was urged to influence colleges and seminaries toward revision of curriculum to include issues of peace and justice.[101]

In summary, the association was being challenged to change its neutral role, to take public positions, to become active in the pursuit of the goals of political activism, especially on the issues of race, the war, and alienated youth.

Herman Wornom presented the recommendations to the board of directors at the December 29, 1969, meeting. The board recognized that if implemented, those decisions would change the nature of the R.E.A., or at least their understanding of that nature or heritage. In good, churchly fashion, the board acted judiciously and adopted a resolution to form a "Committee on the Nature and Future Function of the R.E.A." That fifteen-member committee chaired by Marvin Taylor was called into session on April 19, 1970.[102]

The immediate task for the committee was to respond to the many suggestions of the 1969 convention. The critical issue was of course the question of the R.E.A. becoming more involved in social concerns in an action-political-position-taking body. The other alternative was to continue to serve as a free forum for expression of diverse ideas and options but never to act as a vocal organization on any serious social issue.

The larger problems really involved the broader question as to the future aims, goals, and purpose of the R.E.A. This matter was particularly significant as the association faced the retirement of its general secretary in the fall of 1970 and the potential appointment of a new administrative head at that time. The situation paralleled the crisis of the association after the death of Henry Cope, its first general secretary.

The two most significant leaders of the R.E.A. seemed to have suggested different future directions. Herman Wornom had risked a first political lobby effort without specific board or organization approval. He seemed to be nudging the association into a more activist position. On the other hand, editor Randolph Crump Miller wasted no time informing the association of his viewpoint. He understood the convention resolutions as reflecting a "loud minority, rather than the silent majority on almost all issues."[103] In the postconvention issue he was even clearer: "A convention of such an organization can receive resolutions, but it cannot bind the other individual members. It can hear a variety of opinions. It can provide the basis for discussion in convention and in the columns of *Religious Education*. But it has no power of itself to pressure any religious, social, or political body. Its small staff precludes many activities even when they are plausible. But within these limitations, the R.E.A. does a whale of a job!''[104]

The task for the Futures Committee was right at the heart of the R.E.A. What would be the new direction of the association as it looked forward to the seventies?

The impact of the Wornom years was clearly moderate. With few exceptions, the R.E.A. had followed a middle road, never really involving itself in the critical social issues of the day. Yet the general secretary leaned toward the left. He had suggested as early as 1963 that the difficult social concerns were important and deserved more attention by the journal and the association. He ended his career as general secretary by planning a most controversial convention. And he risked the first political action of any general secretary in his effort to lobby for the cessation of war in East Asia.

The choice for the seventies lay somewhere between Miller's cautious interpretation of the vision of the R.E.A. and Wornom's more socially oriented passion. The future of the association might well finally be determined by that critical decision.

*   *   *   *   *   *

The period of history of the R.E.A. between 1953 and 1970 was one of domestication of the social pedagogical views of the early mentors of the R.E.A. Social values were expressed by a careful attention to the democratic processes of group work within the boundaries of the association. Public issues were never seriously enjoined while the association was busy internally enjoying its greatest period of success. Controversy was no mark of the journal or of the leadership of the association.

Success was everywhere within. The association under the guidance of Herman Wornom was successful in almost every endeavor: in funding a decade of research stimulation, in hosting round tables of great conversation across the land, in calling higher education to its religious tasks. Success was continuing the effort to alert public education to its religious function and to prod religious folks to take seriously the task of education.

Success was ecumenical. It felt good to have more numbers, more religious types, more Catholics in habits, and some without. It felt right to have more Jews and Orthodox on committees and programs. Success was meeting with cardinals and bishops and judicatory presidents and college presidents and university deans. Success was measured in numbers, simple yearly growth of the numbers of members and numbers of convention participants. Success was in the renewal of local chapters and having several new chapters activated throughout this period.

And the grandest success was the 1969 convention. More than 1500 persons attended, the largest number since the twenties. What a paradoxical statistic: The largest successful attendance became the setting for shaking the very foundations of the association. The 1969 convention, though in every aspect successful, served as a public judgmental word to the association. The glaring failures of the R.E.A. were revealed in public, with the association's blessings!

The convention revealed a failure of the association to live by a true vision of a public pedagogy. In an effort to remain neutral the R.E.A. almost lost the prophetic edge of its heritage, that ideal that religion was central to the marketplace of social conflict and resolution. The convention revealed the association's inability to interpret the real world and the concomitant loss of opportunity to speak either of justice or mercy.

The convention called the R.E.A. to task for lack of concern about the oppressed, the minorities, the war, and young persons. The young people reminded the adult R.E.A. members that the essence of the religious task was to keep social conscience alive and acute.

The R.E.A. drew back from the radical notion of honestly attempting to change a whole society, actually attempting to transform America. Surely such a vision was difficult if not impossible in the pluralism of the fifties and sixties, but its loss was also tragic. For with its death went the grand motivational vision, the promised miracle of religion, new truth, new creation, new life—not a bad vision for Jews and Protestants and Catholics in light of the Exodus and Easter events.

But if the vision of the past was blurred, and if the failures of the R.E.A. were out in the open, and if the association had indeed even invited the prophet within its midst, then there was something of the old vitality still alive. And surely there was.

Herman Wornom left a solid platform for the future. He left an association with adequate income and sound budget. He left an association that was truly ecumenical (in terms of Western Christianity, few contacts existed with Eastern Christianity or other world religions) in fact rather than just in theory. He retired with the association at its healthiest point in the past forty years. This servant of moderation had done his job well; he had unified the association into a viable professional organization with every hope for a long future life.

And as his tenure drew to a close, Wornom seemed to sense anew the ideals of the founders. In 1963 he called attention to the "problems of race, morality of nuclear warfare, the social cause of juvenile delinquency." How prophetic that those areas—race, war, and youth—dominated the 1969 convention. It was Herman Wornom who had planned that last convention, riskfully inviting speakers and suggesting topics that were of course controversial. He orchestrated the public challenge to the R.E.A. to renew its public commitment to a social pedagogy.

And it was finally Herman Wornom who risked acting politically in behalf of anti-war lobby. Yes, his action was measured and cautious. What else? But it was, as well, a closing platform for social pedagogy. He had taken the first step in his last step to lead the association back into the arena of a social vision, toward a public pedagogy.

Notes for Chapter V

1. Minutes of the Editorial Committee, May 6, 1963, Herman Wornom, Secretary, R.E.A.F.
2. Paul Tillich, *The Shaking of the Foundations* (New York: Charles Scribner's Sons, 1948), p. 11.
3. Minutes of the Executive Committee, July 15, 1951, O. M. Walton, Recording Secretary, pp. 1–2.
4. *Religious Education* XLVII (May–June, 1952), p. 178.
5. Ibid., "A Letter from the New General Secretary," p. 180.
6. For a sense of dramatic increase in renewable income over the first ten year Wornom period, see "Memorandum of R.E.A.'s Past and Potential Income," n.d.; covers years 1952–1963, R.E.A.F.
7. Herman E. Wornom, "The Larger Task of Higher Education in Dealing with Religion," an address to the Indiana Council on Religion and Higher Education, Saturday, April 27, 1957, R.E.A.F., p. 1.
8. Herman Wornom, "The Religious Education Association," reprinted from *Religious Education: A Comprehensive Survey*, ed. Marvin J. Taylor (New York: Abingdon Press, 1960), pp. 364–365.
9. Ibid., p. 365.
10. "Schedule of H. E. Wornom for Trip to Cambridge, March 25–27, 1962," R.E.A.F.
11. Herman Wornom, interview held January 24, 1981, New York, New York.
12. Minutes of R.E.A.'s Development Committee, September 17, 1963, p. 2. "It is understood that once the lay committee is formed we will have a luncheon meeting to make plans for each of the members to secure at least four other laymen to make contributions ranging from $50.00 to $200.00 each per annum." Wornom argues as well that the early R.E.A. never generated large numbers of lay members. Though probably true, the rhetoric and appeal to all common educators was clearly a priority of Harper and his colleagues. Herman Wornom interview held January 24, 1981.
13. James J. Gallagher to Brother Gregory Nugent, May 3, 1967, R.E.A.F.
14. Herman Wornom to Mr. James J. Gallagher, May 3, 1967, R.E.A.F.

15. "The Religious Education Association Lay Membership," n.d., R.E.A.F. The membership card was used to solicit lay contributions.

16. Herman Wornom, interview held January 24, 1981, New York, New York.

17. See Wesner Fallaw to Herman Wornom, April 28, 1965 and Herman Wornom to Wesner Fallaw, April 29, 1965, R.E.A.F.

18. Herman Wornom to Oswald Bronson, president; Philip Scharper, chairman of the board; Rabbi Simon Greenberg, chairman, executive committee, May 11, 1970, R.E.A.F.

19. Margaret Mary Meyer, O.P. to Herman Wornom, May 19, 1970, R.E.A.F.

20. Joe Davis Heacock to Herman Wornom, May 18, 1970. R.E.A.F.

21. Sheldon Lewis and Bob Gurmankin, Jewish Students for Peace, to Herman Wornom, May 15, 1970, R.E.A.F.

22. James J. Doyle to Herman Wornom, May 14, 1970, R.E.A.F.

23. Minutes of the Committee on Religion in Higher Education of the R.E.A., April 22, 1954, R.E.A.F., p. 4.

24. Ibid., p. 4.

25. "A Decade of Developments in the Religious Education Association," n.d., R.E.A.F.

26. "Persons Who Plan to Attend the New York Roundtable of the Religious Education Association at Columbia University, November 26 & 27, 1954," R.E.A.F.

27. "Memorandum," untitled, written by Ellis L. Philips, Jr., November 30, 1954, R.E.A.F.

28. "Issues Raised at Chicago Regional Roundtable Requiring Further Study," n.d., no author, R.E.A.F.

29. Walter Houston Clark to Herman Wornom, December 6, 1954, R.E.A.F.

30. Herman Wornom, "The Larger Task of Higher Education in Dealing With Religion," an address to the Indiana Council on Religion and Higher Education, April 27, 1957, p. 10. Wornom's best essay on the question of higher education and religion; "Critical Issues of Religion in Public Higher Education" was published in *Religious Education* LIV (January–February, 1959), pp. 97–107. Wornom's article grew out of the "National Consultative Conference on Religion in the State University" held at the University of Michigan. His article highlighted issues raised by that conference, yet was not breaking any new ground in terms of theory or ideas. The essays of that conference were published under the title *Religion and the State University* (Ann Arbor: The University of Michigan Press, 1958), Erich A. Walter, editor.

31. "Proposals for a Study of the Place of Religion in the Curricula of State Institutions of Higher Learning," n.d., but sometime after 1958, p. 11, R.E.A.F.

32. John Peatling, "Research and Religious Education," *Religious Education* LXXIII (Special Edition September–October, 1978), p. 112. Peatling convincingly argues that the R.E.A. made significant progress in research during the fifties and sixties. That success was due at least in part because of Wornom's dogged persistence.

33. "Survey of Research in Religious and Character Education, 1959," assembled by Leonard A. Stidley, Jr. *Religious Education* LIV (May–June, 1959), pp. 235–268.

34. Form letter from R.E.A. office, April 24, 1959, R.E.A.F.

35. Document attached to form letter from R.E.A. office, April 24, 1959, R.E.A.F., pp. 27–29.

36. See memo "Reports on Three Conferences of Social Science Consultants on Research Problems in Religious and Character Education," held at Union Theological Seminary, New York City, June 13–14, July 4–5, July 18–19, 1959 and *Highlights of*

Recommendations for Research, ed. Herman E. Wornom, reprinted from *Religious Education* LV (January–February, 1960), pp. 49–68.

37. "Three Achievements in the Program of the Religious Education Association During 1959," n.d., no author, but obviously Herman Wornom, R.E.A.F.

38. Research Supplement to *Religious Education* LVII (July–August, 1962), pp. S.1–S.174.

39. *Research Plans in the Fields of Religion, Values and Morality and Their Bearing on Religious and Character Formation,* ed. Stuart W. Cook, (New York: R.E.A., 1962).

40. Herman Wornom, "Findings as to the Value of the Research Planning Workshop Sponsored by the Religious Education Association Held at Cornell University, August 18–29, 1961," unpublished manuscript, R.E.A.F., pp. 12–18.

41. "Highlights," pp. 3–4.

42. "Transcript (First Draft) of Minutes of Strategy Committee R.E.A. New York Office," November 22, 1961, pp. 16ff. R.E.A.F.

43. Ibid., p. 22.

44. "Research Department and Director of Research for the Religious Education Association," March 19, 1964, unpublished manuscript, n.d., no author, R.E.A.F.

45. Specifications for a Director of Research for the Religious Education Association," unpublished manuscript, n.d., no author, R.E.A.F.

46. Herman Wornom, "Director of R.E.A. Research Department," typed manuscript, R.E.A.F.

47. Charles G. Williams, Lilly Endowment, Inc. to Merton Strommen, March 22, 1966, R.E.A.F.

48. Merton P. Strommen, ed., *Research on Religious Development: A Comprehensive Handbook* (New York: Hawthorn Books, Inc., 1971).

49. See minutes of executive committee during the years of 1968–1969. R.E.A.F.

50. Transcript minutes, November 22, 1961, p. 19. R.E.A.F.

51. P. E. Kretzman, "Lutheran Religious Education Provision for Religious Education in the Evangelical Lutheran Church of the United States," *Religious Education* X (February, 1915), pp. 5–15.

52. Herman Wornom to Cardinal Samuel Stritch, Chicago, July 7, 1954, R.E.A.F.

53. Memorandum of Attendance at National Convention of the Religious Education Association, Palmer House, Chicago, November 20–22, 1966, n.d., R.E.A.F. Unpublished manuscript of two pages.

54. Mother Gabrielle Husson, president, Newton College of the Sacred Heart, Newton, Massachusetts, to Herman Wornom, November 28, 1966, R.E.A.F.

55. "Proposed Letter to High School Principals," from C. Albert Koob, n.d., but sometime during 1967, form letter, unpublished manuscript, R.E.A.F.

56. Rev. Hughbert H. Landram to Herman Wornom, June 29, 1954, R.E.A.F.

57. Herman Wornom to Cardinal Stritch, July 7, 1954, R.E.A.F.

58. "Stritch Cautions on 'Unity' Session, Forbids Chicago Catholics to Participate in Meeting of World Church Council," *New York Times,* July 8, 1954, R.E.A.F.

59. Letter from Herman Wornom to Cardinal Stritch, July 8, 1954, R.E.A.F. In an interview with Wornom January 25, 1981, he made clear that his intention was simply to affirm the Cardinal's right to his viewpoint. I suggest the Cardinal might have derived another meaning, the literal sense of Wornom's letter.

60. Letter from Cardinal Stritch to Herman Wornom, August 27, 1954, R.E.A.F.

61. Letter from Herman Wornom to Cardinal Stritch, September 11, 1954, R.E.A.F.

62. Letter from Cardinal Albert Meyer to Herman Wornom, October 24, 1960, R.E.A.F.

63. "Philosophy of Education and Religious Values—A Symposium," *Religious Education* XLVII (November–December, 1953), pp. 369–422.

64. Kendig Brubaker Cully, "Two Decades of Thinking Concerning Christian Nurture," *Religious Education* LIV (November–December, 1959), pp. 481–489.

65. William Clayton Bower, "Recent Trends in Christian Education, An Appraisal," *Religious Education* LV (July–August, 1960), pp. 243–247.

66. Interview with Randolph Crump Miller, September 5, 1977, New Haven, Connecticut.

67. Cully, "Two Decades of Thinking Concerning Christian Nurture," p. 484.

68. James Michael Lee's remarks in honor of the retirement of "Randy" Miller as editor of the journal. R.E.A. Anniversary Convention, Chicago, Illinois.

69. Randolph Crump Miller, "Christian Education As a Theological Discipline and Method," *Religious Education* XLVIII (November–December, 1935), p. 413.

70. See Sara Little's "Randolph Crump Miller: Theologian-Educator," *Religious Education* LXXIII (September–October, 1978), pp. 67–68. For the most part, I am in agreement with Little's analysis, especially on the issue of Miller's consistency. Process theology is almost of necessity the result of Miller's lifelong commitment to relationships and theological compromise. He was and is a prophet of unity!

71. Randolph Crump Miller, *Christian Nurture and the Church* (New York: Charles Scribner's Sons, 1961), pp. 48–64 and *A Symphony of the Christian Year* (Greenwich, Conn.: Seabury Press, 1954), pp. 133–139, 154–160, 161–167. Miller's shift from Coe is significant. Religious education takes place in the church for the democracy. The state is no democracy of God, rather it is secular but still the location for Christians to attempt to live out their Christian convictions. Miller wants to save the social importance of education but abandon the notion that society was the place of the kingdom of God.

72. Author's survey conducted by Mary Jo Ostermann, student at Garrett Theological Seminary, Chicago. Winter, 1978. Results are in author's possession.

73. *Religious Education* LIX (January–February, 1964), pp. 3–120. This symposium was a high point of the entire decade. The articles are inclusive and open in their positive witness. This symposium represents the best of Miller's efforts. It is the rare exception to deal with real problems within the context of the journal's educational task.

74. Planning Committee for the Observance of the 50th Anniversary of the Religious Education Association, no date, attached to a letter dated April 29, 1953, from Herman Wornom to Rev. O. M. Walton, R.E.A.F.

75. Herman Wornom to Rev. O. M. Walton, April 29, 1953, R.E.A.F.

76. Sponsors for the 50th Anniversary Observance of the Religious Education Association, attached to letter from Herman Wornom to Rev. O. M. Walton, April 29, 1953, R.E.A.F.

77. "Primary Asking Budget for the 50th Anniversary Observance Program of the Religious Education Association," attached to "Minutes of the Board of Directors," February 9, 1953, R.E.A.F.

78. "Proposed Budget for 50th Anniversary Observance Program of the Religious Education Association," attached to letter from Herman Wornom to Rev. O. M. Walton, February 4, 1953, R.E.A.F.

79. Herman E. Wornom to Stanton Belfour, executive secretary of the Pitenirn-Crabbe Foundation and consultant to the Howard Heinz Endowment, January 21, 1953, R.E.A.F. And Stanton Belfour to Herman Wornom, April 13, 1953, R.E.A.F.

80. Promotion brochure, "The Place and Adequacy of Religious Education in Our

Times,'' November 8–10, 1953, University of Pittsburgh, Pittsburgh, Penn., p. 10., R.E.A.F.

81. Minutes of the meeting of the Board of Directors of the R.E.A., November 9, 1953, O. M. Walton, Secretary, R.E.A.F.

82. Hugh Hartshorne, ''The Program and Influence of the R.E.A.,'' *Religious Education* XLIX (March–April, 1954), pp. 106–108.

83. Minutes of the meeting of the Board of Directors of the R.E.A., November 9, 1954, O. M. Walton, secretary, R.E.A.F., p. 2.

84. Eugene Carson Blake, ''Strategies for Making Adequate Provision of Religious Education for All Our Young,'' *Religious Education* XLIX (March–April, 1954), p. 103.

85. Theodore A. Gill, ''For Religion in Particular,'' *The Christian Century*, November 25, 1953, p. 1351.

86. Herman Wornom, ''A Program for Exploration and Discovery,'' *Religious Education* XLIX (March–April, 1954), pp. 108–112.

87. Mildred McAfee Horton, ''Many Means to the Highest Value,'' *Religious Education* XLIX (March–April, 1954), pp. 124–128.

88. Theodore Gill, ''For Religion in Particular,'' p. 1353.

89. Minutes of the Meeting of the Executive Committee of R.E.A., April 2, 1953, R.E.A.F.

90. Letter from Herman Wornom to the Executive Committee of R.E.A., April 4, 1969, pp. 1–2, R.E.A.F.

91. Memorandum from Herman Wornom, April 10, 1969, R.E.A.F.

92. David R. Hunter to Herman Wornom, April 9, 1969, R.E.A.F.

93. Herman Wornom to David R. Hunter, April 11, 1969, R.E.A.F.

94. ''Members of the 1969 Convention Program Planning Committee,'' n.d., R.E.A.F., attached to ''Agenda for Advisory Committee for Program for R.E.A.'s 1969 Convention,'' March 9, 1969.

95. Randolph C. Miller, ''Editorial,'' *Religious Education* LXV (January–February, 1970), p. 4.

96. Alvin Pitcher, ''White Racism, Black Development,'' *Religious Education* LXV (March–April, 1970), pp. 86–89.

97. Jesse Jackson, ''Christianity, The Church and Racism,'' *Religious Education* LXV (March–April, 1970), p. 90.

98. Ibid., p. 98.

99. Herman Wornom to Sergeant J. S. Brown, Human Relations Detail, Chicago Police Department, Chicago, November 15, 1969, R.E.A.F.

100. Whitney Young, ''Working Together for Our Common Humanity,'' *Religious Education* LXV (March–April, 1970), p. 144.

101. ''The Religious Education Association: Recommendations Made by Seminars of R.E.A.'s Convention,'' Palmer House, Chicago, Illinois, November 23–26, 1969, R.E.A.F., pp. 1–7.

102. Herman Wornom to members of the Board of Directors of the Religious Education Association, March 12, 1970, R.E.A.F.

103. Randolph Crump Miller, ''Editorial,'' *Religious Education* LXV (January–February, 1970), p. 2.

104. Randolph Crump Miller, ''Editorial,'' *Religious Education* LXV (March–April, 1970), p. 83.

Epilogue

Another uniqueness of the R.E.A. is its commitment to the religious
and moral education of the public, and hence an historic willingness
to engage in painful dialogue around the most volatile issues related
to that end. That potential is yet to be realized.[1]

John Westerhoff, 1982
Editor, *Religious Education*

There are no immediate lessons to learn from a specific historical
interpretation of particular historical events. While history is assuredly
related in the facts of the past, history shares subjectivity with the arts,
journalism, or storytelling. What really happened in the past is rarely
clearly evident, nor does the past have an immediate relationship to the
present or future events. What history contributes modestly to the present is similar to other metaphors for meaning. History participates in
demythologizing the past. History purges erroneous memory and attempts to objectify our reflections on the past by relating the facts, data,
artifacts of recorded memory to human understanding. History is interested in truth (insofar as humanly possible), not in supporting some
particular idealogy or social bias. Yet history remains a human story, we
understand history because we are human, we are always related to our
stories. They create our "webs of reality."

Historical interpretation always raises questions of connections. The
story I have shared argues on the side of historical continuity, while
acknowledging discontinuity which always enhances the context and
character of the central plot line. Healthy traditions are of necessity
rooted in stories, tales that highlight the relationships between origins
and being. Because we are human we need individually and collectively
to rehearse our memories. History attempts to clarify and purify those
sometimes clouded recollections. Insofar as possible historical explanation makes plausible human connections. The history of the R.E.A. is a

192

story essentially filled with continuity. The data compel this interpretation.

The central question of religious education finally revolves around the definitional meaning of religion. Is religion a category of human experience that is primarily related to all of life, or is religion a special separate part of human experience, preserved for institutional jurisdiction? Is religion related to all of the aspects of human society or exclusively the domain of the professional, the religious, the cleric/rabbi, church or synagogue? Where is the place of religious experience: marketplace, political assembly, town square, or chancel, schoolroom, and family hearth? What are the goals of religious life: privatism, self-fulfillment, personal integration, individual well-being, or do the goals of religion have to do with the larger questions of social relationships, public policy, and cultural mythology? And what is the viewpoint of piety; is the focus on the solitary soul, the desert mystic, the isolated charisma of individual prayer, or is the devotion of religion a public piety, a worldly service, a vocation of politics and creativity which participates in the whole of creation? Or is the domain of religion both, private and public?

I have argued that the R.E.A. evolved around that central discussion: what are the goals, aims, contents and arenas of religious life and how are those values nurtured? The data reveal that the early vision of the R.E.A. leadership was deeply committed to a view about religion and religious nurture that was as broad as life itself. Religious education was a public function, a social paideia, a progressive attitude about the salvation of a culture. Gradually that broad perspective became more narrowly defined. The domestication of those values became increasingly ecclesiastical. Social goals shifted to a more provincial vision of church education, rather than the education of the public. The placement of the context for such education became the church/synagogue rather than the public educational ecology of the earlier vision.

Though our historical account of the R.E.A. ended with 1970, the R.E.A. and the larger profession of religious education has continued to evolve through the last decade. The literature of religious education continues to grow, in fact there seems to be a renaissance in the area of professional religious education theory and practice. Leadership in religious education is more evenly shared between Protestants and Catholics and, to a lesser degree, the Jewish community. In fact, one might make the case that the recent theoretical dialogue has shifted from the Protestant religious educator to the American Catholic religious education theorist. Even a cursory reading of *Religious Education* over the past decade illustrates that changing emphasis in leadership.

This development among theorists within the profession and the

R.E.A. does not, however, parochialize the basic central question of religious education. There is a new kind of "catholicity," ("broad, in sympathy, tastes, or interests") about the concerns of religious education. The questions and theories of religious education are as diverse as the pluralism of religious life in North America. What unifies the profession is the pursuit of fundamental theory. What is the essence of religious education?

A brief selective survey of current religious education theory can serve to exhibit that continuing debate through the seventies until the present. Harold Burgess, professor of Christian education at Asbury Theological Seminary, in a very useful text, *An Invitation to Religious Education* (1975), describes four theoretical approaches to the foundation question of religious education. In his "traditional theological approach" he lists Protestant Evangelicals, Frank Gaebelein, Lois LeBar, Harold Carlton Mason; Catholic religious educators Josef Andreas Jungmann, Johannes Hofinger, Marcel van Caster, and others. The design and aim of these theorists is primarily church education conceived in traditional theological terms, all more-or-less doctrinal or confessional.

Burgess' second cateogry, the "Social Cultural" approach, includes the following theorists: George Albert Coe, William Clayton Bower, Ernest Chave, George Herbert Betts, Sophia Lyon Fahs, and others. Interestingly Burgess does not identify any contemporary religious educator in this theoretical position. The educators listed above were all part of the early R.E.A. leadership. They reflect the R.E.A. original vision of a public pedagogy.

Burgess defined his third category as "Contemporary Theological." This group includes a large collection of religious educators: H. Shelton Smith, Randolph Crump Miller, Lewis Sherrill, Gabriel Moran, D. Campbell Wyckoff, Sara Little, Iris Cully, Howard Grimes, and others. The central focus of these religious educators is "church education" though more generally related to social concerns than the "traditionalists."

Burgess' final category of religious education is called the "Social Science" approach to religious education. In this arena Burgess places only one religious education theorist, James Michael Lee. According to Burgess the main emphasis of Lee's work has to do with the teaching act itself. Lee is concerned about the "modification of student behavior," and his theory addresses the structure of instruction itself, normed by the canons of social science. Lee "professionalizes" the act of religious education (instruction), concentrates on the behaviors of teaching and learning, and attends primarily to process as well as content.[2]

One might take issue with Burgess' categories, whether each author is properly placed in the correct theoretical position. Or one might choose a different organization structure altogether. For example: C. Ellis Nelson's book *Where Faith Begins* clearly situates the center of religious education in the local parish, while theorists such as John Westerhoff, William Kennedy, Robert Lynn, Thomas Groome, or Jack L. Seymour all tend to see religious education more generally related to the public or political arena of life. Seymour is the most recent theorist to appeal to a larger public context for religious education. Drawing on the resources of church historian Martin Marty's *Public Church* and Lawrence Cremin's *Public Education,* Seymour advocates a new public paideia, a "Christian education ecology." Seymour's historical studies inform his theoretical viewpoint. There are interesting parallels between his notions and those of the early R.E.A. mentors.[3]

Another group of contemporary religious educators deal with a perspective much more specific, having to do exclusively with special problems of the profession, rather than focusing upon the larger philosophical questions related to society or culture. For example James Fowler's work with faith development stage theory really illuminates one aspect of religious nurture, how faith matures through a lifetime of changes. Fowler's research monitors the natural development of faith in the same way as Lawrence Kohlberg's work explains the cognitive aspects of moral development.[4]

Other recent theorists identify a specific population for their theoretical attention. The work of Maria Harris, Michael Warren, or D. Campbell Wyckoff with youth ministry are all illustrative of religious educators' concern for a particular public, rather than the broader question of public policy.[5] Another emerging group of women religious educators now identify feminist concerns as a critical agenda for religious education. For example, the work of feminist religious educators, Letty Russell, Susan Thislethwaite, or Clarisse Croteau-Chonka all apply a feminist's critique to the question of religion and education.[6]

The R.E.A. has provided and continues to provide a free forum for these diverse persons and those kinds of theoretical exchanges, though I have argued always with a bias toward the more public vision. There is probably no question that the contemporary issues of religious education reflect the pluralism of contemporary American life, as well as the broad diversity of contemporary theological opinion. The journal of *Religious Education* is continued public testimony to that growing diversity. It is likely true as well that contemporary religious education thought and practice is more diversified than in earlier periods, particularly than in the first two or three decades of the R.E.A. Movement was a more appropriate metaphor for those decades than it was for the seventies or will be for the eighties. There is no general unified "movement" in contemporary religious education today. Rather there is a great deal of pluralism and apparent vitality as evidenced by the last decade of published literature in the field.

This book is dedicated to that dialogue. What the history of the R.E.A. does is provide a modest background and public access to substantial data which might enrich that present debate. In a very real sense the thesis of this book is one theoretical perspective. It is my hope that this account of that history might serve in some way to stimulate that continued conversation about the broad goals of religious education, particularly the question of the public's religion and the paideia and praxis that nurture that social reality.

Notes for Epilogue

1. John H. Westerhoff III, "Scripture and Education: Challenges Facing Religious Educators," *Religious Education* LXXVII (September–October, 1982), p. 474.

2. Harold William Burgess, *An Invitation to Religious Education* (Birmingham, Ala.: Religious Education Press, 1975), pp. 13–16.

3. See C. Ellis Nelson, *Where Faith Begins* (Richmond, Va.: John Knox Press, 1967); Thomas H. Groome, *Christian Religious Education: Sharing Our Story and Vision* (San Francisco: Harper & Row, 1980); and Jack L. Seymour, *From Sunday School to Church School: Continuities in Protestant Church Education in the United States, 1860–1929* (Washington, D.C.: University Press of America, Inc., 1982). See especially pp. 10–24 and 155–169.

4. James W. Folwer, *Stages of Faith: The Psychology of Human Development and the Quest for Meaning* (San Francisco: Harper & Row, 1981); Lawrence Kohlberg, *The Philosophy of Moral Development: Essays in Moral Development* (San Francisco: Harper & Row, 1981).

5. Maria Harris, *Portrait of Youth Ministry* (New York: Paulist Press, 1981); Michael Warren, *Youth and the Future of the Church: Ministry with Youth and Young Adults* (New York: Seabury Press, 1982); D. Campbell Wyckoff and Don Richter, eds., *Religious Education Ministry With Youth* (Birmingham, Ala.: Religious Education Press, 1982).

6. See discussion of this topic in *Religious Education* LXXVI (July–August, 1981). See especially articles by Susan Thislethwaite, pp. 391ff, and Clarisse Croteau-Chonka, pp. 369ff, as well as "Essay Review: Feminist Books for Religious Educators," pp. 447ff.

Index of Subjects

197

Index of Names